INTEGRATING ECOFEMINISM, GLOBALIZATION, AND WORLD RELIGIONS

ROSEMARY RADFORD RUETHER

ROWMAN & LITTLEFIELD PUBLISHERS, INC.
Lanham • Boulder • New York • Toronto • Oxford

ROWMAN & LITTLEFIELD PUBLISHERS, INC.

Published in the United States of America
by Rowman & Littlefield Publishers, Inc.
A wholly owned subsidary of The Rowman & Littlefield Publishing Group, Inc.
4501 Forbes Boulevard, Suite 200, Lanham, Maryland 20706
www.rowmanlittlefield.com

PO Box 317
Oxford
OX2 9RU, UK

British Library Cataloguing in Publication Information Available

Library of Congress Cataloging-in-Publication Data

Ruether, Rosemary Radford.
    Integrating ecofeminism, globalization, and world religions / Rosemary
Radford Ruether.
        p. cm. — (Nature's meaning)
    Includes bibliographical references and index.
    ISBN 978-0-7425-3530-5

    1. Globalization—Religious aspects. 2. Ecofeminism—Religious aspects. I.
Title.

    BL65.G55R84 2005
    201'.7—dc22   2004016839

Printed in the United States of America

♾™ The paper used in this publication meets the minimum requirements of
American National Standard for Information Sciences—Permanence of Paper for
Printed Library Materials, ANSI/NISO Z39.48-1992.

INTEGRATING ECOFEMINISM, GLOBALIZATION, AND WORLD RELIGIONS

Nature's Meaning

Series Editor: Roger S. Gottlieb, Professor of Philosophy, Worcester Polytechnic Institute

Each title in Nature's Meaning is created to have the personal stamp of a passionate and articulate spokesperson for environmental sanity. Intended to be engagingly written by experienced thinkers in their field, these books express the comprehensive and personal vision of the topic by an author who has devoted years to studying, teaching, writing about, and often being actively involved with the environmental movement. The books will be intended primarily as college texts, and as beautifully produced volumes, they will also appeal to a wide audience of environmentally concerned readers.

Integrating Ecofeminism, Globalization, and World Religions, by Rosemary Radford Ruether

Environmental Ethics for a Postcolonial World, by Deane Curtin

I dedicate this book to the student leaders of
TREES (Theological Roundtable on Ecological Ethics
and Spirituality) of the Graduate Theological Union,
at Berkeley, California,
especially Whitney Bauman,
my TA for the course in Ecofeminist Theology
in the years 2002, 2003, and 2004,
and Eileen Mary Harrington,
who developed and co-taught with me the course
on Ecofeminism and Globalization in the spring of 2004.

CONTENTS

INTRODUCTION

This volume knits together three concerns: corporate globalization and its challenges, interfaith ecological theology, and ecofeminism. Corporate globalization represents the dominant system of economic power that has emerged since the Second World War, backed up by military intervention by the United States. In the last decade there has emerged increasing protest against this system of power, exposing it as aggravating environmental destruction, disabling authentic democracy, undermining cultural diversity, destabilizing social integrity, and increasing the gap between rich and poor worldwide.

The term "globalization" calls for a brief definition at the outset of this book. The term can simply mean any of the many phenomena linking human populations together across the globe, such as global communication, mixing of cultures and populations through migration, and progressive political movements seeking a more just world order. In the fourth chapter of this book I will detail more of these positive expressions of global interconnections. But the focus of critique in this book is a particular type of centralized and top-down globalization, manifest in transnational corporations and financial institutions. It is this phenomenon, to be defined in greater detail in chapter 1, which I call "corporate globalization."

World religions and their relations both to women and to ecology are other major areas of examination in this volume. In the last decades of the twentieth century the major world religions each began to grapple with the possible harm that their traditions may have caused to the environment and to search for the positive elements in their traditions for an ecologically affirming spirituality and practice. Women and men also have extended feminist theologies into a relationship to the earth. They have asked how the hierarchies of gender in religion and culture have been correlated with the hierarchies of human over nature. They have begun to imagine a different way of interrelating human and nature as an interdependent matrix of life.

In this volume I examine each of these concerns and their interrelationship with each other. The book is divided into four large chapters on (1) defining globalization and its problematic effects, (2) the greening of world religions, (3) ecofeminist theologies and ethics, and (4) alternatives to corporate globalization: is another world possible? Each chapter is subdivided into smaller sections that address different aspects of the four issues. The book does not intend an exhaustive treatment of these enormous problems, but it provides a basic introduction to them for a beginning student, with resources for further reading and study. A website list has also been provided with the major websites on these issues, particularly those used in this volume.

In chapter 1, "Corporate Globalization and the Deepening of Earth's Impoverishment," I focus on defining corporate globalization and critiquing its deleterious effects. I begin by tracing its roots in European colonialism and neocolonialism back to the sixteenth century. I then discuss the emergence of the Bretton Woods institutions, the World Bank, the International Monetary Fund, and the World Trade Organization, as the major organizations of economic governance on behalf of the transnational corporations. After an excursus into increasing ethnic and racial conflict generated by globalization, I look at several key issues of environmental degradation and resource control: air pollution and climate change, industrial agriculture, and the privatization of water.

I then turn to the question of women and how globalization and religious fundamentalisms are aggravating their traditional subordination in patriarchal societies and the exploitation of their labor and sexuality. The chapter ends with a delineation of two major forms of ideology that appear quite different and yet are interacting to justify the dominant economic system and its U.S. military enforcement: the neoliberal appropriation of classical economics and American apocalyptic messianic nationalism.

The second chapter turns to the "Greening of World Religions." In this chapter I show how each of the major world religions has been challenged to critique patterns that may have contributed to environmental destruction and to recover environmentally friendly traditions. This work was reflected particularly in the series of conferences on the world religions and ecology sponsored by the Harvard Center on World Religions in the mid-1990s, each of which resulted in a major book. These studies included Hinduism, Jainism, Buddhism, Confucianism, Daoism, Judaism, Islam, and Christianity, as well as indigenous religions.

After showing how the scholars of each of these world religions have sought to lift up the environmentally friendly potential of their traditions, I ask how has gender, as well as race and class, been a factor in their view of nature? These issues were largely neglected in these conferences and volumes. Yet, in fact, most of these religions have patterns that justify the domination of women, both in the religious practices and in society. Hierarchies over lower-class and slave people and marginalized races are also factors in many of the world's religions. From an ecofeminist and ecojustice perspective it is essential for the religions to deal with this interface between domination of nature and social domination.

A second problem of the world religions is the failure to make real connections between theory and practice. It is one thing to have a beautiful theory about the sacrality of mountains, rivers, the earth, and the energy that sustains the cosmos. But have these theories actually been translated into an ethical practice to avoid deforestation of mountains, pollution of waters, and care for the earth? How have each of the world religions responded in practice to the modern destruction of nature unleashed by industrialism? In order for the world's religions to become helpful players in the struggle for environmental health, this gap between theory and practice must be bridged.

The third chapter addresses explicitly the movements of feminist theory and theology that explore the interface between the domination of women and the domination of nature. After defining the major ideas of ecofeminism, I turn to a series of ecofeminist religious thinkers in various contexts and areas of the world. I first discuss two major North American neopagan thealogians and religious leaders, Starhawk and Carol Christ. Starhawk is also important as a major grassroots organizer against globalization. I then look at several representatives of African ecofeminism, including the leader of the Green Belt movement, Wangari Maathai; then two Indian ecofeminists, a physicist of Hindu background, Vandana Shiva and a Christian, Aruna Gnanadason; then the Latin American context with the leading ecofeminist theologian, Ivone Gebara, and the Conspirando network which has been deeply influenced by her.

After this whirlwind tour of third world ecofeminists, I return to North America to discuss historian of science Carolyn Merchant and theologian Catherine Keller. I conclude by exploring some of the commonalities that connect the thought of these many ecofeminist thinkers, rooted partly in intercommunication with each other, and partly due to the fact that all are critiquing a common global system and seeking an alternative vision to it.

The final chapter, "Alternatives to Corporate Globalization: Is a Different World Possible?" addresses the challenges to the present system and asks whether they are sufficient to represent real change. I open the chapter with three movements that initiated the protest against globalization: the Zapatista movement in Chiapas, Mexico, that erupted on the day that the North American Free Trade Agreement was to go into effect; the direct action street protests against the World Trade Organization and other Bretton Woods institutions that erupted in Seattle in 1999 and have continued worldwide at each of the major meetings of these bodies; and finally the World Social Forum, which gathers nongovernmental organizations (NGOs) from around the world to envision an alternative to this dominant system. The slogan of this Forum, "another world is possible," I have converted into the leading question of this chapter and book.

The chapter then goes on to discuss several examples of both direct action protest and organizing of alternative forms of economic and social life. This includes the movements of Indian farmers to protest genetically modified seeds, as well as the international farmers' organization, Via Campesina. Two examples of protest against privatization of water and electricity from Bolivia and South Africa are then discussed, as well as the long struggle against World Bank–sponsored megadams in India. I then turn to the anti-sweatshop movement in the United States, and its particular expression on American university campuses. Several movements for alternative agriculture are then delineated: the landless farmers' movement in Brazil, the Movimento Sem Terre; the community-supported agriculture movement in the United States; and the fair trade coffee initiatives.

The question of how women are affected by globalization, discussed in chapter 1, is then picked up again here. In this chapter I discuss how women particularly are organizing and providing major leadership for the anti-corporate globalization movement, both within larger movements, such as the *Sem Terra* movement in Brazil and the anti–dam movement in India, and also in predominantly women's groups. This latter area includes several cooperatives in Nicaragua, a multiservice group in a squatter community in Guatemala, and a mothers' movement in Sri Lanka. Religious inspiration is important in several of these movements, Christian, Hindu, and Buddhist. The NGO gathering in Beijing, China, at the United Nations women's meeting, became a kind of world festival of networking for these many women's movements.

The chapter concludes with two major discussions. One is how anti-corporate globalization thinkers are beginning to envision ways to diminish and dismantle the major institutions of corporate global power: the transnational corporations, the Bretton Woods institutions, and the U.S. military. This discussion leads to the question of alternatives to these institutions. How can we begin to imagine a redesigned world in the spaces that open up as these dominating powers are impeded in their global reach? Finally I pick up the issue discussed at the end of chapter 1, namely, the justifying ideologies of this system. I ask how the ruling theories of neoliberal economics can be rethought in a way that integrates interhuman and environmental ethics and spirituality.

Finally, the heresy of American messianic nationalism is tackled. The American churches particularly, in concert with world Christian bodies and other religions, are called on to repudiate this religious ideology of militarist imperialism and to reaffirm a more truthful and life-giving way of understanding issues of God, nation, good, and evil. The book ends with a short conclusion in which I discuss how ecofeminist spirituality and ethics across world religions might begin to express themselves concretely in communities of sustainable life.

1

CORPORATE GLOBALIZATION AND THE DEEPENING OF EARTH'S IMPOVERISHMENT

In this chapter I will discuss the deepening crisis of the impoverishment of the earth's people and the earth itself by the aggressive expansion of corporate globalization. I will first define the meaning of corporate globalization and its development in the post–World War II era, although with roots back into Western colonialism from the sixteenth century. I will also touch on how this deepening poverty, contrasted with fabulous wealth for elites, is fueling ethnic conflict both locally and globally, often exacerbated by religious differences.

I will then look at several key aspects of this impoverishment of both the earth and the majority of its people: air pollution and climate change; the undermining of local sustainable farming and the commodification of the gene pool of plants, animals, and humans; the privatization of water; and population explosion and its collision with the war on women's reproductive rights by conservative religion. The various aspects of how women are disproportionately the victims of corporate globalization will be elaborated. Finally I will discuss the ideologies of both corporate globalization and American imperial aggression with their marriage of neoliberal and Christian fundamentalist thought.

COLONIAL ROOTS OF GLOBALIZATION

We need to start this discussion by some definitions of what is meant by the term globalization. For me, what is being discussed today as "globalization" is simply the latest stage of Western colonialist imperialism. We need to see these current patterns of appropriation of wealth and concentration of power in the West, now especially in the hands of the elites of the United States, in this context of more than 500 years of Western colonialism.[1]

1

Western colonialism can be divided into three phases. The first phase from the late fifteenth century to the early nineteenth century ended with the independence of most of the colonies in the Americas. The second stage, from the mid-nineteenth century to the 1950s, saw the dividing up of Africa among the European nations, as well as most of Asia and the Middle East. England emerged as the great nineteenth-century imperialist nation, creating the empire on which the sun never set. But the aftermath of the Second World War saw the Dutch, French, and English exhausted by the devastation of their home countries and no longer able to afford the direct occupation of these vast colonial territories.

Thus the 1950s saw a process of political decolonialism in which flag independence was conceded to many of these territories in Africa, Asia, and the Middle East. A few colonial powers refused to let go, such as the Portuguese in Angola and Mozambique. Local white settlers tried to block African majority rule, as in Rhodesia and South Africa, and this sparked long bloody revolutionary struggles. But the general pattern that emerged from 1950s and '60s decolonialization was neocolonialism, not popular majority rule. England and France sought to negotiate relations with their former colonies that conceded control over foreign policy and economic wealth to the white settlers and former colonial rulers. The masses of people in former colonies remained impoverished and exploited.

The United States emerged from the Second World War as the strongest world military power and quickly assumed a role of reinforcer of the neocolonial system of control by the West. Third world liberation movements, seeking to throw off neocolonial hegemony over their nations' foreign policy and wealth, often adopted a socialist ideology and allied with the socialist world against continuing Western domination. In response, the West, led by the United States, made anticommunism the ruling ideology of its foreign policy.

The critique and rejection of communism, as defined in Marxist-Leninist states in the first half of the twentieth century as a viable alternative to capitalism, are complex phenomena. The adoption of police-state repression of dissent and totalitarian political organization are certainly worthy of criticism by those concerned with democratic liberties. Yet communism, even in its more repressive expressions, also offered some elements of economic egalitarianism that were attractive to those concerned with justice as well.

But the Western ideological use of anticommunism did not allow a balanced discussion of these ambiguities. Rather anticommunism functioned as a black-and-white rhetoric intended to create a totally negative impression of anything labeled "communism." This ideology was used to justify an attack on any social and political system emerging from the third world that would more justly distribute wealth and political power to the majority. By demonizing communism as atheistic totalitarianism, and pretending to be the champion of "democracy," the West masked the fact that what this crusade was mostly all about was the maintenance of neocolonial Western-controlled capitalism and the prevention of genuine locally controlled political and economic democracy.

With the collapse of the Soviet Union and the emergence of the United States as the overwhelming leader of global military and economic power, the third phase of colonialism built during the Cold War is now coming into greater visibility. This takes the form of a bid for U.S. imperial rule over the rest of the world, not only over the third world, but also seeking to dominate the Middle East and to divide and marginalize the European Economic Union. Britain, ever ambivalent about submerging itself as a small island nation within the European community, seeks to attach itself to the coattails of this American empire, and thus maintain its own global reach. This I think explains the desperate loyalty of Tony Blair to American military adventures around the world.

GLOBALIZATION, THE BRETTON WOODS INSTITUTIONS, AND GROWING POVERTY

To understand this third phase of colonialism, dubbed "globalization," one must look not only at its military expression, concentrated in the hands of the U.S. Armed Forces, but also at the economic institutions that have been built over the last fifty years to control the wealth of the entire planet. This effort to concentrate economic power in the hands of international and particularly of U.S. elites also demands the marginalization of the United Nations. For U.S. elites, the UN must be prevented from operating in any way as a world body that gives equal voice to the third world or indeed to any nation other than the United States. The world system that has been built as the global extension of U.S. hegemony is what is called the Bretton Woods institutions: the World Bank, International Monetary Fund, and, since 1995, the World Trade Organization.

The World Bank and the International Monetary Fund (IMF) were established in 1944–1947 to rebuild war-torn Europe. They are funded by contributions from member nations, with the United States, with 20 percent of its funds, as the largest donor. The G-8 nations, the United States, plus England, France, Germany, Italy, Canada, Japan, and Russia, monopolize the funding and control the decisions. As Europe quickly rebuilt itself, these financial institutions turned to lending for what came to be called "development" of the third world, actually to consolidate control over the economies of the third world by the West. In the 1970s, continued U.S. military spending, the rise of multinational corporations, and the sudden rise of oil prices by OPEC, the Organization of Petroleum Exporting Countries, caused huge funds to be built up in international banks. Under Robert McNamara's leadership (1968–81), the former secretary of defense who designed such murderous projects as the electronic battlefield in the Vietnam War, the policy of the World Bank became the pushing of high-volume, low-interest development loans to the third world.[2]

McNamara favored large development projects, such as huge dams. Some of these former colonial states lacked the political and economic capacity to use such large loans for effective national development. Many of these states were in the hands of dictatorships, such as Marcos in the Philippines, who used such funds for showy projects or stashed them in personal bank accounts. Many projects remained unfinished, with the benefits going to multinationals and national elites, not to the local people. Masses of people were displaced by projects such as dams, without ever being appropriately resettled. Little attention was paid to environmental devastation. The mounting debts accrued from such loans began to cause an international debt crisis. This was manifest in 1982 when Mexico announced that it could not pay its debts. International banking institutions feared a general renunciation of debts by poorer nations.

The response to this debt crisis by the international banking system was to shape the program of Structural Adjustment (SA) aimed at forcing third world countries to pay their debts at the expense of internal development. The formula of Structural Adjustment entailed devaluation of local currency; the sharp rise in interest rates on loans; the removal of trade barriers that protected local industries and agriculture; the privatization of public sector enterprises, such as transportation, energy, telephones, and electricity; and the deregulation of goods, services, and labor, that is, the removal of minimum wage laws and state subsidies for basic foods, education, and health services for the poor. Accepting this package of Structural Adjustment was mandatory in order to receive new loans to repay debts. Each country was directed to focus on one or two traditional export commodities, such as coffee, to earn money in international currency (dollars) to repay debts, at the expense of the diversification of agricultural and industrial production for local consumption.[3]

The World Bank and IMF blamed the governments of third world countries for their poor record in development and debt payment. The claim was that local governments were inefficient, wasting money in subsidizing local services. SA programs were billed as "austerity" measures that would cause temporary "pain" (to whom?) but would soon cause the whole economy to adjust and prosper. The reality was largely the opposite of these rosy predictions. By focusing on stepped-up production of a few export products, such as coffee, the international market for such products was glutted, the prices fell, and so even though the countries were producing and exporting more, they were earning less on their exports.

Local wages also fell, while prices rose, especially with devaluation of currency which overnight made the same money worth a half to a tenth of what it had before. Government subsidies on food, basic commodities, health, education, and transportation were all cut or eliminated, meaning that meeting all these basic needs became much more expensive, often out of the reach of the poorer classes. For example, in post-Sandinista Nicaragua free local health clinics and centers for popular adult education were closed down. Local hospitals no longer had funds to provide medicines and repair equipment. Those going to the hospital often found they had to go out and buy the medicine they needed in pharmacies. Schools were privatized and became very expensive, and even state schools raised tuition beyond the reach of an increasingly impoverished majority. The gains in literacy and health access under the revolutionary regime were rapidly lost. The result was rising poverty, malnutrition, unemployment, homelessness, especially of children, crime, and the turn to drugs for money.[4]

Pushing high-interest loans to repay debts under these conditions of Structural Adjustment created a spiraling upward of the debt trap, even as the poverty of the countries supposed to repay these debts was spiraling downward. Poor countries were able to pay only 30–40 percent of the interest on the loans, with the rest added to the principal owed, so that even though the countries continued to squeeze their resources to repay their loans, their debts mounted year by year. Thus Structural Adjustment had the effect of creating a net extraction of wealth from poor to rich countries, or rather to international banks. For example, in 1988 $50 billion more was paid by poor countries to banks than were actually loaned to them from banks.

Structural Adjustment also had other major effects. By dismantling trade barriers, local production was devastated. Flooded by cheap products from multinational corporations, local industries and agriculture went out of business. In Nicaragua, peanut farmers and a local peanut butter industry could not compete with Skippy's peanut butter from the United States and went out of business. In Korea, rice farmers were put out of business by cheap rice imports from the United States and lost their land. All this was defended as simply the appropriate workings of market laws. Yet large multi-nationals enjoy subsidies and tax breaks from their governments, while lo-cal industries in third world countries were not similarly allowed to protect their industries and agriculture. American rice is cheap, not because Amer-ican farmers are more efficient, but because these farmers and multinational rice distributors are subsidized by the U.S. government.[5]

Why did third world governments take such loans in the first place? Even more, why did they accept these conditions for repayment that were devastating their economies? Basically, for three reasons. Although the ma-jority of people were suffering, the wealthy elites, who controlled the gov-ernments favored by the United States, were prospering. Development loans were a major way for them to cash in on enormous profits. Second, the economists in these governments were trained in the same schools of eco-nomics as those of the World Bank and accepted these theories of market neoliberalism as unquestioned dogma. Finally, any government that resisted the SA package would be made into a pariah, isolated and denied further loans and markets. This was the strategy toward Nicaragua which brought down the Sandinista government and which has been applied for more than forty years against Cuba. These strictures were enough to bring most third world governments into line.[6]

This system of global control by international financial institutions and corporations is being greatly extended since 1995 by the World Trade Or-ganization. The WTO sets market rules that not only prevent any trade bar-riers that protect local industries, but also enforce new rules that extend the ability of such corporations to exploit local wealth, such as TRIMS and TRIPS, that is, Trade-related Investment Measures and Trade-related Intel-lectual Property laws. These new market rules prevent local governments from protecting their own financial institutions and property ownership against takeovers by foreign corporations. They allow corporations to patent the genetic properties of seeds, plants, and even human DNA, preventing lo-cal farmers from producing their own seeds and plants that have been part of local agriculture for thousands of years. Corporations are also buying up watersheds and aquifers, and forcing local people to pay for water that they formerly used free from their own wells and streams.[7]

These market rules of the WTO function on behalf of the unac-countable economic power of transnational corporations. The growth of these huge corporations as a major world power is key to this system of global capitalism. In the 1880s corporations in the United States won the legal status of persons. In the 1950s and 1960s they uprooted themselves from accountability to local communities. The 1980s to the present have seen their concerted effort to dismantle any national or international laws that would regulate their "freedom" of movement and investment.

One major effort to prevent such regulation of transnational corporations was the Multilateral Agreement on Investment (MAI) that was negotiated in secret between 1995 and 1998 by the Organization for Economic Cooperation and Development, an organization representing the transnational corporations. The MAI sought to limit the legal ability of governments at all levels (local, provincial, and national) to regulate foreign investment and the activities of foreign-based corporations. National borders could thus become totally permeable to large corporations who could enter any country and buy up their businesses, banks, and other assets. Governments would not be permitted to pass laws to protect their national assets, businesses, and banks, regulate labor conditions, prevent human rights abuses or environmental damage. Although international outcry prevented this agreement from being accepted, investment liberalization is still the operating agenda of the World Trade Organization, which continues to seek to incorporate its rules into its trade regulations.[8]

Deregulation in trade and investment has also been accompanied by unregulated speculative trade in money. This is made possible by the integration of the world stock market into one system which can be accessed through electronic communication. Such financial speculation does not invest in any actual development; it simply profits from money exchanges. Thus with the flick of a computer signal billions of dollars can be moved around the world, buying stocks and bonds when the market goes up and selling when it goes down, creating vast profits for unaccountable financial traders, but throwing entire countries and regions of the world into financial crisis. The Asian financial crisis that hit Thailand, Japan, and Korea in 1997–1998 was partly caused by such speculative trade in money.[9]

This global system of transnational corporations and the Bretton Woods institutions means third world governments have largely lost their national sovereignty, their right or ability to pass laws to protect their own national industries or shape their own development and foreign policies. Through international banking institutions, global corporations, representing the interests of rich elites in dominant nations, rule the world.

The gap between rich and poor has steadily grown, with some 85 percent of the wealth of the world in the hands of some 20 percent of the world's population, much of that concentrated in the top 1 percent, while the remaining 80 percent share out the remaining 15 percent and the poorest 20 percent, more than a billion people, live in deep misery on the brink of starvation.[10] In 1960 the richest 20 percent had thirty times the wealth of the poorest 20 percent; by 1995 this gap had grown to eighty-two times. The 225 richest people in the world have a combined wealth of over $1 trillion, equal to the annual income of the poorest 50 percent of humanity or 2.5 billion people, while the richest three people have assets that exceed that of the forty-eight poorest nations. This means, in terms of absolute levels of poverty, that in 1999 almost half of the world's population was living on less than $2 a day, and more than 20 percent of the world, 1.2 billion people, on less than $1 a day, according to World Bank figures.[11]

GLOBALIZATION AND ETHNIC CONFLICT

One aspect of the effects of corporate globalization that has been little discussed, either by its defenders or its critics, is how the gap between rich and poor is fueling ethnic conflict within and between nations. In many ex-colonial nations of Asia, Africa, and Latin America, European settlers or ethnic minorities with special advantages of education and entrepreneurial skills have been the overwhelming recipients of the wealth created by globalization, while the impoverished majority are primarily indigenous peoples. In South Africa whites long monopolized land, mining, industrial wealth, and education, while keeping the black majority poor and disenfranchised. With the end of apartheid whites privatized state enterprises and thus continued overwhelmingly to monopolize wealth, even though no longer controlling all political power.[12]

In Zimbabwe a small number of whites continue to control 70 percent of the land. This is the best land with highly productive export agriculture. The black government that came into power with the end of white monopoly rule agreed not to redistribute land for ten years. But with increasing government corruption, together with increasing poverty for the black majority brought about by Structural Adjustment policies, the Mugabe government is using the resentment against whites to fuel murderous takeovers of white land, killing or expelling white farmers and their black laborers. Since these mobs have little ability to run such farms, the result is further economic disaster for the country.[13]

In many other parts of Africa and Asia, ethnic minorities, such as Lebanese in West Africa, Indians in East Africa, and the Chinese in Burma, have had the skills and connections to profit enormously from globalization, while the majority of the local people have fallen into deeper misery. These wealthy minorities may become the targets for the frustrated rage of the poor majority, especially when stirred up by demagogic popular leaders.

These attacks may begin with selective nationalizations, seizing the businesses and properties of these wealthy elites. But under conditions of intensifying conflict mobs can be stirred up to murder, rape, and pillage the persons and property of wealthy ethnic minorities, including local businesses run by members of these groups who are not themselves the big plutocrats, but are nevertheless wealthier than the indigenous people and more accessible to their rage. The wealthy minority may be expelled from the country as a group, destroying important sectors of the economy run by these groups.[14]

Chinese-American law professor Amy Chua has detailed this grim story in *World on Fire: How Exporting Free Market Democracy Breeds Ethnic Hatred and Global Insecurity* (2003).[15] Chua exposes the fallacy of the American identification of free market globalization and democracy. American foreign policy has assumed the compatibility, if not identity, of the two. American imperial adventures abroad, most recently in Afghanistan and Iraq, have sought to dismantle state-controlled economies to allow corporate takeovers by American businesses charged with "rebuilding the country," while at the same time imposing American-style "free elections," based on universal suffrage.

In many cases this is a formula for exacerbated ethnic conflict as long-suppressed majorities held in check by ruling minorities rise and use the vote to take power, targeting the former ruling groups, as well as Americans who are seen as foreign invaders that are further impoverishing the country. Increasingly, Americans themselves are becoming a global "ethnic minority" whose businesses and embassies become targets for global rage of those who feel humiliated by American wealth and power.[16]

This combination of neoliberal "free markets" and "free elections" based on universal suffrage, ironically, contradicts actual American history. American white elites have always been very chary of giving the American poor, especially its major ethnic minority, African Americans, free access to the vote. After the Fourteenth Amendment formally enfranchised black males (the vote for women took another fifty years), Jim Crow laws, as well as property and literacy requirements, were imposed that effectively disenfranchised blacks, as well as much of the poorer classes. Today the United States continues to elect its leaders by minority vote dominated by middle- and upper-class whites. This is done by complex disincentives to vote, outright disenfranchisement of certain groups (those with felony convictions), and the domination of elections by the extremely wealthy. The result is that there is little likelihood of electing state or national leaders that represent real alternatives to the hegemonic political and economic ideology.[17]

The New Deal put in place some elements of a welfare state, minimum wage laws, social security, unemployment compensation, and workplace protection, that modified the conflict between wealth and poverty in the United States. This safety net is far less developed in the United States than in Western Europe and has been greatly undermined with the reign of neoliberal economic thinking from the Reagan years to today. But even so the undermining of public social services imposed on poor countries as part of Structural Adjustment goes beyond what American elites impose on their own people. Moreover American businesses and agriculture remain subsidized and protected, even as corporate leaders demand the dismantling of such protections and subsidies in poor countries under the ideology of "free trade."

This unacknowledged conflict between laissez-fair free trade that impoverishes the majority and "free elections" by universal suffrage that enfranchises them has been typically played out in U.S. foreign policy by various strategies that assure "free markets," while preventing populist figures from being elected. One way this has been done, since the beginning of the American colonial empire with the Spanish American War in 1898, has been to sponsor dictators that provide open markets to American business interests while repressing popular dissent. When democratization movements succeed in electing a populist figure, such as Salvador Allende in Chile in 1973, the United States, together with local elites, have created coups that put a repressive dictator in place.[18]

In some cases local elites have collaborated with a local strongman to create a dictatorship that represses dissent while opening the country to free trade. The IMF and the United States have generally supported such arrangements. Although the United States prefers "free elections" and a "free press," it usually does so in a way that seeks to assure that only leaders favorable to U.S. interests have a chance to be elected. The ambivalence toward "free elections" in 2004 in American-occupied Iraq is an example of this double message. The United States wants to justify its invasion as bringing "democracy" to Iraq, while preventing the previously repressed Shi'ite majority from coming to power. There is, of course, no guarantee that the victory of the Shi'ite majority would not itself scapegoat the minority but previously favored Sunnis, as well as curtail the liberties of women. But the U.S. leaders are primarily concerned to prevent an Islamic populist regime from coming to power that would deny U.S. corporate access to Iraq resources.[19]

Those who seek alternatives to globalization need to be much more cognizant of the ethnic factor in the division between rich beneficiaries and impoverished victims of free trade policies and the danger of a backlash against globalization turning into genocidal crusades against privileged lo-

cal minorities. Reasoned struggles to change the system that is impoverishing the majority can be deflected into symbolic targeting of privileged
groups and their institutions. Ethnic and religious differences between privileged groups and the poor majority add racist and religious rhetoric to such
backlashes, with easy appeal to enflamed emotions.

Targeted groups generally respond with heightened security and expanded discrimination against "enemies," perceived as members of the opposition group, ethnicity, and religion. The U.S. response to the 9/11 attacks
on the two symbolic targets of the World Trade Center and the Pentagon
is the obvious case in point. Those who seek a deepened democracy as part
of an alternative to globalization need to define what kind of democracy
they are talking about. This is an issue to which we will return in the fourth
and final chapter of this book.

Having defined something of the meaning of corporate globalization
and engaged in a brief excursus on the dangers of ethnic conflict hidden in
this global development, I now turn to a discussion of a series of dimensions
of corporate globalization. How does corporate globalization connect with
air pollution and climate change? What is its connection with industrialized
agriculture? What are its connections with corporate efforts to monopolize
control over water? Given the focus on women in this study, how is gender
a particular factor in worsening poverty and oppression exacerbated by corporate globalization? Finally, how is corporate globalization justified by a
mixture of ideologies, religious and secular?

AIR POLLUTION AND CLIMATE CHANGE

With modern industrialization, fossil fuels, coal, petroleum, and natural gas,
became the primary sources of energy, accounting for almost 80 percent of
the fuels used to power the industrial system. The burning of these fuels releases gaseous byproducts, particularly carbon dioxide. Nitrogen oxide
comes especially from fertilizers, while herds of cattle and rice paddies emit
methane gases. Carbon dioxide is now 30 percent higher in the earth's atmosphere than in preindustrial times; nitrous oxide is 19 percent higher.
These gases in the atmosphere are causing acute respiratory problems in
many cities, not only in the West, but in big cities worldwide.

Gases new to the earth's atmosphere, chlorofluorocarbons and other
chlorinated substances, are released by aerosol cans, air conditioners, and re-
frigerators. Bromide atoms come from halons in fire-extinguishing equipment and methyl bromide from pesticides. In the 1970s it began to become

apparent that these chemicals were causing holes in the ozone layer. At the stratospheric level (fifteen miles) the ozone layer deflects ultraviolet light from the sun. When holes in the ozone layer allow these ultraviolet rays to penetrate the earth, there are a variety of damaging results. Humans, especially with fair skin, experience increased skin cancers, and the elderly increased cataracts. The rays also damage the immune system, reducing defenses against infectious and fungal diseases. Radiation causes loss of plankton in the seas, affecting their ability to remove carbon dioxide from the atmosphere and affecting the marine food chain.[20]

When these dangers were first revealed there was widespread skepticism, but by the mid-1980s alternative technologies were emerging to replace some of the culprit technology. Thus in 1985 governments committed themselves to the Vienna Convention for the Protection of the Ozone Layer. Freezes by the mid-1990s and then phaseout of consumption of these substances by 2010 to 2015 were fairly readily agreed upon. It has been far more difficult to find a ready response to the recent data showing that many of these gases are trapping heat in the lower atmosphere, thus causing a slow global warming.

The earth receives an enormous quantity of energy in the form of sunlight. A naturally occurring layer of greenhouse gases allows the sunlight to pass through to be absorbed by the earth. These are then reflected back at longer heat wavelengths. Greenhouse gases absorb some of this heat, trapping it in the lower atmosphere. Without these gases the earth would be frozen and lifeless. But when greenhouse gas concentrations increase, more heat is trapped, causing temperatures to rise.[21]Although the concentration of these gases has varied over earth's history, causing fluctuations of temperature, a delicate balance of these gases in the atmosphere has kept these temperatures within a range that allows life to flourish (averaging about 57.2°F).[22] Since the nineteenth century and particularly in the second half of the twentieth century and into the twenty-first century, the vastly increased burning of fossil fuels has increased the percentage of greenhouse gases in the atmosphere beyond the range of natural occurrence, causing the 1990s to be the warmest decade of the last millennium. Average temperature increase in the twentieth century is about 1.4°F. In some areas, such as the poles, the rise as been as much as 9°F. Estimations are that if nothing is done about greenhouse emissions, global temperature rise could be as much as 5.4°F by the late or even mid-twenty-first century.

The effects of such a rise of temperature would have a dramatic impact on world climate. To mention a few likely results, climate will (and is already becoming) more erratic, with droughts and then violent downpours and flash floods. Melting polar icecaps and warmer waters will cause sea levels to rise, flooding coastal areas and causing entire island nations to disappear beneath the seas. Salts from the seas could creep up rivers and flood aquifers, diminishing the fresh water supply that is already scarce for agriculture and human consumption. Prolonged heat can change the pattern of propagation of birds and plants and cause mosquitoes to survive longer and at higher altitudes, thus causing outbreaks of mosquito-borne diseases, such as malaria and dengue fever. Agriculture will be severely stressed due to higher temperatures, drought, and floods in the tropics, while the Northern zones could profit from a longer growing year (although they would also be affected by a lessened snow fall).[23]

In order to stabilize greenhouse gases at their present level and prevent further rises, it is estimated that human-caused emissions (especially from burning fossil fuels) should be cut 70–80 percent. But the world politics of such agreements to cut emissions quickly became highly controversial. Such emissions are very unevenly distributed around the world, with wealthy industrial nations being the primary polluters, while poor nations, who cause relatively little emissions, would be the primary victims of such warming. The United States, with 4 percent of the world's population, accounts for 36.1 percent of the world's carbon dioxide emissions. Canada, Australia, Western Europe, the former Soviet Union, and Japan also have a high level of emissions. Altogether the industrialized world contributes up to 90 percent of greenhouse gases.[24] Thus deep cuts in emissions of these gases must come primarily from these industrialized countries, especially from the United States. Clearly the implication of such cuts is the phasing out of fossil fuels as the primary source of mechanical energy. The oil-producing countries, while not high polluters themselves, were also reluctant to accept this result, since it would cut into the primary source of their wealth.

The first line of defense of the industrialized nations, especially the United States, against such conclusions was to dispute the findings that temperature changes were caused by humans. The science was declared doubtful and inconclusive. By the mid-1990s scientific data had greatly improved, decisively confirming the reality of human causes of temperature rise. But coalitions of car manufacturers and oil companies banded together to continue to claim that the science was inconclusive, although such arguments were becoming increasingly discredited.[25]

The United Nations Convention on Climate Change was signed at the 1992 Earth Summit and entered into force in March 1994. It committed the signing nations to stabilize the concentrations of greenhouse gases at their 1990 level. There are 181 nations, as well as the European Union, party to this agreement. But by 1995 it became apparent that this agreement was inadequate and negotiations for a legally binding protocol began, culminating in the 1997 Kyoto Protocol, which committed the industrialized and former Eastern bloc nations to reduce their greenhouse emissions to 5.2 percent below 1990 levels during 2008–2012. The United States has consistently acted as the spoiler at these meetings, arguing for the inconclusiveness of the data, the unfairness of the cuts demanded of such high polluters as itself, and the need to lower the level of cuts and provide more trade-offs between high and low polluters, although the United States remained a party to the agreement during the Clinton administration.[26]

Then in March 2001 the new administration of George W. Bush abruptly withdrew from the negotiating process, citing the unfairness of the distribution of cuts. Despite this boycott by the United States, and even spurred by anger at the U.S. attitude, most nations persisted in the negotiations, with 178 nations reaching agreement on key details of the agreement in July 2001 in Bonn, Germany.[27] Nevertheless most climate scientists see the cuts agreed on as inadequate to address the problem and few industrialized nations have actually met their quotas of cuts so far. The United States actually increased their total emissions of carbon dioxide by 18.1 percent between 1990 and 2000. Japan, Canada, and Australia also increased their emissions, although the European Union decreased theirs by 1.4 percent. Russian emissions dropped by a dramatic 30.7 percent primarily due to the slowdown of its economy.[28]

Fossil-fuel burning industrialization is clearly on a collision course with the planet itself, with increasing disfunctionality due to arise in the next decades. What would it mean for the world economy to withdraw from its primary dependence on fossil fuels? Clearly a whole new world of new technologies, based on clean renewable energies, await development. Solar and wind energy, biomass, and hydrogen can power the machinery presently dependent on fossil fuels without the destructive impact on the health of the environment. The two-thirds world, often with abundant sunshine, could be aided to move directly to such renewable energy for its development, bypassing fossil fuels. Both a healthier and more equal world could emerge, although some of the effects of the present rise of greenhouse gases will linger in the atmosphere for some time.[29]

The problem then is one of a clash between the greed of the super-wealthy, who profit short term from the present fossil fuel economy, and planetary needs of both most humans and other living things. Yet the United States and other nations, who continue to cling to petroleum energy (and

fight world wars over it, as in Iraq), may soon be left behind by more inno-
vative parts of the world who are moving more creatively toward new technologies based on clean, renewable energy sources. This clash between fossil
fuel energy and global warming, with its implications for gross injustice to
poorer nations, will undoubtedly be key to issues of whether a "better world
is possible" in the twenty-first century. Small island nations threatened with
annihilation by rising seas have particularly voiced their alarm. In the words
of Maumoon Abdul Gayoom of the Alliances of Small Island States, "So let
me say this to the world: watch what happens to us, the small island states.
The threats we face today will not be limited to us alone. . . . Whatever our
fate tomorrow will be your fate the day after" (March 27, 1995).[30]

GLOBALIZATION AND INDUSTRIAL AGRICULTURE

Industrial agriculture has been growing in the United States, especially since
the Second World War. It has become the model of agriculture promoted
by U.S. agribusiness companies worldwide, with the support of the World
Bank and more recently the World Trade Organization. Traditional agriculture, in which farmers saved seed for the next sowing, shared seed with
neighboring farmers, built soils by integrating into them animal and plant
wastes, interspersed several crops in the same field for natural weed and pest
control, left hedgerows along the fields and rotated fields to allow them to
lie fallow periodically, integrated plants with raising animals and sold produce primarily in the local community, is seen as "primitive" and incapable
of providing the food needs of the world today.

The Fatal Harvest Reader: The Tragedy of Industrial Agriculture, edited by
Andrew Kimball, criticizes the global effort of agribusiness to supplant tra-
ditional methods of farming under the headings of "Seven Deadly Myths of
Industrial Agriculture."[31]

Myth 1: "Industrial agriculture is needed to increase food supply to keep
up with expanding population." In fact, adequate food to feed the world is already being produced. The primary reason that a growing number of humans
are hungry is because they are poor and unable to buy the food they need.
Industrial agriculture has greatly added to this poverty by driving out local
farmers and thus making more and more people dependent on buying high-
priced imported food, rather than growing it locally themselves.

Myth 2: "Industrial agriculture produces food that is safe, healthy and
nutritious." In fact, industrial agriculture is producing food that is increasingly unhealthy and unsafe because of the heavy use of pesticides to grow

it and irradiation to kill the pathogens created by long transportation chains and unhealthy ways of raising and slaughtering animals. It is made to look good by coloring added to meat and fruit, but it is often flat tasting and lacking in nutrition compared to locally produced organic food.

Myth 3: "Industrial agriculture provides cheap food and so is affordable for all." In fact, food grown by industrial agriculture is enormously expensive, if one factors in the costs of seeds, artificial pesticides, fertilizers, machinery, packaging, processing, and transportation, plus the damage it is doing to human and environmental health. It appears cheap only because of government subsidies and the passing along of these hidden costs to the public.

Myth 4: "Industrial agriculture is efficient, growing far more food per acre than traditional agriculture." In fact, industrial agriculture appears efficient only because it is based on single crops grown on huge acreage planted from edge to edge. But the damage it causes to the soil and environment means that output per acre drops after time and is maintained only by increased inputs of fertilizers and pesticides that only exacerbate the problems. Small organic family farms appear inefficient because they grow a variety of crops and animal products, but they actually produce two to six times more per acre than large industrial agribusinesses.

Myth 5: "Industrial agriculture is giving us far more choices in our food." In fact, modern supermarkets appear to offer a great variety only because long transportation chains are bringing food from all over the world without regard to local seasonal production. Also competitive packaging of products, such as breakfast cereals, appears to offer many choices, but their contents are largely identical. But industrial agriculture is actually destroying the enormous variety of species of foods, such as the thousands of types of rice, potatoes, corn, beans, fruits, and vegetables that have been bred by local farmers over the centuries, reducing the world's food supply to a dangerously narrow monoculture of a few species.

Myth 6: "Industrial agriculture protects the environment and wildlife." In fact, industrial agriculture is rendering our soil, air, and water highly polluted, threatening the very survival of adequate food production. By continually destroying the habitats of diverse varieties of plants and animals, as well as poisoning water and soil through pesticides, it is a major cause of extinction of hundreds of thousands of species of plants and animals.

Myth 7: "If industrial agriculture has problems with continually expanding healthy and abundant food, these can be fixed by biotechnology." In fact, biotechnology is greatly exacerbating these problems, threatening dangerous health consequences to humans and the environment, as well as further destruction of local sustainable farming.

The truth of this critique of industrial agriculture and its advancement into biotechnology can be made clear by a brief review of some of the data (which can be found in much greater detail in the current critical literature).[32] First, something about artificial fertilizers and pesticides. Interestingly enough, most of these chemical inputs were first developed in the First and Second World Wars, as nerve gases and material for bombs to kill humans and destroy foliage. Their use in agriculture expresses a mentality of looking at nature as something to be conquered and subdued, rather than as a living world that humans work with and within.[33]

Soil fertility is based on organic humus as a teeming community of living organisms. Organic farming renews and builds humus by decomposing plants and animal wastes and integrating them back into the soil. Artificial fertilizer, by contrast, is based on isolating the chemicals of plant fertility, such as nitrogen, phosphorous, and potassium, and applying them directly to the soils. This actually destroys soil biodiversity, diminishing the nitrogen-fixing bacteria and making soil less porous and more in need of water. Adding more water and chemicals increases this problem and causes soil erosion, draining nutrients off the soil and the chemically laden water into rivers. This causes nitrogen-choked waters that shut off oxygen and asphyxiate aquatic life.

From the farms of the Great Plains of the United States this runoff drains into the Mississippi Delta, forming a vast dead zone. It also contaminates aquifers and contributes to greenhouse gases. Ingested in humans, it reduces oxygen in human blood, causing the blood disease myoglobinemia. Enormous energy is used to produce this form of nitrogen (some 2200 lbs of coal to produce 5.5 lbs of nitrogen).[34]

Pesticides, also developed originally for war use, kill insects by such methods as blocking the nerve-impulse enzyme. But they also kill birds, fish, reptiles, mammals, as well as injuring humans or killing them in high doses. Cancers, and neurological, reproductive, and developmental damage, are some effects of pesticides on humans. It is estimated that from 3 to 25 million people are injured by pesticide use worldwide, especially farmworkers who come into direct contact with these substances.[35] In India, where forced incorporation into industrial agriculture caused the bankruptcy of many traditional farmers, money lenders encouraged farmers to commit suicide to pay their debts out of their liquidated assets; hundreds did so by swallowing pesticides.[36]

Corporate industrial agribusiness creates a global system of food trade that demands a vast transportation system. It is estimated that the food that appears on an American dinner plate has traveled an average 1300 miles.[37]

Often this trade results in ships passing one another with the same foods, such as India sending grain to the United States, while the United States sends grain to India. In 1998 Britain imported 240,000 tons of pork and 125,000 tons of lamb, while exporting 195,000 tons of pork and 102,000 tons of lamb.[38] Massive infrastructures of superhighways, railroads, ships, and planes are needed for this global food transport. This not only uses a great deal of fossil fuel energy, but also releases an enormous amount of toxics into the air and water. Pests are carried along within this transport system. Various kinds of doctoring and packaging are used to give the food a longer shelf life. Much food is wasted in this process, since only "perfect" fruits and vegetables, without spots or bruises, are allowed to appear on supermarket shelves.[39]

Factory farming of animals has been much criticized. I will only mention a few problems here. The crowding of animals in small spaces, the antibiotics used to prevent them from becoming diseased, and artificial stimulants to make them grow faster and irradiation of meat to kill resulting pathogens all add to the health hazards of meats produced in this way.[40] A recent fiasco of industrial meat production was the outbreak of mad cow disease in Britain in 1999, as well as smaller outbreaks elsewhere. Mad cow disease is caused by feeding herbivore cows animal protein to stimulate growth, derived from dead and often diseased sheep and even other cows. The result was scrapie brain disease that can also be passed to humans as the Creutzfeldt-Jacob brain degeneration disease.[41] Vandana Shiva contrasts what she calls "sacred cow cultures," which respect cows in an integrated system of farming, with "mad cow cultures" that treat cows as simply milk and meat producing machines.[42]

These drastic problems, however, have not suggested to corporate leaders the need to return to more organic, locally produced and marketed methods of agriculture, but rather the creation of a yet more globally integrated system that drives small farmers into bankruptcy. A few giant corporations, such as Monsanto and Dupont, control the entire process of food production and delivery from seeds, fertilizers, and pesticides to transportation, packaging, and delivery.

One way of seeking to either replace local farmers with agribusiness or make farmers dependent on agribusiness giants is the patenting of seeds. Slightly altered seeds are bred by combining traditional varieties, claiming superior characteristics of productivity and nutrition. These are then patented and the agribusiness claims ownership of them. Farmers are then sued by these companies for saving seed from harvests and replanting them; thus these companies seek to make farmers dependent on seed companies for their seed. American patent law allows those who breed a "new" seed to patent it, even if virtually the same seed has existed long before in other countries. Thus a Colorado farmer, Larry Proctor, bred a yellow bean from beans he bought in Mexico and patented it. He then claimed ownership of this bean worldwide, forbidding Mexicans from growing and selling this same bean that they had grown for centuries.[43]

This appropriation not only of seed but all the stages of food production from local farmers, forcing them into dependence as contract labor for corporate giants, is greatly extended by genetic engineering. Genetic engineering of seeds is done by breaking into the cellular structure of plants, forcing DNA from another plant or even an animal into the cell structure, thus producing plants with new characteristics. Viruses and bacteria are used to insert such foreign DNA into the cell. Antibiotic markers test whether the insertion has been successful. Thus human growth genes have been inserted into cattle and fish, fish genes into tomatoes, pesticide genes into corn, even firefly genes into tobacco to cause it to glow in the night![44]

One extraordinary product of such genetic engineering is the "terminator seeds" designed to go sterile after the first planting, thus creating a built-in "police" system to prevent farmers from saving and growing their own seed.[45] Other genetically engineered (GE) seeds are herbicide resistant soybeans that allow the spraying of herbicides on all the other plants between the rows of soybeans without killing the soybean plants. Needless to say the farmers who use these seeds are also dependent on the same company to provide them with the herbicides to be used with these seeds. Another GE seed is one that has a built-in insecticide which then kills insects that try to eat the plant. This is marketed as a "brilliant" way to reduce the use of insecticides.[46]

These genetically altered seeds also have built-in problems. Terminator seeds do not stay within the plants they are intended to produce, but drift to nearby plants and thus could cause mutations of new plants, both wild and domestic, that are incapable of reproducing themselves. Insecticides in plants work for a while, but typically result in new, more insecticide resistant super pests being produced, demanding additional and stronger insecticides. Likewise herbicide resistant plants help spark super weeds immune to the herbicides sprayed on them.[47] Moreover GE foods remain largely untested on humans, and U.S. corporations seek to market them without labeling their origins.[48] A variety of health hazards from them are likely, such as growing resistance to antibiotics that come from the antibiotic markers in such plants. Worldwide protest is rising against the growing and marketing of these seeds, even though there is growing use of them in both U.S. agriculture and global agribusinesses owned by U.S. companies.[49]

The World Trade Organization has largely adopted the perspective of corporate industrial agriculture as the only "way to go" and has adopted rules that reinforce the dependence of farmers on these "gene giant" corporations. Farmers who seed to grow their own seed are fined. The claims of corporations to exclusive rights over patented and GE seeds are upheld by intellectual property laws, forbidding local farmers from continuing to grow the seeds on which such manipulated plants were based, even though such plants originated with these farmers and have been grown by them for centuries.[50] The patenting of seeds and its defense as "intellectual property" of seed companies become a major expression of "biopiracy" of communities' rights to their traditional foods.[51] Global corporate agribusiness is causing a major crisis in the future of the entire human food supply, or what Vandana Shiva and others call the "hyjacking of the global food supply."[52]

THE PRIVATIZATION OF WATER
BY GLOBAL CORPORATIONS

A similar struggle is also shaping up over access and control of fresh water, so essential for the life of the whole earth. Although there is a vast amount of water on earth (some 1.4 billion cubic kilometers), most of it is salty. Only 2.6 percent of that amount is fresh and only a part of that is accessible in lakes, rivers, and aquifers. Fresh water is renewed through the hydrological cycle by which water evaporates, forms clouds, and falls as rain. Some studies have shown that the amount of fresh water on earth is actually decreasing due to human construction of houses and pavements that prevent water from being absorbed into the earth; instead this rain water runs off into seas.[53]

Agriculture uses the lion's share of water, about 65–70 percent, while industry takes 20–25 percent and domestic use 10 percent. With exploding human population, the use of water is accelerating, and many areas of the world and poorer sectors of the population are becoming water stressed. More than one billion people have no access to clean drinking water, and this figure is growing.[54] Human use of water is draining aquifers and lakes, and many rivers no longer flow into the sea. Even more troubling, these aquifers, lakes, and rivers have become heavily polluted though agricultural runoff and dumping of toxic wastes. Lack of access to clean water means that a large percent of the human population are afflicted by waterborne diseases.[55]

Unjust wealth and power also mean that the rich have far more access to water and also pay less for it than the poor. North Americans use 1,280 cubic meters of water per person per year, while Europeans use 694 cubic

meters, Asians 535, Latin Americans 311, and Africans 186. This maldistri-
bution is also found between rich and poor and between races within countries. Apartheid South Africa provided ample water for its white minority,
allowing for green lawns and swimming pools, while the black majority
lacked access to clean water. Although the new democratic government
promised to remedy this situation, it has largely continued. Of the 12 percent of water consumed by households, whites receive more than half, while
16 million black women walk at least a kilometer to carry water in buckets
back to their homes.[56] In many cities in Latin America water is delivered at
reasonable cost to the taps of wealthy households, while the urban poor buy
it by the can from private water carriers who may charge as much as 100
times the rate of the city services. [57]

Growing water scarcity is leading to many tensions between social sectors, regions, and nations. Industry and agribusiness seek to assure themselves of the lion's share of water in ways that deprive small farmers and
towns. Cities compete for water against rural areas. Regions within countries are in tension. There are cross-border tensions, such as between the
United States and Canada. Some areas of the world, such as the Middle East,
have major problems of water scarcity. This may become the spark for conflict, for example, between Israel, Syria, Jordan, and Lebanon, who share a
common water source coming down from Mount Hermon in Syria.

The conflict between Israel and the Palestinians has long involved water. Israel has confiscated most of the water from the Jordan River, siphon-
ing it to large farms in the Negev Desert. In both the West Bank and Gaza
Israel has appropriated most of the water, allowing settlers swimming pools
and green lawns, while leaving the Palestinians water-starved for agriculture
and domestic use. Israelis' per capita consumption of water is more than
three times that of Palestinians.[58] In 2003 Israel began to build a high wall
that enclosed the Palestinians in the West Bank in small enclaves. This wall
does not run along the green line (the truce line of 1949), but invades Palestinian lands, often totally enclosing villages or cutting villages off from their
lands. This wall also runs along the aquifer of the central region of Palestine, thus constituting a seizure of water as well as land.[59]

For large water corporations this growing world water stress is seen as
an opportunity for huge profits. The two largest water corporations are
Vivendi and Suez, both based in France, where water has long been managed by private corporations. These two corporations monopolize about 70
percent of the private water market and own or have a controlling interest
in water companies in 130 countries in all five continents.[60] These water
corporations do not only deliver water, but also control treatment plants for

water purification, transportation, waste management, and the construction of water delivery infrastructures. Vivendi also has a communications arm, which controls television, film, publishing, telecom equipment, and Internet services.[61]

These water giants, and others, such as Bechtel, who are seeking to break into the water market, aggressively define water as a commodity to be privatized and sold for profit. In country after country they seek to own or contract to deliver water services on a for-profit basis, promising the modernization of infrastructures, cleaner water, lower prices, and better service to the whole community. Many cities throughout the world have accepted such contracts, only to find themselves deeply disappointed, but also unable to easily withdraw from such agreements. Since privatized water corporations seek to make a profit, not to serve the community, once in control, they raise prices, lay off many of the workers, and cut off water services to those who cannot pay the inflated costs. But they often do not actually deliver the cleaner water that is promised.[62]

Water corporations envision a bonanza of profit by selling water. This involves international trade in which water will be delivered by tankers and even huge balloons dragged through the ocean. There is also an exploding sale of bottled water, not only to an elite market, but to poorer people who lack access to clean drinking water. Although the bottled water companies promise "pure spring water," they generally take such water gratis from tap water or lakes and sell it with some purification and added minerals. But such bottled water is not necessarily cleaner than the tap water or other sources from which they got it. Bottled water, as well as plans for international trade in water, threaten huge environmental costs in discarded plastic containers and fuels.[63]

The water corporations seek political power over local and state governments by sitting on international business councils and inserting a bias in favor of privatization of water as a commodity into trade rules upheld by regional trade treaties, such as NAFTA, and bilateral investment treaties between countries and the WTO. Thus when a city seeks to withdraw from contracts with a water corporation or prevent their water from being privatized, they are faced with suits that accuse them of putting impediments in the way of profits. The World Bank has also enforced the bias toward privatization of water, threatening indebted nations with denial of loans unless they privatize their water.[64] For such institutions of world trade and finance, corporations have a "right" to profits, while human beings do not have a "right" to water.[65]

WOMEN, POPULATION, ENVIRONMENT, AND RELIGION

Population expansion is a major factor in the worsening of environmental destruction. There is not, of course, a one-to-one relation between expanded human numbers, pollution, and resource scarcity. The high levels of consumption of the industrialized nations are the primary factor in this worsening ecological crisis. Industrialized nations, with the United States at the lead, consume far more water, use far more energy, and emit far more toxic wastes per capita than poor countries. In high-consuming countries, such as the United States, efforts to reduce the environmental impact of this high consumption, such as emissions from automobiles, are undone by the continued expansion of human numbers and the number of vehicles they drive. Yet even poor communities, when they double or triple in size, put a heavy burden on scarce resources. The ecological impact of human communities should be seen as a multiplication of human numbers times their level of consumption and times the technological inputs and waste emissions of their way of life.

Population has been growing exponentially, doubling in fewer and fewer years. In 1850 there were a billion people on the earth. By 1930 this number had doubled to two billion, and again by 1975 to four billion, and in 1999 it surpassed six billion. Although the number of children per family has dropped dramatically in the industrial world, and even in much of the developing world in the 1970s to 1990s, 77 million people continue to be added to the world every year. It is estimated that the 2002 world population of 6.2 billion will expand to between 7.9 and 10.9 billion by 2050.[66] Leveling off human population to replacement or below, that is, two children per family or less, is thus a legitimate concern for environmentalists. But this concern must not be isolated as a numbers game that targets the poor, but should be integrated with environmental justice aimed at reducing the high consumption of the rich and converting all societies to sustainable ways of living.

Too often, however, Western concern with population ignored the gender dimension of this question. It is women who bear the children and do much of the child raising. Hence the status of women is crucial to the question of population reduction. By the 1990s a criticism of population reduction programs that focused only on promoting contraception to poor people had grown in third world countries. Although leaders in this field agreed that many women wanted to reduce the size of their families to two or three children, this could not be accomplished simply by focusing on promoting contraception. Rather population must be seen in a holistic way, integrated with women's education and social empowerment, family and community health, nutrition, and adequate employment. It was found that raising the level of women's education, more than any other factor, was correlated with the reduction of the number of children women bore. This perspective on population and women's development was integrated into the United Nations International Conference on Population and Development in Cairo in 1994. Women's reproductive health and social development was recognized as an intrinsic human right. [67]

The United States was a supportive participant in this conference. At the Cairo conference governments agreed to spend $17 billion to achieve access to reproductive health services for all people by 2015, $10.2 billion of which would go for family planning services and $5 billion for maternal health care, the rest going for prevention of HIV/AIDS. The wealthy nations promised to provide a third of this amount, while developing nations would provide the rest. However wealthy nations have fallen far below their promises, spending less than 40 percent of what they promised, while developing nations have spent close to 70 percent of their goals. The United States, particularly, has fallen far below their promised aid. Particularly under the presidential administration of George W. Bush, the United States has all but repudiated the commitments it made at Cairo.

The Bush administration depends heavily on the Christian Right for support and increasingly has reflected the ideology of the Christian Right in its political and judicial appointments. In December 2000 newly elected President Bush nominated John Ashcroft as his attorney general, a man who, as attorney general and then governor of Missouri, had opposed contraceptive insurance coverage and signed a bill declaring that human life begins at conception. As U.S. attorney general Ashcroft has continued to follow a hard line not only against abortion but also against forms of contraception. For example, Ashcroft has pressured the Food and Drug Administration to deny over-the-counter sales of emergency contraception in drug stores, even though this medication is recognized as safe. He has also subpoenaed private medical records of women who have had abortions, and his Justice Department has argued in court that the law need not honor doctor-patient confidentiality.[68]

In December 2000 Bush also named antichoice Wisconsin Governor Tommy Thompson Secretary of the Department of Health and Human Services. Thomson also opposes abortion and has signed bills declaring that life begins at conception. On Bush's first day in office, January 22, 2001, he restored the global gag rule, that had been dropped by the Clinton administration. This rule denies U.S. funds to nongovernmental organizations if they provide abortion services, counseling referrals, or lobbying to change abortion laws, even if they are using moneys other than that from the United States for these activities.

President Bush has continually appointed antichoice men and women to represent the United States at international population conferences and as judges to circuit courts. For example, he appointed antichoice Michael McConnell to the 10th Circuit Court of Appeals, Dennis Shedd to the 4th Circuit Count of Appeals, Lavenski Smith to the 8th Circuit Court of Appeals, Charles Pickering to the 5th Circuit Court of Appeals, Carolyn Kuhl to the 9th Circuit Court of Appeals, and D. Brooks Smith to the 3rd Circuit Court of Appeals, thus virtually packing all these courts with judges hostile to family planning, to women's reproductive rights, and to abortion, even at the earliest stage of fetal development.

Bush reversed the U.S. support for the 1994 Cairo agreement that all couples and individuals have a right to freely determine the number and spacing of their children and to have the information and means to do so. President Bush sent Christian Right representatives to follow up UN conferences on population and development. The antichoice Christian Right delegates appointed to represent the United States at the Asian/Pacific conference on Population and Development in December 2002 tried to dismantle sex education programs, ban condom use for HIV/AIDS prevention, and block programs intended to prevent and treat unsafe abortions.

The Bush administration's catering to the Christian Right's war on women has also been expressed in other ways. One of his first acts as president was to close the White House office on Women's Initiatives and Outreach created by President Clinton in 1995. Bush also sought to strip contraceptive coverage from the Federal Employees Health Benefit Plan, although this was later restored by Congress. He has continually supported "abstinence only" education funding and has appointed representatives who promote these policies. This has also been applied to HIV/AIDS funding. For example, Patricia Funderburk Ware, who supports "abstinence only" policy to prevent HIV/AIDS, was appointed to head the Presidential Advisory Council on HIV/AIDS.

President Bush has been lauded for his promise of $15 billion in his January 2003 State of the Union address of HIV/AIDS funding for Africa.[69] But in March of that year this funding was effectively gutted by applying the global gag rule to these funds. Thus no agency that received these funds from the United States can counsel on abortion and contraception, including the use of condoms as a method to avoid contracting AIDS. Bush also froze $3 million in aid to the World Health Organization to prevent research on mifepristone, a pill that prevents the implantation of a fertilized egg. $200 million was also cut from funding programs for women's reproductive and maternal health in Afghanistan in August 2002.[70]

Although Bush appointees have supported laws that would establish the fetus as a human being, to be treated as a legal person from the first moment of conception, they have not equally promoted women's health care. Rather women's health is promoted only when they are host carriers of a fetus, but not for them as persons in their own right. For example, Tommy Thompson, as Secretary of Health and Human Services, extended the Children's Health Insurance Program to unborn children at any stage of development, but health care coverage was not extended to women either prenatally or postpartum. These are only a few of the actions taken by the Bush administration against women's reproductive health during the first two years of his presidency. The Bush administration is also very hostile to any form of "gay rights," and has threatened to support a constitutional amendment that would establish the legal definition of marriage as only between a male and a female.[71]

The Bush administration's hostility to women's reproductive rights not only reflects the point of view of the U.S. Christian Right, but also converges with a revival of right-wing or fundamentalist forms of religion around the world. Not only Protestant Christianity, but Catholicism, Islam, and even Buddhism, Confucianism, and Hinduism have seen fundamentalist or extreme conservative movements in the last several decades. In the 1990s this renewal of right-wing forms of religion was studied by teams of scholars brought together by historian Martin Marty, under the rubric of the "fundamentalist project."[72]

These studies found considerable similarities in these movements of conservative religion. Among these similarities is a strong rejection of modern secularism, although not modern technology (which is often used effectively to get across their message). All these movements seek to reinstate a union of religion and state, making strict religious observance of one dominant state religion the law of the land. In other words, they seek a Hindu, Buddhist, Christian, Jewish, or Islamic state, rejecting the modern development of separation of "church" and state. Religious pluralism, differences of religious worldview, both within the established religion and outside it, the tolerance of many religious traditions in the same society, all are rejected. Worsening of women's status is a key aspect of this fundamentalist backlash.

It is often assumed among Western liberals that progress in women's status toward equality with men is an irreversible and inevitable trend in all "modernizing" human societies. It is even assumed by some that "feminism" has largely accomplished its goals and can be left behind as a movement for women's rights. But global figures belie this optimism. In many areas of the world fundamentalist backlash is causing a regression of women's status. This regression is exacerbated by the growing disparity between rich and poor that often targets poor women disproportionately. Thus it is worthwhile to spend some time both on the continuing and even worsening low status of women in many parts of the world and the way in which corporate globalization is exacerbating this regression.

One of the most common characteristics found across all forms of fundamentalism, whether Christian, Muslim, Jewish, Hindu, or Confucian, is an effort to reinstate strict patriarchal norms for family and society. These movements threaten to reverse the tide of liberalization to equalize women's educational, social, and political status. Fundamentalists want fathers and husbands to be strictly dominant over daughters and wives. They believe that men and women should be defined as having totally different natures and roles, rooted in divine law and hence not subject to modification or change. Women should be confined to the home, to child-raising and service to the husband. In Islam this involves the reinstatement of strict codes of dress that cover the female body head to foot and sometimes even the face, shielding the female body from public gaze by any man not the woman's husband. Women are often forbidden to leave the house without a male relative as their escort.[73]

Women's person, body, and sexuality are defined as the property of their husband to be totally at his disposal, not under the woman's own control. This generally involves a rejection of abortion and sometimes even of birth control. It should be noted, however, that not all conservative Islamic regimes are anti-birth control. The Qur'an allows birth control, and the Islamic regime in Iran has drawn on this tradition to promote family planning nationally. Islamic clerics have even issued decrees (*fatwas*) approving family planning methods from oral contraceptives and condoms to sterilization. Family planning, including free contraceptives, has been integrated into primary health care, and men's responsibility for reproductive health has been strengthened. The result has been considerable success in reducing average child bearing in Iran from 5.6 children per couple in 1985 to 2.8 in 2000.[74]

Most fundamentalist religious movements are particularly concerned to cut off what they see as a pernicious corruption of traditional morality that would allow sexual relations outside of marriage or other than exclusively heterosexual relations (although traditional societies have always covertly allowed both of these for men). Ideally they believe that women should not work outside the home, especially in well-paid or publicly prominent professions that might rival the income of the husband or give women economic and social independence. More extreme Muslim fundamentalists even look askance at women's education. The extreme case of such views is found among the Taliban in Afghanistan who sought to forbid any education for women and girls, even at the primary school level. Although these regressive efforts are defended as the reinstatement of "tradition," some of them go beyond what actually existed in the past. Fundamentalism is a modern reactionary movement against secularism that seeks to establish a norm of total subordination of women to men as an unchanging ideal demanded by God.

This shared agenda among fundamentalists against women's reproductive rights, freer forms of sexuality, especially among the young, diverse forms of the family, particularly same-sex marriages, sometimes finds conservative religionists in alliance with each other across religious traditions. For example, at the United Nations conference on Population and Development at Cairo in 1994 the Vatican sought to ally with conservative Muslims to block any approval of artificial contraception, abortion, plural forms of the family, or the rights of women and girls to control their own sexuality. This outreach by the Vatican was not welcomed by all Muslims, however, and several Egyptian clerics issued statements defending the Qur'an's allowance of contraception and family planning.[75]

Religious conservatives have typically objected to international covenants and declarations that seek to eliminate all discrimination against women. They have insisted that such modern Western definitions of gender equality do not apply to religious laws that define women as different from men. For example, Islamic laws that decree that a daughter's inheritance from her parents should be one-half of what is received by sons cannot be challenged on the grounds of discrimination because it is based on divine revelation. Some fundamentalists have adopted the language of cultural relativism and respect for "difference" to insist that diverse cultural traditions toward the relation of men and women in society should be respected as a part of culture, especially when they are grounded in religious tradition. Efforts to define universal standards of gender nondiscrimination that should apply to all cultures are labeled "Western cultural imperialism," and feminists in particular are decried as "Western cultural imperialists."[76] Liberals find it difficult to respond to such arguments that steal postmodern arguments to defend premodern patriarchal societies.

Despite a wide success in promoting the ideal of women's equality as a principle worldwide, women in fact continued to suffer many forms of discrimination and even violence. This is partly a continuation of traditional patterns of patriarchal societies and partly due to a new fundamentalist backlash against modernity that makes women its particular target.

Violence to women continues to be an endemic problem worldwide. In developed countries women live somewhat longer than men, on average eighty years for women, compared with seventy-five years for men. Women predominate among the elderly. Fewer pregnancies and better health care are responsible for this longer life for women. However in Africa life expectancy is dramatically less, and women live shorter lives than men, on average forty-five years for women compared to forty-eight years for men. In Asia women also live shorter lives than men and are underrepresented in the total population, some ninety-five women per one hundred men.[77]

This underrepresentation of women, estimated to be some 60 million women who are missing in the world population,[78] is due to pervasive patterns of violence that begin before birth. In China the one child policy, combined with male child preference, means that there is a high level of female feticide and infanticide, resulting in a marked gender disparity in the total population. Female feticide and infanticide are also common in India and Pakistan. In India and Pakistan women also suffer a high level of violence in the home, together with lesser medical care and nutrition.[79] Ironically, women who are the food managers in the family suffer food discrimination due to social assumptions that men eat first and get the best food, while women eat the leftovers.

In India thousands of women have been killed or severely injured each year in dowry murders or attempted murders. These murders are caused by the high demands put on expected dowries for women, in which the husband and his family collude to murder the new bride in order to obtain a second bride and dowry.[80] Another form of assault on women is found primarily in Africa in the practice of female genital mutilation designed to remove women's capacity for sexual pleasure. An estimated 130 million women have undergone this cutting of their genitals, and another 2 million a year are subject to this practice, which can lead to a lifetime of painful urination, menstruation, and sexual intercourse and increased risk of death in childbirth. "Honor killing" also takes the lives of women in Islamic countries and families. In 2000 as many as 5,000 girls died at the hands of their parents and relatives because they were suspected of having sex or socializing inappropriately with males, or even because they had been raped.[81]

Girls and women are also more likely than men or boys to be sold into slavery, primarily for forced sexual prostitution. This means that hundreds of thousands of girls are sold by the parents, often with the promise that they will be given jobs as domestic servants. However, in fact, these girls are taken to big cities, where they find themselves virtually imprisoned in brothels. There they are subjected to continual sexual use, beaten, and threatened with death if they try to escape.[82] Such forced prostitution exists in high numbers in Asia, but is also found in North America. Dozens of Mexican girls have been brought to the United States with a promise of jobs, but found themselves imprisoned in brothels. In some cases large trucks at truck stops were the venue where these girls' sexual services were made available.[83]

Rape, incest, and battering plague women in all cultures and classes throughout the world. In 1998 the number of reported rape cases in the United States was 3.5 million.[84] There is no accurate account of the incidence of domestic violence, especially when one considers other forms of violence than physical, such as verbal and psychological abuse. It is estimated that some 22 percent[85] of women in the United States experience physical abuse by a husband or partner at some time in their life. In many societies beating his wife is considered a husband's right, upheld by custom and religious law. (One passage in the Qur'an explicitly allows a husband to beat and confine his wife.)[86] Women in many societies expect to be beaten and endure this throughout their marriage.

In addition to physical violence, women experience many other forms of discrimination. These other forms of discrimination are aggravated by patterns of violence and fear of violence. For example, a woman who is being beaten also has a hard time maintaining a steady job. Economically, women work longer hours than men and primarily work without pay. It is estimated that worldwide two-thirds of women's work is unpaid, while 75 percent of men's work is paid.[87]

When women work for pay, they are generally paid less than men. Women average between two-thirds and three-fourths of the average male wage worldwide. In the United States in 1998 the average male wage was $37,196, while the average female wage was $27,304. Men also gain more advantage from education than women. A man with a BA averages $54,524, while a woman with the same degree averages $39,786.[88] These averages mask the actual gender gap in income which is much wider when class and race are factored in. Most women, especially women of color, are clustered in low-paying "pink"-collar jobs, while top CEOs are mostly white males. Women account for only 5 percent of senior staff of the 500 largest corporations in the United States. Female-headed households are more likely to be in poverty than male-headed households. In the United States female-headed households account for a third of the children living in poverty.[89]

Education is also a major area where women still suffer discrimination, particularly in poorer countries. Two-thirds of the 876 million illiterate people of the world are female. In most African and many Asian countries girls are 80 percent less than boys in school enrollment and half of these girls drop out of school after the fourth grade. Although access to high school education is difficult for both men and women in poorer countries, women make up only 2 percent to 7 percent per thousand of those who attend high school and college.

Women also continue to have less civil rights than men. In countries as diverse as Botswana, Chile, Namibia, and Swaziland, married women are legally under the guardianship of their husbands and have no rights to own and manage property. Women also have lesser rights to divorce in many countries. Husbands in Bolivia, Guatemala, Syria, and most Arab countries can restrict a wife's choice to work outside the home. Women are not allowed to drive cars in Saudi Arabia. Women are also greatly underrepresented in government. Nordic nations have the highest percentage of women in parliament, with 39 percent of the seats in the lower and upper houses. But women hold only 15 percent of the parliamentary seats in the Americas, including the United States, and a scant 4 percent in Arab states. In 2000 in Dijbouti, Jordan, Kuwait, Palau, Tonga, Tuvalu, and Vanuatu, no women held seats in legislatures.[90]

These patterns of discrimination against women are aggravated by corporate globalization. Structural Adjustment policies enforced by the World Bank caused deep cuts in government investment in domestic welfare, as we have seen earlier in this chapter. Women typically suffer disproportionately from such cuts in domestic welfare spending. When education is no longer free or subsidized, poor families typically choose to spend their scarce income to educate the boys in the family, while keeping the girls at home to care for the children or sending them to work.

When health needs are no longer subsidized by the government, women are less likely to get the benefits of medical care. Moreover, since women are also the care providers, it is they who take primary responsibility for the sick and dying in the home. Women are usually the ones who take food and provide clean clothes, sheets, and nursing care in hospitals, when these are no longer provided. When health centers are closed down, women recover traditional herbal medicine, growing it in their gardens or gathering it in fields and forests to care for sick family members.

When local farming is wiped out, that sector of subsistence farming traditionally in the hands of women is particularly devastated. In Africa local farming has traditionally been done by women, but international promotion of agriculture goes almost entirely to male farmers with large landholdings that are able to make use of the seeds, pesticides, petroleum-based fertilizers, and mechanized tools of larger agribusiness. As Indian ecofeminist Vandana Shiva has shown, in India women traditionally integrated animals and plants, forests, fields, and home, feeding the animals from foliage from the forests or left over from harvests and using dung for fertilizer and fuel. This sector of sustainable agriculture is wiped out by the mechanized farming promoted by the Green Revolution, resulting in further impoverishment of women and their families, as well as falling water tables and polluted soil, water, and air.[91]

With the devastation of traditional means of survival, it is typically women who pick up the pieces with redoubled work. If water is scarce and polluted, women walk twice as far to carry it back to their homes on their heads. When firewood becomes scarce, women walk farther to carry it back in bundles on their heads. When devaluation causes the value of money to fall precipitously, women plant vegetables and fruits in their yards to produce food to sustain daily life.[92] Women go out to work to clean the houses of the rich. They produce food in their kitchen, weave baskets or create handicrafts, and hawk these goods in the informal market in the streets. If there is rising malnutrition, women create communal kitchens to feed the poorest women and children in the community.

Although this is seldom noticed, women in poor families are often poorer than the adult males of their own families. If there is a little money for a car, a radio, a wristwatch, or new clothes to be had, this is often appropriated by the adult males, while women go without and have to provide the means of daily subsistence for their children and even for adult males who give them little help. At the same time that they are redoubling their labor for daily survival, women are often suffering from the anger of unemployed men because of their loss of status. Women are beaten in their homes and raped in the streets, even as they struggle to provide the means of livelihood for their families. Women often give up food, clothes, and comforts for themselves to provide for their children, putting themselves last.

The displacement of subsistence farmers from their land in Mexico and Central America forced many to emigrate in search of work. The maquiladoras or factories for the assembly of such goods as clothes, electronic goods, and toys have been built in large numbers in free trade zones. One such area is the Mexican side of the U.S.-Mexican border. The preferred laborers in these factories are young women between the ages of sixteen and twenty-six. The low wages and toxic working conditions burn such women out by their late twenties. As we will see in chapter 4, the antisweatshop movement has focused on exposing the oppressive conditions in these factories.

This redoubled labor of women to bridge the gap of survival needs for themselves and their families also impels some women to found women's groups that become sites of resistance to the devastation wrought by globalization. Women form weaving or handicraft cooperatives and market their goods through alternative NGO (nongovernmental organization) networks. NGOs from developed countries and women in poor countries work together to create communal kitchens. For example, in Nicaragua, devastated by Structural Adjustment impoverishment after the fall of the Sandinistas, women created Ollas de Soya in the poorest neighborhoods. They mixed soy flour received from international NGOs with locally grown vegetables and fruits to create nourishing meals for those most threatened by malnutrition, especially pregnant women and small children.[93] In the final chapter when I talk of alternatives to globalization, I will detail some of these survival projects created by women.

As we have argued above, gender is a crucial but often invisible factor in the disparities of wealth and poverty worldwide. Religious fundamentalist backlash is worsening the status of women in many societies, while corporate globalization exploits this low status of women. Ecofeminism seeks to explore these interconnections between the exploitation of women and that of the natural world. But before moving on to a more in-depth discussion of the interconnections of religion, ecology, and women in chapters 2 and 3, I conclude this chapter by turning back to the ideologies that support corporate globalization. How has the secular language of neoliberal economics increasingly become buttressed by a religious rhetoric of apocalyptic warfare borrowed from religious fundamentalism in the late twentieth and early twenty-first centuries?

IDEOLOGICAL JUSTIFICATIONS FOR
GLOBALIZATION AND IMPERIAL WAR

The ideologies that justify this global system of domination, wealth, and impoverishment are a blend of neoclassical economic liberalism, and rhetoric drawn from religious fundamentalisms. I will first delineate neoliberal economic ideology and then describe its reinforcement by religious rhetoric. Neoliberal economic ideology is based on eighteenth-century English liberalism, but represents a narrowing and reduction of its humanism.[94] It is based on a materialist utilitarian anthropology that defines the human being as *homo economicus.* Humans are seen as autonomous rational subjects who act solely to maximize their individual self-interest. This self-interest is assumed to be purely economic, that is, to maximize their economic possessions.

This maximization of economic wealth is equated with human well-being and hence with happiness. The more one has the better off one is. The better off one is the happier one will be. Possessions are also equated with consumption and with domination of nature. The more one consumes the better off one is and so the happier one will be. The earth sets no intrinsic limitations to this endless growth and maximization of wealth. Humans are sovereign over the rest of nature whose capacity to produce wealth is assumed to be unlimited. Humans are also not to be constrained by concerns about the well-being of other people. Altruism, concern for other people, is assumed to interfere with one's own well-being or simply mask what is at bottom self-interest.[95] In this economist culture there is no basis for discussion of anything that might be called "the common good," but only of the self-interest of individuals, defined by instrumental reason.

This drive of every individual to maximize his (sic) self-interest is assumed to be self-regulating. Each person maximizing his own self-interest will be met by others equally seeking to maximize their self-interest, with a resulting harmony of well-being for all, that is, the "invisible hand" of Adam Smith. However, Adam Smith assumed a competitive world consisting of small, relatively equal local producers.[96] This theory has little to do with a world dominated by global corporations that hold the kind of monopolistic power Smith wished to dismantle.

This anthropology, that Cynthia Moe-Lobeda calls *homo economicus, consumens et dominans*,[97] is incorporated into economic theory through several dogmas. The first dogma is that economic growth benefits all humans. This dogma contradicts reality in several glaring ways. First, any economic activity which generates a market price is counted as growth, even if it is destructive activity, such as oil spills which then demand expenditures for clean-up. Depletion of environmental resources is not counted, but treated as an "externality." Cutting down a forest generates profits in lumber and so counts as growth, even though the source of this wealth is permanently undermined.

No account is taken of the distribution of wealth and income. Thus, if the average income and wealth are rising, this is treated as increasing wealth of all, even though this rise is created by the rich becoming much richer, while the poor are getting poorer and the middle class also is losing ground. Moreover if wealth made in one country is then taken out of that country by a transnational corporation, it is still counted as rising wealth within that nation. All economic agents are assumed to be equal, thus ignoring the huge disparity of wealth and power between transnational corporations and local businesses. These myopias create a system of economic theory and calculation that has little relation to reality.[98]

The second dangerous economic myth is the equation of market freedom with human freedom and democracy.[99] The system of maximization of profits of each individual, which presumably results in the harmonization of all self-interests, is claimed to work optimally only if there is no government regulation or outside interference. Thus any regulation of the market must be dismantled in order to create a "free" market. Since the freedom to invest and make money at will is equated with human well-being, freedom, and happiness, any controls over the market diminish human freedom, happiness, and well-being.

This myth again contradicts reality at several glaring points. It ignores the enormous disparity of power between global corporations and local farmers and producers. If they are put out of business by larger corporations, this is not counted as loss of well-being, freedom, and happiness. If farmers are forbidden to grow their own seed and be self-initiating agriculturalists, this is not counted as loss of freedom and well-being. Since these corporations largely control the political process, so-called democratic elections become an exercise in choice between rival plutocrats or representatives of the wealthy. This lack of ability to choose political leaders that represent the interests of the majority of the people is not counted as a loss of democracy.

Corporations also overwhelm the governments of many nations, creating trade rules that forbid national governments from legislating in favor of human rights, just working conditions, and environmental protection, but this is not counted as loss of freedom. The only freedom that counts as freedom and hence as a human right is market freedom, that is, freedom from any constraints on the making of money, even if this is creating severe costs for the well-being of the majority of the people and of the earth.

The third market myth is that this system is natural, normative, and inevitable. This dogma was expressed by British Prime Minister Margaret Thatcher as TINA, "there is no alternative." These market rules are assumed to be built into the very nature of things. They express the "natural law" of how economies must be organized and can only be organized to work optimally. These rules thus become normative and "God-given," in the sense of being in accord with "Nature." They are seen as teleologically redemptive, that is, as expressing the laws of human progress. Only by adhering to these laws can the human enterprise on the earth endlessly progress toward a better and happier world.[100] This market myth denies that neoliberal market economics are actually a human construct. Moreover, it is a system that is causing great harm to the well-being of most humans and is ecologically unsustainable. For these reasons, far from working spontaneously, is must be constantly enforced. Its rules have to be backed by economic coercion in the form of large fines, boycotts, and embargoes against producers and governments that defy these rules. Ultimately it is backed up by military power, by the U.S. military in particular.

This worldview of neoliberal economics is overtly secular and appeals to the truth claims of scientific method, but it is covertly theological. It constitutes a religion with an anthropology, a teleology, and theory of redemption. This secular religion has at least since the post–World War II Cold War become the civil religion of the U.S. political and economic ruling class. Any major deviation from it, critique of it, and quest for an alternative is treated as heresy to be suppressed. With the administration of George W. Bush this civil religion has been supplemented by two other religious rhetorics, patriarchal sexual fundamentalism and messianic nationalism.

We have already alluded to the importance of patriarchal sexual fundamentalism in the Bush administration in the previous section of this chapter on women and reproductive rights. Not only abortion from the first moment of conception, but any form of contraception that might entail prevention of implantation of a fertilized egg, is rejected in the leaders favored by the Bush administration. "Abstinence only" policies reject contraception outside of marriage, even to prevent AIDS. Anything other than traditional heterosexual marriage is frowned upon.

The reasons why this patriarchal sexual fundamentalism has come to be so prominent in this administration are puzzling. Extreme concern for "life" before birth is clearly not matched with any great concern for life after birth! Yet social conservatives would seem to have a stake in reducing the numbers of the poor, preferably before birth, rather than after, even if they are hostile to any suggestion that the rich should reduce their consumption. One can only assume that sexual control over others, women, sexual minorities, youth, has a powerful symbolic and psychological role in the ideology of domination. In making such appeals to "family values" sexual fundamentalism, Bush wishes to establish his credentials as a true, right-thinking Christian with his supporters among patriarchal Protestant and Catholic conservatives.

The critique of American politics in this chapter has focused primarily on the Bush administration. This could give the misleading impression that the policies of this administration are strikingly different from those of earlier administrations, such as that of President William Clinton. In fact the Clinton administration pursued much the same agenda as that of Bush in terms of corporate globalization. What has changed with the Bush administration is more a matter of further extremes of a direction already taken. This is expressed in a more forthright unilateralism and also the adoption of a rhetoric of apocalyptic warfare to justify this unilateralism.

This religious rhetoric, which became prevalent in the Bush administration, particularly after 9/11 (the terrorist attacks on the World Trade Center in New York and the Pentagon near Washington, D.C., on September 11, 2001), adopts the language of messianic nationalism. The proclivity for such messianic nationalism is by no means new with the Bush administration. The United States has long entertained a sense of itself as unique and divinely chosen to be a model and mentor for the rest of the world, both in its economic and political system and in its "way of life." A language approaching holy war has tended to rise whenever the United States launches a war against "enemies." But this rhetoric of holy war has become more blatant with the current "crusade" against "terrorism."

Juan Stam, a Puerto Rican pastor and theologian, has analyzed George W. Bush's religious rhetoric and found that it weaves together the language of apocalyptic warfare with that of a messianic mission.[101] The war against terrorism, first against al-Qaeda in Afghanistan and then against Saddam Hussein in Iraq, is depicted as an episode in an apocalyptic drama of good against evil; the angels of light against the forces of darkness; America, God's chosen people, against God's enemies. This language of apocalyptic warfare against evil assumes an American messianic mission to the world. America in general and Bush in particular are depicted as messianic agents of God in combating evil and establishing good, the will of God, on earth.

This apocalyptic messianic nationalist language was expressed in its most blatant form by General William Boykin, a conservative Protestant Christian charged with the hunt for Osama bin Laden. In speeches to his religious constituency Boykin declared that America is the object of hatred from other nations because we are uniquely a "Christian nation." Boykin went on to claim that "our spiritual enemies can only be conquered when we confront them in the name of God" (i.e., they are actually "Satan"). He then went on to claim that Muslims worship an idol and not the true God. Boykin opined that God has put George W. Bush in the White House at this time to carry out a messianic mission. "We are an army of God raised up for such a time as this."[102]

In other words, George Bush is God's elect messiah put in power to lead the apocalyptic war of God's true people against the demonic forces of the last days. American military conquest, carried out to put the American "democratic" system in place over the rest of the world, will, in effect, "destroy evil" and establish God's reign on earth. Although the Pentagon distanced itself from Boykin's language, they did nothing to counteract it. Significantly, two of Bush's neoconservative supporters, Richard Perle and David Frum, do not hesitate to label the crusade to "win the war on terrorism" as signifying "an end to evil."[103]

Such "hot" messianic apocalyptic language would seem to be very far from the "cool" language of neoliberal economics. But what we see in this administration is that all three of these languages: market freedom as "democracy," sexual fundamentalism, and messianic nationalism, work together in tandem, appealing to different constituencies, but also overlapping and being identified with each other. All three languages of absolutization of "one right way" work together to disempower and silence any discussion of alternatives.

People who advocate alternatives, economically or politically, are not simply regarded as misguided. They are rapidly becoming labeled as traitors, terrorists, and "enemy aliens."[104] The purpose of such combined ideologies is to put any critical discussion of these policies beyond the pale of public American discourse and to disable the very possibility of countermovements. Where the Christian churches are or should be in all this appropriation of Christian language, in what amounts to an American version of the heresy of "German Christianity,"[105] remains to be discussed in our concluding chapter.

NOTES

1. See "The Legacy of Inequality: Colonial Roots," in *Rethinking Globalization: Teaching Justice for an Unjust World*, Bill Bigelow and Bob Person, eds. (Milwaukee, Wisc.: Rethinking Schools, 2002), 31–60; also Edwardo Galeano, *Open Veins of Latin America Five Centuries of the Pillage of a Continent* (New York: Monthly Review Press, 1998); Adam Hochschild, *King Leopold's Ghost: A Story of Greed, Terror and Heroism in Colonial Africa* (New York: Mariner Books, 1998).

2. See Bruce Rich, *Mortgaging the Earth: The World Bank, Environmental Impoverishment and the Crisis of Development* (Boston: Beacon, 1994), 49–106; also Susan George and Fabrizio Sabelli, *Faith and Credit: The World Bank's Secular Empire* (San Francisco and Boulder: Westview Press, 1994), 1–57. Similar material is covered in John Cobb, *The Earthist Challenge to Economism: A Theological Critique of the World Bank* (New York: St. Martin's Press, 1999), 61–89.

3. See Rich, *Mortgaging the Earth*, 186–289; George and Sabelli, *Faith and Credit*, 58–72, and Cobb, *Earthist Challenge*, 90–107.

4. See Sharon Hostetler et al., *A High Price to Pay: Structural Adjustment and Women in Nicaragua* (Washington, D.C.: Witness for Peace, 1995).

5. Critiques of World Bank and WTO policies and structural adjustment abound: see, for example, Ralph Nader et al., *The Case Against "Free Trade:" GATT, NAFTA and the Globalization of Corporate Power* (San Francisco: Earth Island Press, 1993); Kevin Danahern, *50 Years Is Enough: The Case Against the World Bank and the International Monetary Fund* (Cambridge, Mass.: South End Press, 1994); Debi Barker and Jerry Mander, *Invisible Government: The World Trade Organization—Global Government for a New Millennium* (San Francisco: International Forum on Globalization, 1999); Walden Bello, *The United States, Structural Adjustment and Global Poverty* (London: Pluto Press, 1994).

6. See George and Sabelli, *Faith and Credit*, 112–34, 190–296.

7. See Vandana Shiva, *Biopiracy: The Plunder of Nature and Knowledge* (Boston: South End Press, 1997; also Vandana Shiva, *Stolen Harvest: The Hijacking of the Global Food Supply* (Boston: South End Press, 1999); Maude Barlow and Tony Clarke, *Blue Gold: The Battle against Corporate Theft of the World's Waters* (New York: New Press, 2002).

8. See Cynthia Moe-Lobeda, *Globalization and God: Healing a Broken World* (Minneapolis: Fortress Press, 2002), 40–41; also The Council of Canadians, "The MAI Inquiry: Confronting Globalization and Reclaiming Democracy," (Toronto: Council of Canadians, 1999).

9. See Walden Bello, *The Future in Balance: Essays on Globalization and Resistance* (Oakland, Calif.: Food First and Focus on the Global South, 2001), 93–94.

10. A useful primer on global inequality in its myriad dimensions is Bob Sutcliffe, *100 Ways of Seeing an Unequal World* (London: Zed Press, 2002).

11. Moe-Lobeda, *Globalization and God*, 28. On World Bank figures on global poverty, see www.worldbank.org/poverty.

12. For data on continuing inequality in South Africa, see the report of the South Africa Empowerment Commission, 2000, 2001, www.hmfonline.co.za/bee-rep.htm; also Abebe Zegeye, *Our Dream Deferred: The Poor in South Africa* (Pretoria: UNISA Press, 2002).

13. See David Blair, *Degrees of Violence* (London: Continuum, 2002): also Catherine Buckle, *African Tears: The Zimbabwe Land Invasion* (London: Covos Day Books, 2001), and Philip Gourevitch, *We Wish to Inform You that Tomorrow We Will Be Killed with Our Families* (New York: Picador, 1998).

14. Amy Chua, *World on Fire: How Exporting Free Market Democracy Breeds Ethnic Hatred and Global Instability* (New York: Anchor, 2003), 123–45, 163–75.

15. Ibid.

16. Ibid., 229–58.

17. See C. V. Woodward, *The Strange Career of Jim Crow* (New York: Oxford University Press, 1966). On the more recent hijacking of democracy in the United States, see David Korten, "Buying Out Democracy," in his *When Corporations Rule the World* (San Francisco: Berrett-Koehler Publishers, 1995), 141–48; also William Grieder, *Who Will Tell the People? The Betrayal of American Democracy* (New York: Simon and Schuster, 1992).

18. Gary MacEoin, *No Peaceful Way: Chile's Struggle for Dignity* (New York: Sheed and Ward, 1974).

19. Chua, *World on Fire*, 147–62, 289–94.

20. Dinyar Godrej, *The No-Nonsense Guide to Climate Change* (Oxford: New Internationalist Publications, 2001), 37–43.

21. Ibid., 17.

22. Ibid., 12.

23. Ibid., 44–86.

24. Ibid., 104.

25. Ibid., 85–118. See also Seth Dunn and Christopher Flavin, "Moving the Climate Change Agenda Forward," in *State of the World, 2002* (New York: Norton, 2002), 38–50.

26. On the struggle over the accords at Kyoto and particular the contribution of the World Council of Churches to the discussion of climate as a justice issue, see David G. Hallman, "Climate Change: Ethics, Justice and Sustainable Community," in *Christianity and Ecology: Seeking the Well-Being of Earth and Humans*, Dieter T. Hessel and Rosemary Radford Ruether, eds. (Cambridge, Mass.: Harvard University Press, 2000), 453–71.

27. *State of the World 2002*, 29. On the Bonn accords and the refusal of the other nations to accept the U.S. rejection, see Tony Karon, "When it Comes to Kyoto, the U.S. is the 'Rogue Nation,'" July 24, 2001, *Time*, available at www.time.com/world/article/0,8599,168701,00.html.

28. Ibid., 35.

29. Godrej, *No-Nonsense Guide*, 119–36.

30. Ibid., 112.

31. *The Fatal Harvest Reader: The Tragedy of Industrial Agriculture*, Andrew Kimbrell, ed. (Washington, D.C.: Foundation for Deep Ecology, Island Press, 2002), 3–36.

32. Ibid, *passim*; also Vandana Shiva, *Stolen Harvest: The Hijacking of the Global Food Supply* (Cambridge, Mass.: South End Press, 2000); Marc Lappé and Britt Bailey, *Against the Grain: Biotechnology and the Corporate Takeover of Your Food* (Monroe, Maine: Common Courage Press, 1998); Rick Welsh, *Reorganizing U.S. Agriculture: The Rise of Industrial Agriculture and Direct Marketing* (Greenbelt, Md.: Henry A. Wallace Institute for Alternative Agriculture, August, 1997); Helena Norberg-Hodge, *From the Ground Up; Rethinking Industrial Agriculture* (New York: Zed Books, 1993).

33. See Ron Kroese, "Industrial Agriculture's War against Nature"; also Jason McKenny, "Artificial Fertility: The Environmental Costs of Industrial Fertilizers," Monica Moore, "Hidden Dimensions of Damage: Pesticides and Health;" and "Nuclear Lunch: The Dangers and Unknowns of Food Irradiation," in *Fatal Harvest Reader*, 92–105, 123, 134, and 162,

34. McKenny, "Artificial Fertility," 121–29.

35. Moore, "Hidden Dimensions of Damage," 130–47.

36. Shiva, *Stolen Harvest*, 10, 101; also see Bigelow and Peterson, *Rethinking Globalization*, 226.

37. Rebecca Spector, "Fully Integrated Food Systems," in *Fatal Harvest Reader*, 289.

38. Debi Barker, "Globalization and Industrial Agriculture," In *Fatal Harvest Reader*, 257.

39. Ibid., 249–63.

40. Colby, "Nuclear Lunch," ibid., 161–65. Also David Coats, *Old MacDonald's Factory Farm* (New York: Continuum, 1989).

41. See Richard W. Lacey, *Mad Cow Disease: The History of BSE in Britain* (Channel Islands: Cypsela Publications Limits, 1994).

42. Shiva, *Stolen Harvest*, 51–71.

43. See Sandy Tolan, "The Mystery of the Yellow Bean: The Politics of Patenting Foods," in Bigelow and Peterson, *Rethinking Globalization*, 223–26. On patenting law and the history of patenting biological organisms, see Vandana Shiva, *Protect or Plunder: Understanding Intellectual Property Rights* (London: Zed, 2000).

44. Joseph Mendelsohn III, "Untested, Unlabeled and You're Eating It: The Health and Environmental Hazards of Genetically Engineered Food," *Fatal Harvest Reader*, 148–60; also Bill Lambrecht, *Dinner at the New Gene Café: How Genetic Engineering Is Changing What We Eat, How We Live and the Global Politics of Food* (New York: St. Martin's Press, 2001).

45. See Martha L. Crouch, "From Golden Rice to Terminator Technology, Agricultural Biotechnology Will not Feed the World or Save the Environment," see www.edmonds-institute.org/crouch.html.

46. Shiva, *Stolen Harvest*, 79–116.

47. Ibid.

48. Mendelsohn, "Untested, Unlabeled and You're Eating It."

49. Shiva, *Stolen Harvest*, 117–23. See also the Open Letter from the Karnataka State Farmers Association, declaring their intention to burn fields of GE engineered plants: "We Will Reduce Your Fields to Ashes," in Bigelow and Perterson, *Rethinking Globalization*, 228–29.

50. Shiva, *Biopiracy*.

51. Ibid.

52. Shiva, *Stolen Harvest*.

53. Maude Barlow and Tony Clarke, *Blue Gold*, 12. See also Vandana Shiva, *Water Wars: Privatization, Pollution and Profit* (Boston: South End Press, 2002).

54. Ibid., 24; also see Sandra Postel, *Last Oasis: Facing Water Scarcity* (New York: Norton, 1992).

55. Barlow and Clarke, 26–76.

56. Ibid., 56, 69.

57. Ibid., 59.

58. Ibid., 72.

59. For the map of the wall Israel is building in the West Bank, see www.btselem.org. Palestinians in the Tulkarem and Qalqiliya areas have been deprived of about 20 percent of their water by the wall: personal communication from Brother

David Scarpa of Bethlehem University: dscarpa@bethlehem.edu. See also Palestinian Environmental NGO network (PENGON), www.pengon.org.

60. Barlow and Clarke, *Blue Gold*, 85, 107–17.

61. Ibid., 113.

62. Ibid., 102–27.

63. Ibid., 96, 130–52.

64. Ibid., 160–80.

65. On the struggle to define water as a right, not simply a "need," see ibid., xxi–xxiii.

66. *State of the World, 2002*, 129–30.

67. For a comparison of the Cairo Program of Action and the moral teachings of the Catholic Church, see *El Cairo y la Iglesia Católica* (Washington, D.C.: CFFC/CCD, 2004).

68. NARAL e-mail report, February 13, 2004.

69. See Amy Goldstein and Dan Morgan, "Bush Signs $15 Billion AIDS Bill; Funding Questioned," in the *Washington Post*, May 28, 2003.

70. The above information on the Bush administration and reproductive rights came from J. Bernstein, "The Bush Administration's Assault on Women, a Chronology," February 24, 2003, a NARAL paper.

71. Ibid.

72. Martin Marty and R. Scott Appleby edited a series of books on comparative fundamentalisms in world religions in the mid-1990s, published by the University of Chicago Press. For the major volume in the series that touches on gender issues, see *Fundamentalisms and Society: Reclaiming the Sciences, the Family and Education* (Chicago: University of Chicago Press, 1994).

73. See Courtney W. Howland, ed. *Religious Fundamentalisms and the Human Rights of Women* (New York: St. Martin's Press, 1999). Also John Stratton Hawley, ed. *Fundamentalism and Gender* (Oxford: Oxford University Press, 1994).

74. *State of the World, 2002*, 141.

75. See Rosemary Ruether, "An Alliance that Fizzled," *Conscience* 15, no. 4 (Winter 1994–95), 52–53.

76. Rosemary Ruether, "Culture and Women's Rights," *Conscience* 16, no. 4 (Winter 1995–96), 13–15.

77. Bob Sutcliffe, *100 Ways of Seeing an Unequal World* (London: Zed, 2001), secs. 23, 33.

78. *State of the World 2002*, 144

79. Sutcliffe, *100 Ways of Seeing Inequality*, sec. 34.

80. Ranjana Kumari, *Brides Are not for Burning: Dowry Victims in India* (Delhi: Radiant, 1989), also Veena Talwar Oldenburg, *Dowry Murder: The Imperial Origins of a Cultural Crime* (Oxford: Oxford University Press, 2002).

81. *State of the World 2002*, 144.

82. Susan Thistlethwaite and Rita Nakashima Brock, *Casting Stones: Prostitution and Liberation in Asia and the United States* (Minneapolis: Fortress, 1996).

83. There have been numerous cases of Mexican immigrant women forced into prostitution in the U.S.: see Peter Landesman, "The Girls Next Door," *New York Times*, January 25, 2004, sec.6, 30. Also "Immigrants were Allegedly Forced into Prostitution," *Los Angeles Times*, April 9, 2004, B5.

84. *World Almanac 2000*, 906.

85. See "Not a Minute too Soon: Facts and Figures. Domestic and Intimate Violence," www.Uniform.org/campaigns/November25/facts_figures.

86. Surah 4: An-Nisa': 34 reads in the English translation of the Arabic text by A. A. Maududi, "As for those women whose defiance you have cause to fear, admonish them and keep them apart from your beds and beat them." For discussion of this text, see Riffat Hassan, "Feminism in Islam," *Feminism in World Religions*, Arvind Sharma and Katherine Young, eds. (Albany, N.Y.: SUNY Press, 1999), 263–64.

87. Sutcliffe, *100 Ways of Seeing an Unequal World*, sec. 59.

88. *World Almanac 2000*, 151.

89. *State of the World 2000*, 133.

90. Ibid.

91. Vandana Shiva, *The Violence of the Green Revolution*.

92. These remarks are based on my experiences in Zimbabwe in the mid-1990s where Structural Adjustment had cut the value of the Zimbabwe dollar to a tenth its former value and middle-class professors' wives were growing greens in their gardens to have enough to feed their families.

93. These remarks about women's survival strategies in Nicaragua are based on my own trips to that country in the 1990s.

94. On the roots of free market ideology in classical liberalism, see Cynthia Moe-Lobeda, *Globalization and God: Healing a Broken World* (Minneapolis: Fortress Press, 2002), 63–65.

95. Ibid., 59–60.

96. For a critique of the misuse of Adam Smith's idea of the "invisible hand" by global capitalist economics, see Moe-Lobeda, *Globalization and God*, 199, note 67.

97. Moe-Lobeda, *Globalization and God*, 59.

98. Ibid., 148–53. I have followed Moe-Lobeda in the delineation of these "market myths," but with additions of my own comments and organization.

99. Ibid., 153–58.

100. Ibid., 161–63.

101. Juan Stam, "El lenguaje religioso de George W. Bush: Análisis semántico y teológico," *Signos de Vida* (Puerto Rico), June 2003.

102. On General William Boykin's remarks, see Brian Knowlton, *International Herald Tribune*, October 22, 2003; also Odai Sirri, *Aljazeer.Net*, October 19, 2003.

103. Richard Perle and David Frum, *An End of Evil: How to Win the War on Terrorism* (New York: Random House, 2003).

104. Des Moines peace activists were summoned before a federal grand jury linked to antiterrorism surveillance. After an outcry, this summons was dropped. See

article by Tim Schmitt, "Victory," in *Pointblank: Des Moines Metro Area Alternative Weekly*, February 18, 2004.

105. In 1934 Christians in Germany, led by Karl Barth, issued the Barmen Declaration calling for rejection of and resistance to "German Christianity," a Christianity that glorified Hitler as a Messiah and preached racial exclusivism as biblical. See Robert McAfee Brown, *Kairos: Three Prophetic Challenges to the Church* (Grand Rapids, Mich.: Eerdmans, 1990).

2

THE GREENING OF
WORLD RELIGIONS

In 1967 historian of science Lynn White published a challenging article in *Science*, "The Historical Roots of Our Ecologic Crisis."[1] In this article White argued that the Christian religion had played a major role in causing disregard for nature in Western civilization. Specifically, the passage in Genesis 1:26, "Let us create man in our image, after our likeness and let them have dominion over the fish of the sea and over the birds of the air and over the cattle and over all the earth and over every creeping thing that creeps upon the earth," was the source of a claim to unbridled mastery of humanity over nature that is the root of the ecological crisis. White dubbed Christianity "the most anthropocentric religion the world has seen."[2]

White's article was read by environmentalists as a total dismissal of Christianity as having any positive resources for ecology, although White himself was more nuanced. Even the view quoted above was qualified with the phrase, "In its Western form," suggesting that Eastern Christianity might be more nature friendly. He warned that Christianity was complex and contained a variety of traditions. Most specifically he lifted up St. Francis of Assisi as trying to "depose man from his monarchy over creation and set up a democracy of all God's creatures." He also declared that science and technology were so "tinctured with orthodox Christian arrogance toward nature that no solution to our ecologic crisis can be expected from them alone." White believed that an alternative worldview was necessary, and this alternative must be religious. "Since the roots of our trouble are so largely religious, the remedy must also be essentially religious."[3]

This article sent Christian theologians scrambling to defend their traditions from what seemed like an unequivocal condemnation. Jewish and Christian scholars of the Bible began to search their Scriptures for more positive views of the human-nature relationship. White's claim, echoed also in other ecological thinkers, such Thomas Berry, is that the ecological crisis is not simply a matter of poor use of technology. It is rooted in religious worldviews and needs a new religious worldview to heal it. This suggests that all the religions should examine their traditions to find the roots for such revisioning.[4] Westerners have sometimes looked to Asian or indigenous traditions for ecological salvation on the assumption that these religions celebrated the sacrality of nature and the presence of the divine in all things, and so could provide a more ecological cosmology.

The 1980s and 1990s saw a variety of books that began to examine the ecological potential of Christianity and also to compare worldviews of different religions from the perspective of ecology. The volume *Worldviews and Ecology*, edited by Mary Evelyn Tucker and John Grim, both professors of religious studies at Bucknell University,[5] looked at the worldviews of Native Americans, Judaism, Christianity, Islam, Baha'i, Hinduism, Buddhism, Jainism, Daoism, and Confucianism, as well as recent movements, such as process theology, deep ecology, and ecofeminism, for insights on the development of a needed worldview for what Thomas Berry called the "ecozoic age."[6]

In the mid-1990s Tucker and Grim became the organizers of a massive project through the Harvard University Center for the Study of World Religions to examine all the major world religions, including indigenous religions, for their ecological import. This took the form of ten major conferences put on between 1996 and 1998 on ecology in Buddhism, Confucianism, Judaism, Christianity, Islam, Hinduism, Daoism, Jainism, Shinto, and indigenous religions. The conferences assembled hundreds of scholars across these faiths to ponder both their problems and their positive ecological potential. These ten conferences were followed by a culminating gathering that sought to compare the different religious worldviews and put them in dialogue with science and economics on questions of environmental ethics. Each conference issued in a major book published by the Harvard University Press.[7]

In this chapter I survey the major conclusions of these conferences. I show some of the difficulties of assuming a straightforward relationship between the worldviews of particular religions of the world and the treatment of nature. For some thinkers, the primary cause of ecological degradation is not traditional religions, but an aggressive new worldview coming from secular science, technology, and economics that fosters an unbridled consumerism and instrumental view of nature. This modern worldview may or may not have roots in the Bible. Even if one believes that this is not the case, all traditional religious worldviews, whether that of the Abrahamic faiths of human stewardship of nature under God or the Hindu view of the sacrality of the land and its rivers and forests, have so far mounted little protest against the destructive impoverishment of the earth by modern "development." The environmental crisis is itself a new issue created by global industrialization and population expansion, and thus one should not expect ancient religions to have addressed it intentionally. The key issue is then, how do religions translate their worldviews into environmental ethics in practice today?

Although some of the above-mentioned collections of articles on ecology and world religions make connections between worldviews and gender, this topic is not central in these works. Yet more absent is attention to issues of class, race, and cosmology. How religious worldviews correlate the hierarchy of the divine over the human, the spiritual over the material, with the hierarchy of male over female, and with elites over subjugated groups, such as the untouchables in the Hindu caste system, is a question that is mostly ignored in the discussion of how religious worldviews are related to environmental ethics. Do religions impede or promote environmental pollution when they identify ritual impurity or pollution with certain bodily functions, particularly those connected with female sexuality, such as menstruation and childbirth? How is environmental pollution affected by treating human wastes as causing ritual impurity and assigning the tasks of clearing wastes to a lower caste thereby also seen as impure? How is environmental ethics affected when a religion sees relations with people outside its religious group as causing "impurity"? These questions of the religious roots of the relation between human-nature abuse and interhuman abuse need far more careful attention in the conversation about religion and ecological ethics.

Why focus on religion as a key factor in this struggle for a more just and sustainable global society? As we have seen, ecologists initially disregarded religion as almost entirely a negative factor in relation to the natural world. But recently this view has changed dramatically in some quarters, as we shall see in the last section of this chapter. Those concerned with a just and sustainable world have come to realize that religion is a key component in this quest. Precisely because they are the carriers of moral values and symbolic worldviews, religion is key to healing the antiecological worldviews of the past, as White himself suggested.

HINDUISM

In this exploration of religion, ecology, and gender, I start with Hinduism, one of the most ancient traditions and the major religion of the vast subcontinent of India. The roots of Hinduism lie in the Brahmanical texts of the Aryan invaders of India who arrived in successive waves in the early to mid second millennium BCE. The Brahmanical canon consists of the four Samhitas or Vedas (1500–800 BCE) that consist mainly of hymns and sacrificial formulae, the Brahmanas and Aranyakas (1100–800 BCE), and the Upanishads (800–300 BCE) that flow from schools associated with the four Samhitas. Later writings from the classical period included in Brahmanical tradition are the Dharma-Sastras (legal codes), epics (the Mahabharata and Ramayana), the Darsanas or philosophical systems, and the Puranas, or compilations of myths. Six different philosophical schools emerged in classical Hinduism: Inyaya, Vaisesika, Purva-Mimamsa, Vedanta, Samkhya, and Yoga.[8]

Some have questioned whether Hinduism can be seen as a single religion at all, rather than a great melange of different religious tendencies, held loosely together by some reference to Vedic tradition. This tradition itself overlaid earlier cultures going back to the third millennium BCE Harappa culture of the Indus valley. These earlier non-Aryan people were submerged by the Aryan invaders and made lower caste or outcastes in the Hindu system. But the Purana literature (200–300 CE) that cultivates special devotion to particular Goddesses reflects a reemergence of pre-Aryan religious traditions that had never disappeared on the popular level.[9]

The Brahmanical tradition was able to absorb and synthesize many of these new movements with their own traditions, while others, such as Buddhism and Jainism, separated from it and began distinct religions critical of Brahmanism. Modern Hindu reformers of the late nineteenth and twentieth centuries sought to modernize Hinduism and remove practices such as widow burning and refusal of remarriage of widows. But recent Hindu fundamentalist movements have tried to restore what they see as orthodox practices, focusing especially on traditional gender relations, including the occasional practice of widow burning.[10]

India offers a particularly intense example of the ambiguities and contradictions between religious worldview and ecological ethics. Perhaps nowhere is there such an extensive sense of the sacrality of place. Its forests and rivers are seen as holy, even as embodied gods and goddesses. India as a whole is venerated as a sacred land. In Hindu tradition to cross the ocean in travel outside India was to incur ritual pollution, necessitating a ceremony of purification on reentry.[11] But these views of the sacrality of land, forests, and rivers seem to have done little to protect India from vast ecological destruction under the impact of modern development. Its forests have been stripped, its soil depleted, its rivers turned into running sewers.

One can also point to extensive environmental activism in India. A 1993 article reported that over 950 NGOs dedicated to environmental protection existed in India.[12] Activist movements to protest the damming of rivers, causing the flooding of valleys and displacement of villagers, and to protect forests from logging by hugging trees, have been widely reported. Yet many of these environmental movements are not readily connected with Brahmanical elites. They flow more from secular educated middle classes, and from popular groups, including tribal communities outside of orthodox Hindu leadership.[13]

Even such a central religious idea and practice as the sacral purity of the Ganges river, that brings tens of thousands to bathe in its waters every year, does not translate readily into ecological protection of the river. Rather religious practices, such as throwing the ashes of the dead into it, contribute to its pollution. Moreover the religious definition of the river's power to purify rests on a religiomagical concept of purity that resists the ecological problem of its possible pollution by human and industrial wastes and hence the need for humans to act to clean it up. The religious understanding of its purity and the ecological definition of clean and unclean water operate in different spheres of thought that cannot be brought into one framework without deep reinterpretation. Since it is religiously pure, Hindu priests insist it cannot be made impure by human wastes.[14]

The relation between gender and caste hierarchies and Hindu philosophical cosmology also offer poignant contradictions. In few countries in the world are the images of goddesses more prevalent than in India. On every street corner temples great and small celebrate the divine female in her many expressions. Yet traditional Hinduism fostered a strict subordination of women within the family and society. Women were excluded from Brahmanical education in Brahmin families and were stereotyped as both ignorant and a source of ritual pollution through their bodily processes. This impurity of women was linked with the impurity of the Sudras, the lowest of the four castes whose task was to serve the others. Married even before puberty, the Hindu woman was instructed to treat her husband as a god, and to regard herself as blameworthy if he died before her death, even though he was often many years older than she. On his death, she was faced with the choices of offering herself to be burned alive on his funeral pyre or to shave her head and be treated as a marginalized creature in the family.[15]

Modern reform has brought education and equal legal rights to Indian women. A lively women's movement has flourished since the 1970s on both the popular and the university levels. But this movement has uncovered a shocking amount of violence to women in practice, not only the occasional revival of widow burning, but the much more frequent practice of burning an unwanted wife in contrived kitchen accidents in order to obtain a new bride and dowry. Female feticide has been aided by the modern medical practice of amniocentesis to rid a family of unwanted daughters and hopefully to produce wanted sons.[16]

Incorporated young into the husband's family, young brides have traditionally suffered abuse by mother-in-laws, husbands, and even sisters of the husband, and enjoyed little status until they could produce sons that grew old enough to protect them. This family system itself tends to produce a cycle of violence in which the formerly abused bride becomes the abusing mother-in-law to her new daughter-in-law.[17] What does this pattern of abuse of women have to do with the worship of Goddesses?

Tracy Pintchman has attempted a comprehensive study of the idea of the Great Goddess in Hindu cosmology, and its relation to traditional female roles, in her 1994 book *The Rise of the Goddess in the Hindu Tradition*.[18] Pintchman sees this idea emerging gradually in Hindu literature, culminating in the Puranas. Key to the idea of the Great Goddess as cosmogonic power is the synthesizing of three ideas: *prakriti, shakti,* and *maya.* Each of these three terms is complex, with a range of meaning that partly overlaps with the others. *Shakti* generally refers to cosmic energy that activates the cosmogonic process and brings about the various levels of the created or manifest world. *Prakriti* is the matrix or primal materiality out of which the universe is created, itself composed of a dynamic interaction of forces. *Maya* is a particularly slippery term. Often translated in English as "illusion," and seen as expressing a view of the material world as mere delusory appearance from which the ascetic must escape in order to unite the soul (*atman*) with its divine counterpart, Brahman, it also can be seen as creative energy linking *shakti* and *prakriti*.[19]

In the Vedic literature these terms are occasionally imaged as feminine but not systematically identified with a Goddess or Goddesses. The philosophical treatises develop coherent cosmologies that interconnect the three terms. But it is in the Puranas that cosmologies based on the interlinking of *shakti, maya,* and *prakriti* are identified with a Great Goddess. This Great Goddess (*Mahadevi*) is the highest expression of all goddesses and also manifests the essential nature of women. In this cosmology of the Great Goddess, the primal male deity, *Brahman,* or his expressions in *Siva* or *Vishnu,* are seen as a passive power or potentiality. Female *shakti* is necessary to activate this male potential and translate it into cosmogonic activity. *Maya* is the skillful activity of this creative process. It can also be characterized as delusory play of the divine. *Prakriti* is unformed materiality which is thus shaped and formed by divine potentiality, activated by *shakti* and manifesting itself through this activity.

What is notable in this tradition is that the male supreme being is not seen as having inherent capacity for creative action. He must be activated through the female power of *shakti*. The cosmogonic process, and its expression in the many forms of the material world, are female identified. The energy that activates the divine to create, the creative process, and the material base that is shaped are all female principles that together express the Great Goddess. She brings together all three aspects of creation as the creatrix, that which is created and the process of creation.

This Great Goddess is both a benevolent and a destructive force. She can be seen as Durga, protectress of the gods and slayer of demons that threaten the cosmos. She creates, maintains, and destroys the cosmos. As destroyer she is the bloodthirsty Kali with raised bloodied sword, and girdle of severed heads, dancing on the prone body of Siva.[20] Thus she encompasses the cosmic rhythm of life and death which rises as creative activity, is maintained and eventually destroyed to rise again in a new cycle of life and death. Just as the life process on the earth goes through a cycle of life, death, and rebirth, so the cosmos itself is created, maintained, and destroyed in an endless cyclical rhythm. It is the Great Goddess who is the underlying cause and basis of this cosmic process.

Since this Great Goddess is identified both with all particular Goddesses in their different aspects, and also with the essential nature of women, this would seem to suggest that women are very powerful, since they possess the raw material and energy of creativity itself. But Pintchman shows the ambivalence of this concept of divine femaleness. Women embody creative power and its material expression. But, when acting on their own, women are seen as dangerous and potentially destructive. Women's power must be channeled and controlled so as to become an orderly process of creation and maintenance of life. This happens only when women give their power utterly to their male lord, who both is activated through it and controls it.

Pintchman sees this cosmology as closely correlated with the social view of women, especially of women's sexuality, in Hindu society. Men are seen as unable to create on their own. Their potential for creativity must be activated through women's *shakti* or creative energy, but this must also be controlled and channeled through the male to produce the desired outcome, children, especially male children. Married Goddesses and, by implication, married women channel their energy through their husbands and so become the material matrices or mothers of children. Acting on its own, without subjugation to control by the husband, female power becomes wild and destructive.[21]

This view of female cosmogonic power translated socially into both awe and suspicion of female creative power. Women on their own are seen as unreliable and dangerous. They are both necessary for men to create and must be strictly controlled in order not to become violently chaotic. The ontological status of the visible world shares in this ambiguity. It is produced through and expresses the female creative energy, but this process and its product are impermanent and illusory and will disappear or be destroyed in time. This impermanent world produced through female power and expressing female materiality is also a realm of ignorance or delusion that impedes male potential for liberation and union with ultimate reality, trapping it in a cycle of rebirth.

To escape this realm of illusion, the male ascetic must separate from the household, the realm of women, to seek the solitude of contemplative union with the permanent realm of being outside this cyclic process. Although a few women in popular traditions became *bhaktis* (unmarried devotees of a deity), and some have been recognized as gurus in modern times,[22] in traditional Hinduism women generally could not become ascetics living on their own outside the household. Women were seen as incapable of *moksa* or liberation from rebirth. They belong to the realm of impermanence, ignorance, impurity, and delusion. They are doomed to continual rebirth, until they become male and thus able to escape from it.[23]

Such a worldview is highly ambivalent toward the welfare of the material world, just as it is ambivalent about the nature of women. Why care about the pollution of rivers, air, or soil, or the denuding of forests, if all this is illusory, destined to pass, while true reality belongs to a realm outside of this female cosmogonic process? Abuse or disregard for nature and abuse and disregard for women are thus closely correlated and belong to the same worldview. Such a cosmology would seem to be totally antipathetic to an ecological ethic, as environmental ethicist J. Baird Callicott has claimed.[24]

But such a view of the phenomenal world as a female realm of ignorance to be renounced by male ascetics is also capable of reinterpretation. It is not accidental that the leading Indian ecological thinker and activist, Vandana Shiva, is a feminist who claims the Hindu concepts of *Shakti* and *Prakriti* as the basis for her ecological struggle.[25] This is not simply her personal theory, but it also is expressed in environmental action, particularly in movements of women who see their tree hugging and other such mass action to resist environmental degradation as a expression of their *shakti* or female power to protect the world.[26]

Male asceticism also need not disregard natural life. It can be reinterpreted as a separation from and resistance to the world of industrial development that is abusing nature and impoverishing human life. The ascetic becomes a prophetic activist whose fasting and renunciatory lifestyle stand against the "world" of injustice and who leads a mass community movement that opposes logging forests or damming rivers.[27] Although Gandhi's use of the ascetic tradition for a practice of nonviolent resistance to British colonialism, and his cultivation of an alternative village economy, were too early to be explicitly ecological, they are being expanded today to include an environmental ethic.[28]

Thus both the Hindu tradition of ascetic renunciation of the world of delusion, and the imaging of the divine and human "feminine" as expressions of creative and sustaining cosmic energy underlying the phenomenal world, are ideas capable of feminist and ecological interpretation. What is needed are movements to empower women and to enable both men and women to resist destructive development and to defend sustainable relationships with nature. These movements, in turn, can lay hold of many traditional Hindu symbols, such as the sacrality of forests, rivers, and land and the power of Goddesses in and through the creative process.[29] The renunciation of mind-deluding consumption in favor of simple living in harmony with highest reality can express a struggle to create alternatives both to gender hierarchy and to environmental destruction.

JAINISM

The Jain religion goes back to the fifth century BCE to a great teacher, Vardhamana Mahavira, who was a contemporary of the Buddha. Jains claim that this teacher was himself the twenty-fourth in a long line of teachers stretching back hundreds of years.[30] Jainism historically is a rigidly ascetic faith whose key spirituality lies in the liberation of the soul from the bondage of karma that causes continual rebirth in embodied forms, in order to enter a state of eternal bliss. Jains have no creator deity and see the world of souls and bodies as without beginning or end, passing through periodic cycles of decline and rebirth. Their worship focuses on the liberated ones, the great teachers, who have been freed from rebirth.

For Jains the phenomenal world consists of a vast hierarchy of embodied forms, from beings that dwell in air, water, fire, and earth to one-, two-, three-, four-, and five-sensed beings (plants, worms, insects, fish, and birds to mammals) culminating in humans who have all five senses (touch, taste, smell, sight, and hearing) together with rationality. Souls dwell in all these beings and are continually reborn in these different forms. All souls are alike, having the same ontological nature. A soul in a human form may be reincarnated in an insect or a plant. Thus Jains look at the phenomenal world as literally teeming with life, a community of fellow souls.[31]

The goal of life, however, is not to celebrate this community of embodied forms or to promote its welfare per se, but to liberate souls from embodiment. This can happen only in human (or in some sects, male human) embodiment, all other forms having to be reincarnated in a (male) human to be capable of liberation. The path to this liberation is strenuous avoidance of harm to others (*ahimsa*). Violence in thought and word and deed, stealing or taking what is not given, lying, unchastity, and possessiveness all represent passions in the self that must be overcome by rigorous avoidance of these misdeeds. These sins are seen as producing a subtle matter that clings to the soul and causes it to be reborn. By avoiding these passions one cleanses the soul from karma, making possible its liberation from rebirth.[32]

Jains are divided into two orders, monastics, male and female, and laymen and women. Monastics take the most rigorous vows to avoid all harming, not killing or injuring any living thing, including insects or tiny life forms in air and water. Even stepping on grass or touching plants is forbidden. They wear a veil over the mouth to avoid accidentally ingesting a gnat. They possess almost nothing and beg for their food. They depend entirely on the lay community who provide them with vegetarian food carefully prepared to eliminate any living beings (i.e., water must be boiled and strained, and then the vegetables boiled in the boiled water).

Laypeople, the vast proportion of Jains, take more limited vows. They must avoid certain professions seen as involving killing or abuse of animals. They must be vegetarians, avoid lying, unchastity, and possessiveness, and sustain the monastic community that represents their ultimate ideals. Ironically, the effect of these rules for laypeople is that Jains have become concentrated in skilled crafts and trade and become highly successful businessmen. They live primarily in urban areas, rather than in villages. They have also prized education and adapted readily to high-tech modern life.[33]

The Jain view of women is conflicted. Early on women were allowed to become monastics equally with men, thus implicitly acknowledging that females have the same intellectual and spiritual capacity as men for liberation of the soul. From 300 BCE to about 200 CE there were continual debates over whether women in fact are capable of liberation. Jains divided into two sects, the Digambaras who insisted on the total nudity of monks and the Shvetambaras or white-clad monastics. The Digambaras did not admit women as renunciates, claiming that women's "impurity" forbade them to go naked.

The debates between these two sects went far beyond the issue of nudity or dress to the question of female nature. The Digambaras attacked women as sensual, arrogant, and threatening to the renunciate way of life, claiming that women by nature lacked the spiritual capacity for liberation. The Shvetambaras defended the essential equality of women and men and replied that women are capable of the same range of good and evil as men. Even though the Shvetambaras admit women to monastic life—historically there have been several times more nuns than monks in Jainism—they restrict them more than monks. Nuns are not allowed to go out alone, but must always be in pairs. The oldest and most spiritually advanced nun is subordinate to all monks, even the youngest. Their education was limited, and they could not study certain Jain texts.[34]

These rules reveal a continuing assumption of women's sexual unreliability and lack of intellect, even among Shvetambaras. The result is that there has been little intellectual leadership from nuns, although even today their numbers exceed those of males (c. 3400 nuns to 1200 monks). Many Jain women became nuns on becoming widows, this being preferable to the marginalized status of widows in Indian society. Today there is more education of nuns. Some Jain nuns have emerged as intellectual leaders, writers, and speakers, but they are exceptional.[35]

Laywomen among Jains have followed the typical way of life of Indian women. They were expected to be wives and mothers, totally devoted to their husbands and children. The Jain wife had the added responsibility of preparing the food both for the family and for mendicant monks and nuns that conformed to rigorous dietary rules. They also passed on much of the practical tradition to their children, and were more frequent in worship at temples (although their proximity to the images of teachers was sometimes restricted on the assumption of women's impurity, especially during menstruation). Laywomen engaged in frequent fasts as a way of repenting for any sins and gaining merit toward ultimate liberation from embodiment. The doctrine of karma itself among Jains (like Hindus) suggested that having been born in a low social status, either as a woman or as a low-caste or –class person, was itself an expression of sins in a former life. Thus women must continually repent for the very fact of being female.

This Jain worldview offers grave contradictions to any social justice or environmental ethic, much less an ecofeminist ethic that seeks to knit these together (see chapter 3 of this volume on ecofeminism). If oppressive social status is due to past sins of the oppressed person, there is little impetus to change gender or class hierarchies in society. If one seeks to avoid embodied forms of all kinds in order to be liberated from embodiment, this does not create much concern about the welfare of such bodies. Jain social outreach has been expressed primarily in opposing the killing or mistreatment of animals, which has included creating hospices where abused animals, including birds, might be cared for and live out their lives in peace. During famines and droughts, Jains have been involved in creating feeding stations that provided clean vegetarian food for the whole community, Jain and non-Jain alike.

But Jains traditionally have not opposed social systems that produce oppression. In modern times they have embraced the global economy and have not criticized its effects in creating poverty and environmental devastation. In spite of their strong doctrine of *ahimsa* (nonviolence or nonharming) they have not been pacifists and have not opposed militarism, including the Indian development of nuclear weapons.[36]

Yet in modern times, especially among Jain laity in the Diaspora (in Britain and North America), many Jains have embraced an environmental ethic as central to their religious identity. This comes about as the traditional ascetic path becomes less prominent and even incomprehensible to many modern people. In this context the themes of nonviolence, not harming others, vegetarianism, and the belief that the whole world is alive with souls that are part of one living community of which humans are one expression, are translated into a new ethic of concern for the welfare of all embodied beings.[37]

In the *Jain Declaration on Nature*, prepared by L. M. Singhvi, a member of the Indian parliament and published as a booklet in 1992, Jains have presented their core beliefs as the basis of an environmental ethics based on nonviolence, the interdependence of all life forms, the need for manifold perspectives on life (i.e., the need to look at reality from the plant or animal perspective, not simply from human anthropocentric, egocentric, or ethnocentric perspectives), equanimity or balance of all life needs with each other, and compassion or empathy with others that calls for service and care for the needs of others, including plants and animals, equally with those of humans.[38]

Jains have readily joined with other religious groups in supporting global statements of environmental ethics. In Devon, England, Schumacher College, that sponsors a curriculum based on environmental ethics and draws students and lecturers from all over the world, is run by a Jain, Satish Kumar. Kumar is also the editor of the important magazine *Resurgence*, that presents an alternative, environmentally friendly way of life.[39] Thus the Jain tradition today is seeking to make a contribution to the dialogue of world religions on ecological issues.

BUDDHISM

Buddhism originated at the same time as Jainism in India, in the sixth century BCE. But it has become a much more complex tradition with some 360 million adherents worldwide. Dying out in India, Buddhism moved to China, Korea, and Japan, adapting itself to different cultures. It became the major religion of countries such as Tibet, Sri Lanka, and Thailand. Today there are two and a half million Buddhists in the United States, and Buddhism is undergoing new adaptations to the American context.[40]

Buddhism was founded by Siddhartha Gautama (c. 563–483 BCE), born of princely parents, who left the comfort of his father's palace to become a mendicant, seeking liberation from the world of suffering and sorrow. Siddhartha came to reject the Hindu beliefs in a substantive self and ultimate reality (Atman–Brahman) for a conviction that there is no substantive self and underlying phenomenal reality is emptiness (*sunyata*). What exists is a flux of coming to be and passing away in endless interconnections (*pratityasamutpada*).[41]

Suffering is inherent in this reality of impermanence, but it is translated into the personal experience of suffering through egoism and desire. By clinging to the self as if it could become permanent, by seeking to build walls of security to protect oneself from suffering, the self becomes driven by anxiety. Liberation comes through a disciplined meditational practice by which one sees through these delusions, surrenders ignorance, greed, and delusion by gaining insight into the true nature of the self as part of an impermanent flux endlessly arising and passing away in emptiness. The goal of this insight is liberation from desire, creating a serene person who accepts reality as it is. Such an enlightened person can also become generous and compassionate, sympathetic to the suffering of all others.

Siddhartha (Buddha) organized his insights and practice into the form of a monastic community (*Sangha*) which was dedicated to meditational practices designed to lead to this liberating insight into reality in a frugal way of life freed from cravings and desires. Rejecting the extreme asceticism of Jain monks, as well as the libertine life of the world, Buddhist monasticism pursues the middle path of equanimity of mind and moderation in discipline of the body. Like Jains, Buddhist monks depend on the lay community to furnish them with their food, but are not vegetarians, although they do not kill animals themselves.[42]

Like Jains, Buddhists went through protracted debate about the role of women in monasticism. The Buddha is said to have been asked by his foster mother and aunt to found a monastic order for women, but he refused three times, agreeing to do so only after the intervention of his kinsman and constant companion, Ananda. But he insisted that women must live under eight special rules that placed them in a position subordinate to men. Every nun, no matter how elderly and advanced in her practice, must treat every monk, even the youngest, as her superior. The formal ceremonies of the nuns must be carried out under the guidance of the monks' *Sangha*. The monks, not the nuns, set the penances for erring nuns. Nuns can receive *dharma* instructions from monks, but can never teach monks.[43]

The Buddha also said that the *sangha* would be weakened and true Buddhist teaching would die out in 500 years, rather than lasting 1000 years, because of the presence of women in it, thus making the very existence of nuns a kind of bad karma for future Buddhism. Buddhism inherited from Hinduism the idea that being incarnated as a woman is itself an indication of sins in a previous life. Also, since laypeople receive less merit by giving to nuns, nuns' orders have been much less well supported than male orders. Consequently they have tended to fall into social, economic, and intellectual marginality and have died out in many areas.

An exception is China where the female order established in the fourth century CE has lasted in unbroken tradition until today. Through China, nuns' orders were extended to Korea, Japan, and Vietnam and Taiwan, and today to the West. Fully ordained nuns did not spread to some other Buddhist countries such as Thailand, Cambodia, Laos, or Tibet. There some women have shaved their heads and lived as renunciants, although without full ordination. Today nuns' orders are being redeveloped, drawing on ordination through the Chinese lineages. This is a problem since Chinese Buddhists are Mahayanists, and thus their lineages are not acceptable to monks from the Theravada tradition, as in Thailand. Some Buddhist women who have adopted a monastic way of life without full ordination are not interested in obtaining it since it carries with it subordination to the monks, which they prefer to avoid.[44]

Some Buddhist texts have insisted that the female body disqualifies women from certain ranks of existence, such as a Buddha. But there have also been countervailing egalitarian traditions in Buddhism. Some texts, such as the Prajnaparamita Sutras, insist that all such apparent characteristics of the body are illusory and only unenlightened persons believe there is a real distinction between males and females. Stories were told of enlightened women, even girl children, who become Bodhisattvas, to show the absurdity of distinctions, such as sex, in religion. Bodhisattvas are also presented as androgynous, with both male and female characteristics, to show the fluidity of gender.[45] It is said that the path of liberation is the same for men and women. Women are as capable as men of pursuing it.[46]

As Buddhism moved from India to China and Japan, it took on some of the cosmological elements of those cultures. The emptiness into which all things co-arise in interrelationships began to sound less like a void and more like *Tao*, or *Chi*, divine energy that underlies all phenomena. The idea of Buddha-nature as the true state of being into which we are delivered, when we see things correctly, was extended to all nature. Some teachers declared that even rocks and mountains have Buddha nature.[47] There is no split of mind and matter, self and nature, but all are one, in dynamic interconnection. There is no hierarchy of a transcendent male deity outside of the cosmos, or human over nature, but only the flux of impermanent beings in changing interrelationship. This view of reality has been seen in the twentieth century as similar to process philosophy and has been appropriated by environmentalists and deep ecologists as evidence of positive resources of Buddhism for ecology.[48]

Some Buddhists have been skeptical of "green Buddhism" as a modern adaptation to a global crisis that distorts traditional Buddhism.[49] Aspects of Buddhism inimical to ecological concerns are cited, such as the following. Buddhism focuses on the individual spiritual quest through withdrawal into monastic retreat from society. Social problems, including those afflicting nature, such as deforestation and pollution of the air and water, are part of the suffering of impermanence from which the monk seeks detachment. To be anxious about such problems and to seek to change them would seem to be the opposite of the Buddhist path of enlightenment. Rather the monk seeks a serene equanimity in the face of the illusory nature of such problems.

Whether or not such stances have contributed to disconnection from social and ecological evils, what is evident today is that societies with majority Buddhist cultures are suffering as much as any others from the ecological crisis of modern industrial development. Thailand has become largely deforested, and Bangkok is one of the most polluted cities in the world. Many from largely Buddhist countries have blamed this on the invasion of Western styles of development and a Western paradigm of reality that disconnects the human from nature. The solution is seen as reclaiming the traditional Asian values of the unity of the human and nature.[50] But this begs the question of whether worldviews such as Buddhism are also part of the problem or at least do not lend themselves easily to solutions. A spirituality of detachment from suffering as illusory impermanence doesn't readily become an ethic that seeks to change this impermanent flux for the better or that even believes that it can be changed for the better!

Nevertheless Buddhism is being ardently mined as a resource for an environmental ethic. Significant local and international movements to protect and restore nature are arising, claiming Buddhist inspiration. One can cite the Sarvodaya movement in Sri Lanka in which students are mobilized to go to poor villages to work with the people to build roads, clean wells, and dig latrines. This has developed into a broad-based effort to free the country from Western styles of development for local sustainable ways of caring for basic human needs.[51]

In Thailand hundreds of monks together with thousands of laypeople have been involved in activist movements to resist logging and preserve the remaining forests. One ingenious way of linking this struggle with Buddhist symbols has been the ordaining of trees, wrapping trees in the saffron robes of a monk to declare the tree sacrosanct, making it a sacrilege to cut it.[52]

In the United States several Buddhist monastic retreat centers, such as Green Gulch Zen Center and Spirit Rock Meditation center, both in Marin County near San Francisco, and Zen Mountain Center in Apple Canyon in southern California, have made themselves into model ecological communities. They have sought to raise their own food organically, and demonstrate water-saving practices and renewable energy. These ecological practices have been incorporated into the way of life of these communities, so they become an integral element of prayer, meditation, and the seasonal cycles of life for those who live there or come as guests. They also provide both examples and teaching that help people carry such practices into their daily lives elsewhere.[53]

The movement for Engaged Buddhism, pioneered by social activists, such as Sulak Sivaraska of Thailand, has developed a social justice rereading of traditional Buddhist thought. For Sulak, the Buddhist mandate to overcome the clinging of the self to desires needs to be seen in relation to social structures, as well as to individuals. The impulses of greed, hatred, and illusion trap the self in ignorance and suffering and express the global social systems of militarism and trade that are devastating the earth and impoverishing the majority of its people.

Greed is the impulse to endless possessiveness. It is based on a false belief in the possibility of ever expanding "growth" of material goods that is the key to a Western-defined "developmentalism." This ideology of infinite growth is the central ideology of the World Bank and other agents of global capitalism. It is an ideology that ignores the finite limits of the earth. It is creating a world where a small minority of people are excessively wealthy, while the majority fall into poverty and the environment is being stripped of its life-giving capacity.

Greed in turn generates fear and hatred. The rich who concentrate the wealth of the world in their hands feel threatened by the expanding numbers of poor. The poor resent the wealthy. Increasing global animosity is creating an endless cycle of violence that plays itself out locally and globally. This whole system is held in place by ignorance or delusion. The affluent misrepresent what they are doing as ultimately of benefit to all. The poor see more clearly how this wealth and power play out at their expense, but often can see no alternative but to claim "part of the pie," seeking to include themselves in the same path of "development."[54]

For Sulak, Buddhism, as well as other traditional religions, offers the true alternative to this mad rush of greed, hatred, and delusion. We must teach ourselves to withdraw from desires, learn to live simply and share equally with one another. We need to redevelop local communities and their integration with local and regional ecosystems. We need to detach ourselves from the system of world trade backed by militarism of the dominant powers. We need to rediscover our local cultures that traditionally taught us to live within our means and care for our forests, soil, and waters in a sustainable way. In this way Buddhist language and institutions, such as monasteries and ashrams, become instruments of an ethic of ecological justice and sustainable living in local communities.

CONFUCIANISM AND DAOISM

Confucianism and Daoism are the two major native traditions of China. They have sometimes been seen as rivals, with Daoism standing as a critique of Confucianism, but they can also be seen as complementary viewpoints and practices within a larger whole, addressed to the same constituency, the male educated class of China.

Confucianism originated with Confucius who lived from the mid-sixth into the fifth centuries (551–479 BCE). He was primarily a teacher who sought to shape the social and political ethics of the leadership class and to establish an educational system for a moral order in a time of violence and chaos. Although not very successful in his own time, Confucius' thought came to be accepted as the official creed of China. The Confucian canon of four major books, Confucius' *Analects* (or conversations), that of his major disciple, the *Mencius*, with the later writings, the *Great Learning* and the *Doctrine of the Mean*, became the basis for the civil service examination system from the fourteenth into the twentieth century. Confucianism was officially rejected by revolutionary China, but continues to deeply shape family and social patterns in China, as well as in Korea and Japan influenced by China. The Chinese nationalists in Taiwan made traditional Confucianism the basis of law, subordinating the more diverse cultural traditions of the indigenous Taiwanese.[55]

Confucius himself largely avoided divine or religious warrants for his thought, to such an extent that Confucianism has often been seen as a secular humanism, not a religion. But the cosmological assumptions of Confucianism are made more explicit in Neo-Confucian thinkers in the eleventh to nineteenth centuries.[56] Confucianism, like Daoism, has no personified deity or creation story. The universe is generated and sustained by a holistic matter-energy (*Ch'i*) that is in continuous transformational process. This process is neither linear or cyclical, but a continual pulsation of life and death, generation and disintegration. This generative process takes place through the interaction of two vital forces, *yin* and *yang*. Originally these terms referred to the shady and sunny sides of a hill.[57] It came to describe the whole range of dialectical poles in creative processes, cold/heat, damp/dry, passive/active, earth/heaven. These polarities are connected with female/male. As is often pointed out, these are not competitive dualisms. Both aspects are equally necessary. They interpenetrate one another and only through their interaction is life created and sustained.[58]

The self in Confucian thought is not the isolated individual, but the socially constituted self who exists in and through relationships. These interrelationships express one's social location in various contexts, as son or daughter and parents, wife and husband, family and society, rulers and subjects. Confucianism seeks to establish the ethics of duties, deference, and responsibility in each of these roles in relation to the others to whom one is related. Social harmony consists of each person playing the proper rituals of deference and carrying out the duties appropriate to each of these different relationships. Through cultivating this social harmony one harmonized society with the cosmos, with Heaven.

Filial piety is the central ethic for all relations with superiors, ultimately even the relation of humans to Heaven and Earth as one's cosmic parents.[59] Rulers to subjects, husband to wife, parents to children, in turn bear responsibility for careful and wise rule, avoiding any abusive use of power. Such an ethic of right relation is not simply spontaneous, for Confucianism, but the fruit of education and a long process of self-cultivation and refinement. The purpose of the Confucian educational system was to produce this self-cultivated "gentleman" who is the ideal sage, ruler, and civil servant. Harmonious families, harmonious society, harmonious government are the fruit of this process of self-cultivation.[60]

This vision of mutual duties in relationship became embedded in a rigid system of patriarchal hierarchy. It produced a ruling class elite over the masses and fixed views of the female as subordinate to the male in all relationships, as daughter to father, wife to husband, and even mother to elder son. These are defined in the Confucian classic, *Li chi*, as the "three submissions," buttressed by the four virtues appropriate to women, "feminine" modes of virtue, work, deportment, and speech. Feminine virtue focuses on chastity and complete obedience to superiors. Feminine work is confined to domestic work. Deportment and speech indicates cleanliness, and ritual patterns self-abasement and deference.

Women were excluded from the educational system that produced the "gentleman," forbidden outside work or political leadership, denied remarriage as widows, and encouraged to remain chaste even to a preference for death by suicide, rather than sexual violation. Woman's chief task as wife was to produce male heirs, and the birth of daughters was unwelcome.[61]

Reality in Chinese history has always been more complex than this theory. Confucius himself suggested some possibility of social mobility through education in which the intelligent son of the middle class might move up the ladder.[62] Some women of the elite found ways to become educated, to write and teach in the secluded confines of their intimate circles, and China has not been without its powerful queens. But these exceptions take place against the grain. Queens are typically portrayed in Chinese history as cruel and greedy, and perhaps often have been in a system in which their power was not quite legitimate.[63]

In revolutionary China in the 1950s Confucianism represented the ossified class hierarchy that must be swept away to create an egalitarian socialist China. Women were also to be liberated, allowed equal education, work, and political leadership. But China, much like modern societies elsewhere, has tended to create the pattern of the "double workday" for women who must compete as a "man" in society, while also continuing to do much of the traditional work and to maintain a deferential relation to men in the family.[64]

Modern ecologically minded Confucianists or admirers of Confucianism suggest that this tradition has rich resources for an environmental ethic. The sense of the self constituted in and through interrelationship is seen as far superior to the Western view of the isolated self externally related to others.[65] To make this an environmental ethic one must extend this sense of the relational self to the nonhuman community, an extension already suggested by the situation of the relational self in its cosmic context. Moreover Confucianism is an activist tradition in which government leadership to promote harmony is encouraged. This can today be made more explicit as a mandate for the responsibility of governments to establish and enforce laws for the protection of the environment.[66]

Although this potential for an ecological ethic may be there, it does not yet seem to be activated. Republican China has scorned Confucianism in favor of an adoption of a Western style Promethean "man" who conquers nature. Taiwanese environmental NGOs do not look to traditional Chinese philosophies, but imitate Western campaigns for protection of nature. Some temples carry out programs of protection of forests, but these are local rather than national in scope.[67] Ecofeminist Huey-li Li has suggested that Chinese thought generally has yet to recognize the way that the hierarchy of men over women itself distorts the concept of yin-yang into both a social and cosmological hierarchy, stifling the potential of this idea for relationships of mutuality between men and women, humans and nature.[68]

By contrast to Confucianism, Daoism is much more popular with environmentalists. It has been appropriated by deep ecologists as a source of their vision of the ecological self. New Age religion in the West endlessly refers to the "Dao" as a key symbol for their quest for spontaneity, naturalness, and "going with the flow." This Western use of Daoism has been strongly criticized by scholars of Daoism as both ignorant and exploitative of Chinese tradition by those who have little depth of knowledge or respect for the integrity of this tradition in its own historical reality.[69]

Daoism's legendary founder, Lao Tzu, supposedly lived in the sixth century BCE, but the *Tao te ching* he is said to have authored is a composite text that took form in the third century BCE. Many folk practices that are taken into Daoism are much more ancient, going back to Chinese shamanism, while more organized Daoists sects date from the second century CE. Thus what is lumped under the name "Daoism" is a complex of traditions, both popular and esoteric. Despite this diversity, a shared view of the Dao and the path of harmonizing the self with the Dao can be found in the many Daoist traditions.

Daoism shares with Confucianism a nondualistic cosmology, but rejects its activist social ordering. For Daoism, the Dao is simultaneously the unmanifest void of creativity and its shape-shifting manifestation in a continual process of differentiation in multiplicity. The goal of Daoist spirituality is to harmonize the self with the Dao, not through cognitive education and social structure, but through retreat from the world of laws, books, and political systems to reclaim intuitive, spontaneous, and nonaggressive ways of being.

The Daoist way of noncoercive action (*wu-wei*) is not seen as irrelevant to shaping good rulers. Rather it claims that a ruler rules best by ruling least, by letting go of domination and allowing local communities of humans and other living beings to live according to their own ways of being. The Daoist is convinced that human interference based on rational systems of cognition invariably makes things worse. When the ruler guides without appearing to guide, letting living things shape themselves according to their own dynamics, the results are likely to be better. Daoism suggests a how, not a what; a way of living, not a system of knowledge.[70]

The dynamic interaction of *yin* and *yang*, female and male energies, passive and active, is central to Daoism, but in a way that emphasizes their mutual interpenetration, and rejects the Confucian use of them as social hierarchy. In contrast to Confucianism, Daoism gives priority to the *yin*, the female or passive side of the duality, and suggests that *yang* is in some sense grounded in *yin*. In rejecting dominance and analytical forms of cognition for intuitive knowing and noncoercive acting, the Daoist sage cultivates the *yin* side of his being. Lowliness and weakness are said to be stronger than aggressive hardness, just as water appears weak, but can wear away a stone. *Yin* or female energy puts us in touch with the womblike void, the inexhaustible source of life from which all things spring. In the oft-quoted words of the *Tao te ching*,

> The Valley Spirit never dies. It is named the Mysterious Female.
> And the Doorway of the Mysterious Female is the base
> from which Heaven and Earth spring. It is there within us all the while.
> Draw upon it as you will, it never runs dry.[71]

The goal is still the dynamic balance of *yin* and *yang*, but the male of the elite class must retreat from one-sided masculinity in a conscious cultivation of the "feminine" to find wholeness. He needs to retreat from upward mobility and the career ladder of society, reclaim domestic space, respect women, care for children, especially female infants likely to be discarded in the patrilineal system, and respect all sentient beings. Thus Daoism intentionally seeks to reverse the patterns of separation and hierarchy that shape the dominant patriarchal society to return to harmonious communion with the Dao.

Does this make Daoism a protofeminism? One has to exercise caution in taking Daoism out of its social setting which was undoubtedly patriarchal. As Joanne Birdwhistell has pointed out, the ability of the Daoist sage to retreat to his home or mountain hermitage and cultivate feminine modes of being itself reflected his privileged status as an member of the male elite. Women themselves are not necessarily liberated thereby.[72] Nevertheless Daoism comes closer to cultivating male and female equality than other ancient religions that arose in the "axial" age.[73] Women were admitted to Daoist ordination to the seventh grade of perfection, denied only the eighth or last grade. Women are writers of some of the texts of the Daoist canon. They are found among the teachers of male as well as female adepts; they headed monasteries and are found in the ranks of the celestial immortals, or those who have achieved full enlightenment.[74] Daoism established spiritual training for women that allowed them to put aside their domestic duties for the pursuit of spiritual life.

Of particular interest is the Daoist development of a transformative alchemy of the body that is itself rooted in practices of Chinese medicine designed to remove blockages to the free flow of energy. This path of psychophysical liberation recognized corporal differences of male and female, but in order ultimately to overcome gender differences. The path of liberation begins for men and women with cultivating compassion and kindness for the weak, although women are seen as already more in touch with this way of being than men. It then proceeds with forms of physical transformation that aim at both drawing on and overcoming male and female bodily and social differences. The female must strengthen her bones, while the male must cultivate a more supple spine, thus each compensating for the distortions of their gender socialization.

Psychophysical alchemy then proceeds by focusing on the distinctive male and female bodily hormonal systems in order to subject them to control. This involves the male curbing the unruly power of semen or male procreative power, while women focus on curbing and finally stopping their menstrual flow or "cutting off the head of the red dragon." For women this means returning their bodies to their prepubescent youth and thus halting the process of decay that set in with puberty. As male and female overcome gender differentiation, their training becomes more similar. For both this is described as a pregnancy, gestating and finally giving birth to a spiritual embryo or new self that is restored to harmony with the cosmic Dao. This path of psychospiritual transformation is notable for its lack of body-spirit dualism, its rootedness in the transformation of the body as seat of spiritual power through the body's own energies. It recognizes male and female differences, both biological and socially constructed, but uses these as a path to ultimately overcome difference, psychophysical and social.[75]

If Daoism seems to offer more of an "equal opportunity" for self-transformation than most other axial religions, what of its ecological potential? Is it the ready ally of environmental ethics that some Westerners have imagined? Although Daoism's ideal is restored "naturalness," the harmonization of self and cosmos, it has little use for collective action to change destructive environmental practices of modern industrialism characteristic of Western movements to "save the planet." Its way remains determinedly individual, focused on the transformation of each person, not the transformation of social systems. Yet Daoists traditionally have cultivated forest sanctuaries. Recently they have committed themselves to major projects of tree planting and protection of forests in China.[76]

However, some Daoist thinkers have become highly suspicious of Western environmental rhetoric and practice, smacking as it does to them of Christian-style missionary movements that preach a fallen world that must then be "saved" by coercive methods.[77] In keeping with their own tradition of *wu wei* or nonaction, Daoists suspect that large-scale intervention to "change the world" is likely to do more harm than good.[78] What is needed is to give up egoistic and coercive ways of acting toward other human and nonhuman beings, so that the way of nature can reestablish its own path of life. This is always more in balance than any system that humans can devise and impose on the rest of reality.

A Declaration of the Chinese Daoist Association on Global Ecology outlines the Daoist approach to ecological ethics. Reharmonization of human beings with the Dao means allowing the many things of the natural world to each grow according to its own innate nature. The ecological crisis is seen as rooted primarily in an inflated egoism in which humans have imagined that they can conquer and control nature. The primary path then is not new technology or social organization, but the surrender of this inflated egoism so that humans can resituate themselves in the harmony of each being with the others. This harmony remains in place and is accessible to us, if we would but "let go" of our demands for accumulation, possession, and control.[79]

JUDAISM

The Jewish tradition is a multifaceted development over three thousand years and offers two distinct ways of looking at the relation of God and creation with a certain range of possibilities within each approach. Jewish mysticism, a minority esoteric tradition in Judaism, offers the possibility of seeing divine transcendence coming forth from itself into an immanent self-expression in creation. This is suggested in the sapiential traditions in the Hebrew Bible and in second temple writings. The first century BCE *Wisdom of Solomon* speaks of Wisdom as coming forth from God and becoming the agent and ground of creation.

> She is the illumination that streams from everlasting light, the flawless reflection of the active power of God and the image of God's goodness. (7:25–26)

Sapiential traditions were elaborated in Jewish gnosticisms of the first to third centuries CE and were further developed in medieval Jewish Kabbalah. Kabbalah images the divine One emerging through a series of descending self-expressions into the manyness of the creation. The mystical path of redemption is a process of return to divine Oneness. In this process God can be seen as the innermost being of all that is.[80]

However, mainstream Jewish tradition is resistant to any tendency to break down the strict line between creation and creatures by making creation itself an expression of God. It also wishes to maintain a clear hierarchy of beings within creation, with the human having a special role as image of God and God's representative over nonhuman creation. But this role is in no way a license for abuse of nature. Contemporary ecologically concerned Jews would insist that the human role is that of stewardship, not ownership, of creation. The earth remains the Lord's. We are God's delegates to care for creation and are accountable to God for our stewardship.[81]

Within this view of the God-human and human-nonhuman relation, there are various possibilities in Jewish tradition for celebrating both the sacrality of creation and human restraints in relation to it. Some thinkers make a parallel between revelation of God through creation and the revelation of God in the written Torah. This parallel is first explored in the book of Ecclesiasticus or the Wisdom of Ben Sirach which sees the Wisdom of God poured out upon the whole creation, finding its definitive incarnation in the written Torah. The laws of purity, Kosher food, and Sabbath teach Jews the limitations of use of nature. Nature is not simply there to be exploited ad infinitum. Rather there are limitations on when sex may be enjoyed, what foods can be eaten, how much one should work. These laws teach restraints upon the human appetite toward nature.[82]

Moreover the nonhuman world, animals, plants, celestial bodies, are not simply under human control. They also have their own purposes, their own relation to God. The Book of Job particularly teaches not only the mystery of God, but the mystery of God's creation that goes far beyond human knowledge and control and has a direct relation to God independently of humans. The sphere of human knowledge and control is limited, and other creatures have a better understanding of God.

> But ask the animals and they will teach you; the birds of the air and they will tell you; ask the plants of the earth and they will teach you and the fish of the sea will declare to you. Who among all these does not know that the hand of the Lord has done this? In his hand is the life of every living thing and the breath of every human being. (12:7–10)

Creation should not be exalted as divine, but neither is it our slave. Rather humans and nonhumans are fellow creatures of God. In the words of Abraham Heschel, "the earth is our sister, not our Mother."[83]

Is the privileged role of stewardship over creation as God's image shared equally with men and women, or are men, especially free men, seen as having primacy in this role? The Jewish tradition, like the Christian which depends on it, is ambivalent on this question. There is a considerable increase in overt misogyny in Jewish writings of the early rabbinic period, although this may reflect not so much a worsening status of women, but greater freedom of some elite women to play roles of economic patronage in the community which some men found threatening.[84] The Testament of Rueben (109–106 BCE) condemns women as more "overcome by the spirit of fornication than men" and sternly advises men that "evil are women, my sons, and since they have no power or strength over men, they use wiles of outer attraction that they may draw them to themselves"(5:1–7).

Some Jewish writings of this period reserve the term "image of God" for men alone, while other writings include women equally in the image of God. [85] The Hellenistic Jewish philosopher, Philo, sees the very creation of women as coming about through a fall in which the original androgynous Adam lost control over his body or lower self. With Eve came sex "which is the beginning of iniquities and transgressions and it is owing to this that men have exchanged their previously immortal and happy existence for one that is mortal and full of misfortune."[86] Yet Philo also sees women as having the image of God, understood as the spark of the divine Logos in their souls, and believes that they have an equal capacity for spiritual transformation.[87]

Rabbinic Judaism developed a pattern of religious and social life in which women were systematically located in a separate space and roles from men. This was defined by their greater impurity through their reproductive roles in childbirth and menstruation, as well as the assumption of the dangers of their sexual attraction. They were excluded from the most valued roles of study and teaching of the Torah. Women's task was to free men for study through their economic and domestic support roles. Since it is presumed that these roles take all their time, they are excused from the "time-bound" commandments that men observe.

Women's religious duties included recitation of the prayers that welcomed the Sabbath, attending the *seder* Passover meal, and hearing the book of Esther on Purim. They also were to visit the ritual bath seven days after the end of menstruation, make the Sabbath bread, and light the Sabbath candles. Their role in food preparation meant they had to be expert in the laws of kosher observed in the home. The Jewish wife is simultaneously in-dispensable for the Jewish man to observe his responsibilities, and yet clearly confined to a subordinate and complementary relationship with these male duties. The fact that the very constitution of a *minyan* (quorum) for prayer consists of ten Jewish men, with women not counted, locates women firmly under male headship, not as an autonomous persons in their own right.[88]

All this has been strongly criticized by modern Jewish feminists who have won the equality of women with men in defining a *minyan*, calling girls equally with boys to the Torah, and the right of women to study and be or-dained to the rabbinate in the Reform and Conservative traditions. The Or-thodox, by definition, cling to the traditional rules. Since only Orthodox Ju-daism is recognized in Israel, this has considerable influence on women's status in religious and family law in that state.[89]

The relationship of Judaism to "nature" has a connection with how Jews, as the chosen people of a male transcendent God, positioned them-selves in relation to the Canaanites. These earlier inhabitants of the "prom-ised land" were defined as worshippers of the "gods of nature." The demand that these people of the "land of Canaan" are to be deprived of their land and displaced by conquering Hebrews sets a relation of male monotheists to indigenous peoples, as "pagans" or worshipers of false gods of "nature," that has had an enormous influence in the history of global colonization from ancient times to the present.

Biblical historians today question whether there actually was any such conquest of the land by invading Hebrews coming from exile in Egypt or whether the earlier peoples were actually displaced during the periods of political hegemony of Jews in Palestine.[90] But the importance of this con-quest myth is less a question of its historicity and more with the way it cre-ates a powerful narrative that continues to justify conquest and colonization of indigenous people in later history. This myth has been particularly acted out in the course of Christian missionizing expansion through Europe and later into Latin America, Asia, and Africa.

Jews, from the beginning of the Christian era until the twentieth cen-tury, were displaced from the land of Israel and so had no possibility of us-ing this conquest theology during that time. However, with the founding of the state of Israel in 1948 and its expanding control of land primarily through expropriation of land from the Palestinians, the issue of the rela-tionship of Jewish election and its "right" to the land previously defined as Palestine again becomes acute. Since Palestinians in the twentieth century are primarily Muslims, with a dwindling minority of Christians, one cannot claim the right of Jews to displace them on the grounds that they are worshippers of the "gods of nature." Nevertheless some militant rabbis justify the right of Jewish settlers to displace Palestinian people and take their land by referring to them as "Amelekites." This puts Palestinians in the category of those people who, since the time of Joshua, Jews have had a right to "kill in every generation" (Exodus 17:8–16).[91]

Levitical law contains a rich body of tradition having to do with the conservation of the land, its regular rest and restoration through a weekly Sabbath, a sabbatical year (every seven years), and Jubilee (every fifty years).[92] One wonders whether the neglect of this body of legislation by Jewish environmentalists is not related to the fact that such laws refer specifically to the "land of Israel" and one can hardly implement them without attention to what one is doing to Palestinians and their life in the land. The decision of the editors of the major volume on *Judaism and Ecology* to exclude any attention to the state of Israel, and to focus only on Judaism and ecology in the United States, seems to reflect this pattern of avoidance of the challenge of the Jewish sabbatical tradition for environmental justice in the state of Israel in relationship to occupied Palestinian people and land.[93] This ambivalence is highlighted when some Jewish thinkers question whether the very idea of ecology is a "Jewish agenda."[94]

These remarks are by no means intended to suggest that the maltreatment of Palestinians by the state of Israel today is unique. Rather this maltreatment repeats the patterns by which Western culture has justified the conquest and colonization of earlier indigenous peoples and their land in expanding European empires, a pattern which Christianity itself took over from the Hebrew Bible. The point is that when we consider religion and its relation to ecology and justice, we must give attention to the relationship between the monotheist myth of a chosen people and the conquest of indigenous people. We need to recognize how this religious narrative justifies the displacement of indigenous people from their land, by defining them as religiously and racially inferior and thereby lacking rights to land.

Although some Jewish leaders in the United States have questioned the relevance to Judaism of the ecological agenda, a small but creative minority has sought to lift up Jewish resources for ecology. Jewish environmental NGOs, such as Shomrei Adamah, Keepers of the Earth (1988), have sprung up. In 1993 the Coalition on the Environment and Jewish Life was formed to coordinate U.S. Jewish educational and public policy efforts on the environment.[95] Activists, such as Arthur Waskow, have formed the Shalom Center in Philadelphia. Waskow's work has sought to adapt traditional Jewish observances, such as the Sabbath and Kosher laws, to environmental ethics. Observance of the Sabbath has been redefined as a powerful counter to the consumerist workaholic culture of modern capitalism. Avoiding foods that are produced by exploited labor and under toxic conditions becomes a new way of making food laws relevant to ecological concerns.[96]

These are powerful gestures toward a Jewish environmentalism. But perhaps the full promise of Judaism for ecology will remain delimited until Jews can link ecology and social justice and can connect these concerns with a vision of ecojustice for the peoples of Israel and Palestine, dwelling in peace and justice together in the one land both claim as home.

ISLAM

Islam offers similar patterns for environmental cosmology and ethics to the Jewish tradition, but with some significant differences. Islam rejects the idea that God rested on the seventh day of creation, seeing this as attributing weakness to God. Thus it lacks the tradition of Sabbath rest so important to Judaism. It also does not accept the idea that humans are made in God's image, seeing this as extending divinity to humans.[97] Islam rejects all secondary manifestations of God, such as is suggested by Jewish Kabbalism, and even more by the Christian trinity. God is all-powerful and completely sovereign; the whole creation is directly dependent on God. Some of the Sufi mystical tradition even rejected secondary causes within creation, seeing everything that exists as directly created by God from moment to moment.[98] Islamic mysticism draws on a Neoplatonic emanational model of the God-creation relationship to suggest that God's being overflows into creation and thus God's spirit is present within it. The spiritual task is to return from this diffusion into union with God.[99]

Islam stresses the unique role of the human as vice-regent of God in rule over the creation. Although this idea can be stated in a way that sounds like unlimited dominion, environmentally concerned Muslims stress those passages that define it as stewardship. God alone has dominion over creation. Humans are given vice-regency as a burden, not a privilege.[100] They are strictly accountable to God for right conduct and will be judged on their proper discharge of their duties. Although Islam has a strong belief in the future immortality of humans, either rewarded in heaven or punished in hell, eschatology is not based on asceticism or a view of the present world as unreal and unimportant. Rather eschatology functions as moral accountability to God for obedience to God's law (*shari'a*). Islamic environmentalists stress that right care for the earth is an integral part of those duties for which we will be judged on the last day.[101]

Although humans are superior and intended by God to rule all others even from before the creation of the world, the plants and animals are by no means to be seen as simply the slaves of humans, much less as lifeless mechanical instruments. Rather all nature praises God and is the theater of divine glory. Islam can even speak of the creatures of nonhuman nature as each having their own *umma* or community with their own purposes and relation to God. To destroy a species of plant or animal is to destroy a whole chorus of God's worshippers and thus to deeply offend God who made them and loves them.[102] The nonhuman world can be said to be naturally "Muslim" or submissive to God, obeying God's law by their very nature. Nature can also be seen as a parallel to the Qur'an, revealing God's word and will. One can read God's will through nature, as well as through written revelation.[103]

Only humans can become alienated from God and thus must learn to become obedient to God through moral and spiritual discipline. Islam (like Judaism) does not have a doctrine of the Fall. Humans can become out of touch with God, but they don't lose their true human nature which is to be in harmony with God. They can be awakened to this true nature and learn to live in accordance with it through transforming grace that ever streams forth from God's mercy, walking in the ways of God's commandments manifest in the *shari'a*.[104]

Perhaps no world religion is so embattled on the question of women and gender roles as contemporary Islam, although forms of fundamentalism that stress the restoration of traditional subordination of women are also present in Christianity and Judaism and even Hinduism and Confucianism.[105] Yet Muslims today insist that the Qur'an defends women's full equality before God. Women simply have different rules than men in society, but that does not make women spiritually inferior.[106] There are occasional virulent outbursts of misogyny in the tradition and from fundamentalists today who declare that women are inferior mentally, morally, and physically, more prone to fornication, and will be the majority of those who go to hell. Only by strict control that separates women from any public role or space and confines them to their homes under the power of father or husband can women be kept in check.[107]

Yet Muslim feminists insist that these demands are not truly representative of the original spirit of Islam as intended by the prophet Mohammed. The Qur'an does declare that men are above women and are responsible for their maintenance, but Muslim feminists claim that this is simply a reasonable division of labor that allows women to devote their energies to child care. Western feminism is seen as "emancipating" women into the world of paid work, causing men to abandon their responsibilities. Women find themselves having to do double duty as both breadwinners and as sole parents.[108]

The Qur'an allowed a man up to four wives, if he could maintain them all equally. Men were also allowed to divorce their wives by simply pronouncing them divorced three times, while a woman had great difficulty initiating a divorce. Yet women also had control of their dowries and managed their own money. Although a daughter only inherited half of what a son inherited from their parents, she did not need to support dependents with this money, and therefore did not require as much money as the man who had to support a wife and children.[109]

Particularly fraught today is the issue of Muslim dress. Fundamentalists insist on a full *burka* that covers a woman from head to toe, including her face, having only eye slits or a network patch that allows the woman to see, but not to be seen. Islamic feminists insist that Islam calls only for modest dress, meaning not exposing arms and legs and covering the hair and neck with a scarf. Far from preventing women from functioning in public for work or study, this allows the women to be present in these places without being harassed by men. It also is seen as a way that women proclaim their identity as Muslim.[110]

Some extreme fundamentalists, such as the Taliban in Afghanistan, have sought to turn back the clock on any modernization of women's role, rejecting female education even on the primary level and any work outside the home. Other societies, such as Egypt and Iran, that wish to be both Islamic and modern, seek a balance between what is seen as the extremes of Western "emancipation" that abandons role differences and strict repression of women. Women wear some version of "modest" dress in public, but are encouraged to pursue higher education and work, particularly in areas seen as especially appropriate to women, such as women's education and medical care of women and children.[111]

With few exceptions the connection between women's subordination and the impoverishment of nature is not drawn by (male) Muslim environmentalists.[112] Rather they tend to see the root of the problem as a Western view of science, technology, and unlimited consumerism that has disrupted the sustainable relation of human and nature of traditional society. Islamic societies have come to suffer extreme pollution and ecological devastation because they have bought into this model of modernity. Islamic fundamentalists follow the same path of modern technological "development," while seeking to reverse the "decadent" social patterns in relation to women and sexuality they see as coming from the West.[113]

The corrupting influence of the oil economy on Muslim cultures, how the struggle for oil between East and West has fed into fundamentalist apocalyptic violence, would certainly be another area that would need to be explored here, although there is little mention of this in this volume.

Islamic environmentalists wish to criticize both fundamentalism and secularity and to recover a model of balanced and sustainable care for nature as human responsibility before God. They want to promote this ethic, not only in personal conduct, but in the official legal codes that govern society. To make environmental law into *shari'a* is necessary if this law is to become mandatory for Islamic nations.[114] Yet they admit that neither Islamic religious authorities or governments seem to be presently taking the ecological crisis very seriously or to be able to mount effective mandates to change the present course of ecological devastation.[115]

CHRISTIANITY

Christianity is the religion against which Lynn White directed his charges of being the cause of the ecological crisis. Yet many Christians in the beginning of the twenty-first century are deeply involved in ecological thought and action. The World Council of Churches has declared "peace, justice and integrity of creation" as its threefold social agenda. Most denominations have made statements proclaiming that the ecological crisis is a serious issue in which Christians need to be involved as an expression of their faith.[116] This abundance of work on ecological ethics and theology by Christians does not, in my view, reflect the superiority of Christianity as an ecological worldview, but the fact that Christianity is the largest of the world religions with almost two billion members worldwide and possesses an abundance of institutional resources for such involvement. Also many Christians feel that they have a need to turn around a global devastation for which their religion and its derivative Western worldview and global power are largely responsible.

Christian tradition married the Hebraic and Greek philosophical traditions of antiquity and so brought together the command of the Hebrew Bible to have "dominion" over the earth with the Greek philosophical hierarchy of spirit over matter. It sees God the Father as uniquely and definitively incarnated in "his son," a human male. The Christian ascetic tradition that defined its ideals until modern times sees this physical world as ephemeral. The spiritual journey of redemption is directed toward an escape from material life into communion with a transcendent God to be perfected only after death. These traditions represent strong incentives both to dominate the earth and to disconnect one's own identity from the body and material existence.

Yet Christianity also has countervailing traditions that modern ecological Christians are seeking to recover. Drawing on the Jewish Wisdom tradition, Christ as divine Logos creates and sustains the whole cosmos and brings it into communion with God. In the words of Paul's letter to the Colossians, "In him all things were created in heaven and on earth, visible and invisible, whether thrones or dominions or principalities or authorities, all things were created through him and for him, He is before all things and in him all things hold together" (Col. 1:16–17). In this theology, the whole of creation can be seen as sacramental,[117] a visible bodying forth of God's word and spirit or, in the words of Sallie McFague, as God's body.[118]

In Christian tradition, drawing on Genesis 1, all of creation is "very good." Evil and disruption occur because of human disobedience to God, not because of the evil nature of creation. Moreover in Christ all things are renewed and brought to fulfillment, not only human individuals or the church, but all creation. Thus the Christian mission to redeem the world must today be understood as including a redemption of the world from ecological abuse caused by human ignorance and sin. Although redemption is God's work that is a gracious gift to undeserving humans, yet humans redeemed in Christ also become copartners with God in overcoming personal and structural sin and bringing in a Kingdom of God in which all humanity together with nature dwells in justice and peace.[119] These are some of the mandates upon which Christians draw for an ecological theology and ethics.

Christianity, as much or more than other world religions, has harbored a misogynist inferiorizing view of women. The early Christian writers interpreted the Genesis 2–3 story of Eve and the expulsion from paradise as a woman-blaming myth. Woman, according to traditional Christian theology, was both created subordinate to man by God's design at the beginning, but also took the lead in disobeying God and causing the Fall and the advent of evil in the world. Women do have the image of God or a spiritual nature capable of redemption, but they are physically, morally, and mentally inferior and lack that part of the image of God having to do with dominion. Redemption for women, then, has to do with their voluntary acceptance of their subordination to male headship, even if it includes injustice and abuse. Through patient suffering they will redeem themselves, and perhaps their spouses as well, and ascend to equal spiritual glory in life after death.[120]

Yet since the seventeenth century Western Christians have been involved in a reinterpretation of this tradition that vindicates the equality of the sexes. The Quakers in the second half of the seventeenth century revised the creation and Fall story to insist that men and women were created perfectly equal "in the beginning" and the Fall came about through the "usurpation of power of some over others." Thus the powerful (dominant males) are the chief culprits for the Fall; from this usurpation of dominating power flows all violence and oppression between humans.[121]

This view was picked up and developed by the founders of American feminism in the nineteenth century, most of whom, like Sarah and Angelina Grimké, Lucretia Mott, and Susan B. Anthony, came from the Quaker tradition.[122]

Contemporary Christian feminism takes for granted both the inherent equality of the sexes and the view that the subordination of women is a social construction that is fundamentally unjust and contrary to our true potential as men and women. Women in the United States gradually won equal education, access to professions, the vote, and civil status through the "eighty years and more" of the first feminist movement from 1836 to 1921. Moreover most U.S. Protestant denominations accepted women's ordination between the 1850s and 1980s. Women's studies and feminist theology have become fairly well established in American universities and theological seminaries.[123]

Christianity has also been an exclusivist and aggressively missionizing religion. From its earliest years it took as its mandate the command of Jesus according to Matthew 28:18–20: "All authority in heaven and on earth has been given to me. Go therefore and make disciples of all nations, baptizing them in the name of the Father and of the Son and of the Holy Spirit and teaching them to observe all that I have commanded you, and lo, I am with you always, to the close of the age."

This command to convert all peoples of the world to Christianity was coupled with the idea of *terra nullius*. By papal decree all lands held by non-Christians were declared unoccupied or "empty" land which could be appropriated by invading Christians as part of their mission to convert all peoples to Christ.[124] This view theoretically applied to people of all other world religions, but it has been used with particular rigor toward those people seen as "pagans" or "nature worshippers" who live in what were interpreted as "primitive" societies.

These indigenous peoples are today being recognized as having precious cosmologies and practices of sustainable relations between humans and nature. But they have been subjugated to genocidal uprooting from their land and destruction of their cultures for five hundred years by an aggressive combination of Christian mission and colonialism. Today they are

the target of new colonizing and commodification by multinational phar-
maceutical companies that see their lands and traditions as possessed of valuable resources for food and medicine.[125]

In the light of this heritage of genocidal violence and expropriation of
the lands of non-Christian peoples throughout the globe, it is with difficulty
that Christians enter into real dialogue with other religions and cultures. It
is still very controversial among Christians to accept the view that Christianity is simply one human religion among others, no more valid than Islam, Judaism, Hinduism, or Buddhism, or even the local worldviews of
Mayan Indians in Southern Mexico and Guatemala or the Shona people of
Zimbabwe.[126] Equality of human religious cultures is also problematic for
other Abrahamic monotheists, Jews and Muslims. Thus the kind of dialogue
among equals between world religions and even with "local" religions,
sponsored by the Harvard conferences and volumes, has hardly been taken
on board by leaders of most world religions. The Parliament of the World's
Religions, which has been meeting since 1993 (held first in 1893), seeks not
only interfaith dialogue, but the construction of a global ethic shared by the
world's religions. Yet this movement is still a marginalized effort, ignored by
major Christian bodies, including the World Council of Churches.[127]

What then can be said about the "greening of world religions" in the
light of the Harvard project of conferences and publications? There seems
to be some consensus about what religious attitudes lend themselves to
abuse of nature. Highly individualistic religious views that concentrate
solely on the salvation of the individual "soul" taken out of its social and
even corporal contexts are unhelpful. Mandates for unlimited domination
that see the (elite male) human as having all power over the rest of nature,
and the right to manipulate the rest of nature without regard to its own
ecosystems, are problematic. Religions that are highly otherworldly, deem-
ing this world as ephemeral and without intrinsic value, from which the soul
should escape to eternal life or await an imminent destruction followed by
a heavenly world, are not helpful.

Unfortunately it is exactly these patterns of thought that are on the rise
today through fundamentalist religious revivals in the Christian and Muslim
worlds particularly. Moreover the ideology of the dominant scientific and
market economy has secular versions of at least the first two worldviews, in-
dividualism and unlimited domination, if not the third view of ascetic or
apocalyptic escape from the earth. The retrieval of ecological potential in
world religions is still very much an expression of small and often marginal
groups within each faith tradition that scarcely makes its way into effective
communication, much less action, at the level of local practice, as Muslims,

Christians, and Jews, Jains, Buddhists, and Hindus gather to hear their preachers or carry out their rituals.

Nevertheless such efforts are hardly to be decried as useless. They are important first steps to identifying the positive resources for environmental ethics in each religious tradition. Moreover they express in various ways actual organizing among people of different faith traditions who see themselves given an additional inspiration and mandate through their faith to engage in preventative or restorative action. People of faith are involved in such efforts as blocking timber companies from cutting down forests, replanting devastated forests, and banning or limiting the release of chemicals into the atmosphere that is causing global warming. People of many faiths have devoted their energies to a worldwide effort to craft a World Charter for Nature, hopefully to be accepted by all nations through the United Nations, that would commit the world's people to more just and sustainable ways of living.[128]

If there is some consensus on what religious stances tend to allow or promote abuse of nature, are there some suggestions through these studies of what worldviews are more conducive to an ecological ethic? Should all religious people seek to emphasize those views that see nature as sacred, as permeated by divine energy, as overcoming any split between matter and spirit, God and nature? It is evident from these studies that religions which see nature as divine, as embodied deities, or as permeated by the divine do not have a better track record of ecological protection than those who see God as a transcendent creator who mandates humans to care for nature, not to abuse it.

What seems to be necessary is some view that the nonhuman world has its own integrity, its own dynamic of life and renewal of life. Humans need to respect the way in which the natural world sustains its own life, which is also the basis for sustaining human life. Whether religious communities see this self-sustaining ecology of nature as created by God or as the self-expression of immanent divine being is perhaps less important than that they actively cultivate respect for nature's own life and see themselves as having to harmonize their own behavior with it. They need to question and reject a view that simply turns the natural world into "commodities" to be used in any way that leads to short-term profit, even though this means long-term disaster for nature, including humans. Humans are within, not outside of, this self-sustaining ecosystem of the natural world. They can only survive themselves by sustaining it.

World religions not only need to create theological or religious visions to respect this self-sustaining life of nature within which humans subsist, but also to promote action to prevent abuse and to restore more harmonious patterns. Here world religions differ considerably on the ways in which they mandate preventative or restorative action. Some traditions, such as Daoism, are highly resistant to activist interventions in nature by humans, and advise an "inaction" that aims at letting nature restore itself. Others, such as Christianity, Islam, and Confucianism, are stronger on socially organized efforts, including the establishment of legal sanctions to curb evil and command good.

It seems to me that effective ecological action probably requires a careful balance and synthesis of both stances. Banning harmful action, such as pouring toxic chemicals into the air, water, and soil, demands not only individual actions but also collective requirements carried out on a political level. Such bans aim at allowing the air, water, and soil to resume their more self-generating capacities for healthful life. Forest management today recognizes that the best policy is not to put out every fire or kill animals once seen as harmful predators, but rather to allow managed fires, and introduce predators that have been killed off, reestablishing patterns by which forests manage themselves.[129] In other cases self-sustaining relations to nature mean discovering how soil fertility, water regeneration in aquifers, and "good air" are themselves produced by natural cycles. Farming and other production must seek to integrate human use of nature into these patterns of natural self-management.[130]

What religion introduces into these practices is the cultivation of sensitivities of reverence, love, and empathy with the natural world that draw us to concern for it. Such concern then calls us to act ecologically as moral duty and as redemptive hope, as obedience to God and alignment of ourselves with divine imperatives for a more peaceful and just world. Effective religious motivation for ecological action may often result in a kind of synthesis of religious traditions. Christian traditions of activism and missionizing may find themselves inspired to a more contemplative restraint through encounter with Asian traditions, such as Daoism. Contemplative traditions, such as Buddhism, inspired by a Western liberation theology, may take on more militant collective action, such as is found in the development of socially engaged Buddhism in Thailand and Vietnam.

This does not mean that some new universal faith that merges the religions of the world will or should emerge. Rather it means that a world religion, while affirming its distinctive identity and tradition, may borrow useful aspects from another religion or rediscover these potentials in its own tradition through dialogue and mutual engagement with other faiths.

World religions have yet to become effective major players in the struggle for an ecologically just and sustainable world. But the potential is there, and there has been extraordinary movement in this direction in the last decade. Secular environmentalists, such as the World Watch Institute researchers for the annual *State of the World Report*, have retreated from an earlier tendency to dismiss religion as only a part of the problem and no part of any solution to ecological crisis. The 2003 edition of this report contained a major article on "Engaging Religion in the Quest for a Sustainable World" that discussed these conferences and volumes on world religions and ecology.

The author, Gary Gardner, outlined what he saw as the vital resources that world religions contain that could be of enormous importance for effective ecological action. These are: (1) religious teachings mandate respect for nature; (2) they have moral authority to transmit such worldviews through preaching, teaching, and media of communication at the disposal of religious institutions; (3) they have major constituencies of billions of people organized in local communities; (4) they have material resources, buildings, money-gathering capacity, and other means of collective power; and (5) they have community-building capacity to promote motivated groups seeking to live their lives individually and communally in an ecologically sustainable way.[131]

Some secular environmentalists are awakening to the enormous potential of religious communities to provide resources in people and organizations, and to nurture deep emotional, ethical, and spiritual motivation to transform lives and to oppose unjust and violent ways of living represented by the dominant systems. The making of alliances between different religious constituencies across faith traditions and between secular and religiously inspired environmentalists is thus on the horizon, awaiting new ways in which these communities can begin to join hands across the world.

NOTES

1. *Science*, vol. 155 (March 10, 1967), 1203–7. Reprinted in *This Sacred Earth: Religion, Nature and Environment*, Roger S. Gottlieb, ed. (New York: Routledge, 1996), 184–93.

2. Ibid., 189.

3. Ibid., 192, 193.

4. Thomas Berry, *The Dream of the Earth* (San Francisco: Sierra Club Books, 1988); see also his recent book, *The Great Work* (New York: Bell Tower, 2000).

5. *Worldviews and Ecology* (Lewisburg, Pa.: Bucknell University Press, 1993).

6. See Thomas Berry, "Into the Future," in Gottlieb, *This Sacred Earth*, 414.

7. *Buddhism and Ecology: The Interconnection of Dharma and Deeds*, Mary Evelyn Tucker and Duncan R. Williams (Cambridge, Mass.: Harvard University Press,

1997). *Confucianism and Ecology: The Interrelation of Heaven, Earth and Humans,* Mary Evelyn Tucker and John Berthrong, eds. (Cambridge, Mass.: Harvard University Press, 1998). *Christianity and Ecology: Seeking the Wellbeing of Earth and Human,* Rosemary Ruether and Dieter Hessel, eds. (Cambridge, Mass.: Harvard University Press, 2000). *Hinduism and Ecology: The Intersection of Earth, Sky and Water,* Mary Evelyn Tucker and Christopher Key Chapple, eds. (Cambridge, Mass.: Harvard University Press, 2000). *Daoism and Ecology: Ways within a Cosmic Landscape,* N.J. Girardot, James Miller, and Liu Xiaogan, eds. (Cambridge, Mass.: Harvard University Press, 2001). *Indigenous Traditions and Ecology: The Interbeing of Cosmology and Community,* John A. Grim, ed. (Cambridge, Mass.: Harvard University Press, 2001). *Jainism and Ecology: Nonviolence in the Web of Life,* Christopher Key Chapple, ed. (Cambridge, Mass.: Harvard University Press, 2002). *Judaism and Ecology: Created World and Revealed Word,* Hava Tirosh-Samuelson, ed. (Cambridge, Mass.: Harvard University Press, 2002). *Islam and Ecology: A Bestowed Trust,* Richard C. Foltz, Frederick M. Denny, and Azizan Baharuddin, eds. (Cambridge, Mass.: Harvard University Press, 2003). The volume on Shinto and Ecology and the culminating conference volume are still to appear.

8. For an overview of this literature, see V. Raghaven, *The Indian Heritage,* 2nd edition (Bangalore: Indian Institute of World Culture, 1958),

9. See Tracy Pintchman, *The Rise of the Goddess in the Hindu Tradition* (Albany, N.Y.: SUNY Press, 1994), 117–18.

10. See John S. Hawley, "Hinduism: *Sati* and Its Defenders," in *Fundamentalism and Gender,* John S. Hawley, ed. (New York: Oxford University Press, 1994), 79–110.

11. Traditional Hinduism saw travel across the seas outside India as causing ritual pollution and mandated a ceremony of purification on return.

12. From N. Patrick Peritore, "Environmental Attitudes of Indian Elites: Challenging Western Post-Modern Models," in *Asian Surveys* 33 (1993), 807, cited in Christopher Key Chapple, Introduction, *Hinduism and Ecology,* xxxiii.

13. For accounts of the protest of the damming of the Narmada river and the Chipko movement to prevent logging by hugging trees, see the articles by William F. Fisher, "Sacred Rivers, Sacred Dams: Competing Visions of Social Justice and Sustainable Development Along the Narmada;" Pratyusha Basu and Jael Stilliman, "Green and Red, Not Saffron: Gender and the Politics of Resistance in the Narmada Valley," and George A. James, "Ethical and Religious Dimensions of Chipko Resistance," in *Hinduism and Ecology,* 401–50, 499–530.

14. See Kelly D. Alley, "Separate Domains: Hinduism, Politics and Environmental Pollution," in *Hinduism and Ecology,* 355–87. Also Alley's article, "Idioms of Degeneracy: Assessing Ganga's Purity and Pollution," in *Purifying the Earthly Body of God: Religion and Ecology in Hindu India,* Lance Nelson, ed. (Albany, N.Y.: SUNY Press, 1998), 297–330.

15. See Katherine Young, "Hinduism," in *Women in World Religions,* Arvind Sharma, ed. (Albany, N.Y.: SUNY Press, 1987), 59–103.

16. See Gabriele Dietrich, *Reflections on the Women's Movement in India: Religion, Ecology and Development* (Dehli: Horizon India Books, 1992). Also Katherine Young,

"Hinduism," in *Today's Women in World Religion*, Arvind Sharma, ed. (Albany, N.Y.: SUNY Press, 1994), 85–135.

17. Katherine Young, "Hinduism," in *Women in World Religion*, 80–84.
18. Tracy Pintchman, *The Rise of the Goddess in the Hindu Tradition*, 61–105.
19. Ibid., 185–214.
20. David Kinsley, *Hindu Goddesses: Visions of the Divine Feminine in the Hindu Tradition* (Berkeley: University of California Press, 1986), 116–31.
21. Pintchman, *The Rise of the Goddess*, 199.
22. See Vasudha Narayanan, "Brimming with *Bhakti*, Embodiments of *Sakti*: Devotees, Deities, Performers, Reformers and Other Women of Power in the Hindu Tradition," in *Feminism and World Religions*, Arvind Sharma and Katherine K. Young, eds. (Albany, N.Y.: SUNY Press, 1999), 25–77.
23. Young, "Hinduism," in *Women in World Religions*, 68–70.
24. See J. Baird Callicott, "Hinduism," in *Earth's Insights: A Survey of Environmental Ethics from the Mediterranean to the Australian Outback* (Berkeley: University of California Press, 1994), 44–53.
25. Vandana Shiva, *Staying Alive: Women, Ecology and Development* (London: Zed, 1989), 38–42.
26. See George James' remarks on "Chipko and the Feminine" in his article on the Chipko Movement in *Hinduism and Ecology*, 516–18.
27. See James on "Chipko and the Ascetic Ideal," ibid., 514–16.
28. For the Gandhian roots of the development of an indigenous Indian environmental ethic, see the two articles by Vinay Lal and Larry D. Shinn in *Hinduism and Ecology*, 183–244.
29. For a feminist interpretation of the Goddess Kali, see Lina Gupta, "Kali the Savior," in *After Patriarchy: Feminist Transformations of World Religions*, Paula Cooey, William R. Eakin, and Jay McDaniel, eds. (Maryknoll, N.Y.: Orbis Press, 1991), 15–38.
30. For an overview of Jainism, its history, doctrines, and literature, see *Sources of the Indian Tradition*, William Theodore de Bary, ed. (New York: Columbia, University Press, 1958), 39–92.
31. See Kristi L. Wiley, "The Nature of Nature: Jain Perspectives on the Natural World," in *Jainism and Ecology*, 35–59.
32. See Nathmal Tatia, "The Jain World View and Ecology,", also John Cort, "Green Jainism? Notes and Queries toward a Possible Jain Environmental Ethic," ibid., 3–18, 63–94.
33. Padmanabh S. Jaini, "Ecology, Economics and Development in Jainism," ibid., 141–56.
34. See Padmanabh S. Jaini, *Gender and Salvation: Jaina Debates on the Spiritual Liberation of Women* (Berkeley: University of California Press, 1991).
35. For a general overview of female status and roles in Jainism, both nuns and laywomen, see Nalini Balhir, "Women in Jainism," in *Women and Religion*, Arvind Sharma, ed. (Albany, N.Y.: SUNY Press, 1994), 121–38. For a detailed anthropological study of Jain laywomen in one community, see Mary Whitney Kelting, *Singing*

to the Jinas: Jain Laywomen, Mandal Singing and Negotiation of Jain Devotion (Oxford: Oxford University Press, 2001).

36. For a skeptical treatment of the translation of Jain tradition into claims of being an ecological ethic, see Paul Dundas, "The Limits of a Jain Environmental Ethic," in *Jainism and Ecology*, 95–117.

37. See Anne Valley, "From Liberation to Ecology: Ethical Discourses among Orthodox and Diaspora Jains," ibid., 193–216.

38. "The Jain Declaration on Nature," ibid., 217–24.

39. Satish Kumar's article on his mother and the traditional Jain way of life she exemplified is in *Jainism and Ecology. Resurgence* magazine can be contacted through Ford House, Hartland, Bideford, Devon, EX39 6EE, UK, or at www.resurgence.com. Schumacher can be contacted at The Old Postern, Darlington, Devon, TQ9 6EA, UK.

40. On American Buddhism, see the chapters by David Landis Barnhill, Stephanie Kaza, and Jeff Yamauchi, in *Buddhism and Ecology*, 187–265. The conversion of American women to Buddhism is creating a significant feminist reinterpretation of Buddhism teachings and practice. See Sandy Boucher, *Turning the Wheel: American Women Creating the New Buddhism* (San Francisco: Harper and Row, 1988).

41. See Callicott, *Earth's Insights*, 57–60; also Arthur L. Herman, *An Introduction to Buddhist Thought* (Washington, D.C.: University Press of America, 1984).

42. On Buddhism, animals, and vegetarianism, see Christopher Chapple, in *Buddhism and Ecology*, 137–38.

43. See Nancy Schuster Barnes, "Buddhism," in *Women in World Religions*, 107–8; also her article on "Women in Buddhism" in *Today's Woman in World Religions*, 142.

44. Nancy Schuster Barnes, "Women in Buddhism" in *Today's Woman in World Religions*, 139–45.

45. Barnes, "Buddhism," *Women in World Religions*, 118–20.

46. See Rita Gross, "The Dharma Is Neither Male nor Female: Buddhism on Gender and Liberation," in Leonard Grob, Riffat Hassan, and Haim Gordon, eds. *Women and Men's Liberation: Testimonies of Spirit* (New York: Greenwood Press, 1991), 105–28.

47. Callicott, *Earth's Insights*, 88; also Paul Ingram, "The Jeweled Net of Nature" and Graham Parkes, "Voices of Mountains, Trees and Rivers: Kukai, Dogen and Deep Ecology," in *Buddhism and Ecology*, 75–81 and 111–25.

48. Ingram, "The Jeweled Net of Nature," 82–83.

49. See Ian Harris, "Buddhism and the Discourse on Environmental Concern: Some Methodological Problems Considered," and Ruben L. F. Habito, "Mountains and Rivers and the Great Earth: Zen and Ecology," in *Buddhism and Ecology*, 377–96, 165–67.

50. See Ian Harris' critique of Suzuki's work, ibid., 338–39. Also D. T. Suzuki, *Zen and Japanese Culture*, 2nd edition (London: Routledge and Kegan Paul, 1959).

51. Callicott, *Earth's Insights*, 227–32; also Joanna Macy, *Dharma and Development: Religion as Resource in the Sarvodaya Self-Help Movement* (West Hartford, Conn.: Kumarian Press, 1985).

52. Callicott, 232–34. On monasticism as an instrument in the struggle against deforestation in Thailand, see Leslie E. Sponsel and Poranee Natadecha-Sponsel, "A Theoretical Analysis of the Potential Contribution of the Monastic Community in Promoting a Green Society in Thailand," *Buddhism and Ecology*, 45–61.

53. See Stephanie Kaza, "American Buddhist Response to the Land: Ecological Practices at Two West Coast Retreat Centers," and Jeff Yamauchi, "The Greening of Zen Mountain Center: A Case Study," in *Buddhism and Ecology*, 219–64.

54. See Sulak Sivaraksa, *A Socially Engaged Buddhism* (Bangkok: Thai Inter-religious Commission for Development, 1988); also his *Seeds of Peace* (Berkeley: Parallax Press, 1993).

55. See Barbara Reed, "Women and Chinese Religion in Contemporary Taiwan," in *Today's Woman in World Religion*, 232–34.

56. See the article by Mary Evelyn Tucker, "The Philosophy of Ch'i as an Ecological Cosmology," in *Confucianism and Ecology*, 187–207. Tucker expounds the cosmological thought of three Neo-Confucian thinkers, Chang Tsai (1020–1071 CE), Lo Ch'in-Shun (1465–1547 CE), and Kaibara Ekken (1630–1714).

57. Toshio Kuwako, "The Philosophy of Environmental Correlation in Chu Hsi," in *Confucianism and Ecology*, 161.

58. See Theresa Kelleher, "Confucianism," in *Women in World Religion*, 165–66; also Joseph A. Adler, "Response and Responsibility: Chou Tun-i and Confucian Resources for Environmental Ethics," in *Confucianism and Ecology*, 136.

59. See Mary Evelyn Tucker, "Ecological Themes in Taoism and Confucianism," in *Worldviews and Ecology*, 157.

60. See John Berthrong, "Motifs for a New Confucian Ecological Vision," in *Confucianism and Ecology*, 237–63.

61. Kelleher, "Confucianism," *Women in World Religions*, 135–59. See also Lü Hsiu-Lien's 1974 *New Feminism* critique of Confucianism in Taiwan, in Barbara Reed, "Women and Chinese Religion in Contemporary Taiwan," in *Today's Woman in World Religions*, 227–32.

62. See "Confucius," in *Sources of the Chinese Tradition*, William Theodore de Bary, Wing-Tsit, and Burton Watcon, eds. (New York: Columbia University Press, 1960), 20–21.

63. On the complexity of the Confucian tradition toward women's education and political power, see Terry Woo, "Confucianism and Feminism," in *Feminism and World Religions*, 110–47.

64. See Miriam Levering, "Women, the State and Religion Today in the People's Republic of China," in *Today's Woman in World Religions*, 171–224.

65. See J. Baird Callicott, *Earth's Insights*, 79–85.

66. See Mary Evelyn Tucker, "Ecological Themes in Taoism and Confucianism," in *Worldviews and Ecology*, 158; and *Confucianism and Ecology*, passim.

67. See Robert P. Weller and Peter K. Boll, "From Heaven-and-Earth to Nature: Chinese Concepts of the Environment and Their Influence on Policy Implementation," in *Confucianism and Ecology*, 313–40.

68. See Huey-li Li, "Some Thoughts on Confucianism and Ecofeminism," ibid., 293–311.

69. See Jordan Paper, "'Daoism' and 'Deep Ecology': Fantasy and Potentiality"; also "What Can Daoism Contribute to Ecology," in *Daoism and Ecology*, 3–21, 71–74.

70. See Roger T. Ames, "The Local and the Focal in Realizing a Daoist World," ibid., 265–82.

71. *Tao te Ching* VI; Arthur Waley, *The Way and Its Power: A Study of the Tao te Ching and Its Place in Chinese Thought* (New York: Grove Press, 1958), 149.

72. Joanne D. Birdwhistell, "Ecological Questions for Daoist Thought: Contemporary Issues and Ancient Texts," in *Daoism and Ecology*, 37–38.

73. Karl Jaspers has defined the "axial age" as the period of the 6th–5th centuries BCE in which the Greek philosophers, the prophets of Israel, Zoroaster in Persia, the Buddha in India, and Confucius in China all flourished. See his *The Origin and Goal of History* (New Haven, Conn.: Yale University Press, 1953).

74. See Barbara Reed, "Taoism," in *Women in World Religions*, 161–82, and Karen Laughlin and Eva Wong, "Feminism and/in Taoism," in *Feminism in World Religions*, 151–55. Miriam Levering, in "Women, the State and Religion Today in the People's Republic of China," in *Today's Woman in World Religions*, describes the roles played by Daoist women in lay and monastic life in China today, 201–11.

75. For the female path of alchemical development, see Laughlin and Wong, ibid., 164–72.

76. See *Daoism and Ecology*, 368–70.

77. See "Change Starts Small: Daoist Practice and the Ecology of Individual Lives," in "A Roundtable Discussion with Liu Ming, René Navarro, Linda Varone, Vincent Chu, Daniel Seitz, and Weidong Lu, *Daoism and Ecology*, 379.

78. See Liu Xiaogan, "Non-Action and the Environment Today: A Conceptual and Applied Study of Laozi's Philosophy," *Daoism and Ecology*, especially his discussion of how the aggressive efforts of Greenpeace to stop the killing of seals destroyed the Inuit Eskimo way of life, 318–20.

79. "A Declaration of the Chinese Daoist Association on Global Ecology," Zhang Jiyu, in *Daoism and Ecology*, 361–71.

80. Arthur Green, "A Kabbalah for the Environmental Age," in *Judaism and Ecology*, 13–16.

81. See David Novak, "The Doctrine of Creation and the Idea of Nature," and Lenn E. Goodman, "Respect for Nature in the Jewish Tradition," ibid., 155–75, 227–59.

82. See Eric Katz. "Judaism and the Ecological Crisis," in *Worldviews and Ecology*, 55–70; also Shalom Rosenberg, "Concept of Torah and Nature in Jewish Thought," in *Judaism and Ecology*, 189–225.

83. Abraham Heschel, *Man Is Not Alone* (New York: Farrar, Straus and Young), 115. See Edward K. Kaplan, "Reverence and Responsibility: Abraham Joshua Heschel on Nature and the Self," in *Judaism and Ecology*, 407–21.

84. See Rosemary R. Ruether, *Women and Redemption: A Theological History* (Minneapolis: Fortress Press, 1998), 28–29.

85. The first century CE *Books of Adam and Eve*, for example, see only Adam as made in God's image, not Eve. Ibid., 27–30.

86. Philo, "On the Creation of the World," 53.

87. See Philo's "On the Therapeutae," in Nahun N. Glazer, ed. *The Essential Philo* (New York: Schocken, 1971), 311–30.

88. Denise L. Carmody, "Judaism," in *Women in World Religions*, 183–206.

89. Denise L. Carmody, "Today's Jewish Woman," in *Today's Woman in World Religions*, 245–66. Also Ellen M. Umansky, "Feminism in Judaism," in *Feminism and World Religions*, 179–213.

90. See Norman K. Gottwald, *The Politics of Ancient Israel* (Louisville, Ky.: Westminster John Knox Press, 2001), 166–67. On the exodus story as appropriated by Saul as a national charter myth of new royal power, see Karel van der Toorn, *Family Religion in Babylonia, Syria and Israel: Continuity and Change in the Forms of Relious Life* (Leiden: E. J. Brill, 1996), 291–302, 349–51, 375–76.

91. Rosemary R. Ruether and Herman J. Ruether, *The Wrath of Jonah: The Crisis of Religious Nationalism in the Israeli-Palestinian Conflict*, 2nd edition (Minneapolis: Fortress Press, 2002), 180.

92. See Rosemary R. Ruether, *Gaia and God*, 211–13.

93. The essays in this volume concentrate entirely on ecological views of Judaism in the West, mainly the United States. Israel is largely ignored and the Palestinians are never mentioned. See Introduction by Hava Tirosh-Samuelson, xxxvii.

94. Ibid., xxxiv, lvi; also in this volume, Mark X. Jacobs, "Jewish Environmentalism: Past Accomplishments and Future Challenges," 458–59.

95. An overview of these developments of Jewish environmentalism in the United States can be found in the article by Marx X. Jacobs, ibid.

96. Arthur Waskow, *Down-to-Earth Judaism: Food, Money, Sex and the Rest of Life* (New York: William Morrow, 1995); also his "What Is Eco-kosher?" in *This Sacred Earth: Religion, Nature, Environment*, Roger S. Gottlieb, ed. (New York: Routledge, 1996), 297–300.

97. Roger E. Timm, "The Ecological Fallout of Islamic Creation Theology," *Worldviews and Ecology*, 84 (citing the Qur'an 50:38 and 42:11).

98. L. Clarke, "The Universe Alive: Nature in the *Masnavi* of Jalal al-Din Rumi," in *Islam and Ecology*, 41.

99. Ibid., 53.

100. See Ibrahim Özdemir, "Toward an Understanding of Environmental Ethics from a Qur'anic Perspective," Mawil Izzi Dien, "Islam and the Environment: Theory and Practice," Saadia Khawar Khan Chishti, "*Fitra*: An Islamic Model for Humans and the Environment," and Othman abd-ar-Rahman Llewellyn, "The Basis for a Discipline of Islamic Environmental Law," in *Islam and Ecology*, 25–27, 109–10, 75–76, 190–91 and *passim*.

101. Timm, *Worldviews and Ecology*, 89–90 on ecology and Muslim eschatology.

102. See Seyyed Hossein Nasr, "Islam and the Environment: Theory and Practice"; also Ibrahim Özdemir, in *Islam and Ecology*, 96, 23.

103. Ibrahim Özdemir, ibid., 8–9, 16–19.

104. Saadia Khawar Khan Chishti, "*Fitra*"; also Abdul Aziz Said and Nathan C. Funk, "Peace in Islam: An Ecology of the Spirit," in *Islam and Ecology*, 67, 71–73, 172–74.

105. See Courtney W. Howland, ed. *Religious Fundamentalisms and the Human Rights of Women* (New York: St. Martin's Press, 1999). Also John Stratton Hawley, ed., *Fundamentalism and Gender* (Oxford: Oxford University Press, 1994) and Martin E. Marty and R. Scott Appleby, eds. *Fundamentalisms and Society: Reclaiming the Sciences, the Family and Education* (Chicago: The University of Chicago Press, 1993).

106. See Saadia Khawar Khan Chishti, *Fitra*, in *Islam and Ecology*, p. 78. For an extended argument on the equality of the sexes in the Qur'an, see Riffat Hassan, "Feminism in Islam," in *Feminism and World Religion*, 248–78.

107. There is an extensive new literature on women under the Taliban. See Rosalind Russell, "Behind the Burqa," in *Afghanistan: Lifting the Veil* (Upper Saddle River, N.J.: Prentice-Hall, 2002), 172–203; Batya Swift Yasqur, *Behind the Burqa* (Hoboken, N.J.: John Wiley, 2002); and Rosemarie Skaine, *The Women of Afghanistan under the Taliban* (Jefferson, N.C.: McFarland, 2002).

108. See Jane I. Smith, "Islam," in *Women in World Religions*, 249–50. Verse 2:228 of the Qur'an says that men are a step above women and verse 4:34 that men are the protectors of women because God has given preference to the one over the other and men provide support for women.

109. Jane I. Smith, ibid., 237–39.

110. Ibid., 240–42, also Jane I. Smith, "Women in Islam," in *Today's Women in World Religions*, 303–25.

111. Ibid., 304–8, 312–16.

112. An example of an ecofeminist Islamic reflection is Nawal Ammar, "Ecological Justice and Human Rights for Women in Islam," in *Islam and Ecology*, 377–89.

113. On the relation between Western scientific ideology and colonialism, see Seyyed Hossein Nasr; also Mawal Izzi Dien and Kaveh L. Afrasiabi, in *Islam and Ecology*, 88–93, 112–16, 286–90.

114. Othman Abd-ar-Rahman Llewellyn, "The Basis for a Discipline of Islamic Environmental Law," *Islam and Ecology*, 185–247.

115. See Richard C. Foltz, "Islamic Environmentalism: A Matter of Interpretation," in *Islam and Ecology*, 249–79.

116. William Somoplatsky-Jarman, Walter E. Grazer, and Stan L. LeQuire, "Partnership for the Environment among U.S. Christians: Reports from the National Religious Partnership for the Environment," *Christianity and Ecology*, 573–90.

117. Rosemary R. Ruether, *Gaia and God*, 229–37.

118. Sallie McFague, *The Body of God: An Ecological Theology* (Minneapolis: Fortress Press, 1993).

119. See Rosemary Ruether, "Ecojustice at the Center of the Church's Mission," in *Christianity and Ecology*, 603–14.

120. Rosemary Ruether, *Women and Redemption*, 71–77, 92–97, and 122–26.

121. Ibid., 137–42.

122. Ibid., 160–74.

123. Rosemary Ruether, "Christianity and Women in the Modern World," in *Today's Woman in World Religions*, 267–301.

124. See Stephanie Fried, "Shoot the Horse to get the Rider: Religion and Forest Politics in Bentian Borneo," *Indigenous Traditions and Ecology*, 74–75.

125. Darrell Addison Posey, "Intellectual Property Rights and the Sacred Balance: Some Spiritual Consequences from the Commercialization of Traditional Resources," in *Indigenous Traditions and Ecology*, 3–23.

126. For an overview of the major Christian theologies of religious diversity, see Paul Knitter, *Introducing Theologies of Religion* (Maryknoll, N.Y.: Orbis Press, 2002).

127. I have attended the meetings of the Parliament of the World's Religions in Chicago (1993), Capetown, South Africa (1999), and Barcelona, Spain (2004). In July 2003 I attended a consultation on ecofeminism at the World Council of Churches in Geneva. When I mentioned the work of the World Parliament to the leaders of the women's and integrity of creation desks at the WCC, this movement was dismissed as marginal to the majority of those in different world religions and unimportant.

128. On the World Charter for Nature, see International Secretariat, c/o University for Peace, PO Box 319, 6100 San José, Costa Rica; also info@earthcharter.org, www.earthcharter.org.

129. On "natural" forest management, see Alan Thein Durning, "Redesigning the Forest Economy," *State of the World*, Lester R. Brown et al., eds. (New York: Norton, 1994), 22–40.

130. See Brian Halwell, "Farming in the Public Interest," in *State of the World Report, 2002* (New York: Norton, 2002), 51–73. Also Jeffrey A. McNeedly and Sara J. Scherr, *Common Ground, Common Future: How Ecoagriculture Can Help Feed the World and Save Wild Biodiversity* (Gland, Switzerland: World Conservation Union, 2001).

131. See Gary Gardner, "Engaging Religion in the Quest for a Sustainable World," in *State of the World, 2003* (New York: Norton, 2003), 152–75.

3

ECOFEMINIST THEA/OLOGIES
AND ETHICS

Ecofeminism has emerged in the late twentieth century as a major school
of philosophical and theological thought and social analysis. The word
"ecofeminism" was coined in 1972 by Francoise d'Eaubonne who developed the "*Ecologie-Féminisme*" group, arguing that "the destruction of the
planet is due to the profit motif inherent in male power." Her 1974 book
Le Féminisme ou la mort (Feminism or Death) saw women as central to bringing about an ecological revolution.[1]

Ecofeminism sees an interconnection between the domination of
women and the domination of nature. This interconnection is typically made
on two levels: ideological-cultural and socioeconomic. On the ideological-
cultural level women are said to be "closer to nature" than men, more
aligned with body, matter, emotions, and the animal world. On the socioeconomic level, women are located in the spheres of reproduction, child raising, food preparation, spinning and weaving, cleaning of clothes and houses,
that are devalued in relation to the public sphere of male power and culture.
My assumption is that the first level is the ideological superstructure for the
second. In other words, claiming that women are "naturally" closer to the
material world and lack the capacity for intellectual and leadership roles justifies locating them in the devalued sphere of material work and excluding
them from higher education and public leadership.

Many ecofeminist thinkers extend this analysis from gender to class,
race, and ethnic hierarchies. That is, devalued classes and races of men and
women are likewise said to lack capacity for intellect and leadership, denied
higher education and located socially in the spheres of physical labor as serfs,
servants, and slaves in households, farms, and workshops. The fruits of this labor, like that of wives in the family, are appropriated by the male elites as the
base for their wealth and freedom to exercise roles of power and culture.

These male elites are the master class who define themselves as owning the dependent classes of people.

This ruling class inscribes in the systems of law, philosophy, and theology a "master narrative" or "logic of domination" that defines the normative human in terms of this male ruling group. For Plato the divine Artisan fashioned human souls from the remnants of the world soul and placed them first in the stars to contemplate the eternal ideas. Then they are placed in bodies on earth and commanded to control the passions that flow from the body. If they succeed, they will discard the body and return to their star in the heavens. If they fail to do so they will be reincarnated as a woman or a "brute." They must then work their way through successive reincarnations back to the form of an elite male to finally win release from the cycle of rebirth.[2] For Plato, the elite Greek male is the normative human.

René Descartes, a major philosopher for early modern European thought, deepened the dualism between mind and body, seeing all bodily reality as mere "dead matter" pushed and pulled by mechanical force. The mind stands outside matter contemplating and controlling it from beyond. In modern liberal thought essential humanity corresponds to rationality and moral will. Humans are seen as autonomous egos "maximizing their self-interests" who form social contracts to protect their property and in which their individual pursuit of profit can be guided by an "invisible hand" to the benefit of the larger society. Although such views of the self claim to define the generic "human," what is assumed here is the male educated and propertied classes. Dependent people, women, slaves, workers, peasants, and colonized peoples are made invisible. They are de facto lumped with instrumentalized nature.[3]

This master narrative, with its logic of domination, has structured Mediterranean and Western societies for thousands of years. Since the sixteenth century it has been extending its control throughout the globe, eliminating smaller indigenous societies with alternative, more egalitarian and nature-sustaining social and cultural patterns. Most other urban civilizations and religions, such as Hinduism in India, and Confucianism in China, also developed patriarchal ideologies with similar social expressions, as we have seen in our survey of world religions. But even these earlier patriarchal worldviews, which retained some sense of the sacrality of nature, are being subordinated in the twentieth and twenty-first centuries by the one triumphant master narrative of Western science and market economics.

How do ecofeminists envision a transformation of this deeply rooted and powerful ideology and social system? Some feminists have objected to any link between the domination of women and that of nature, seeing this as reduplicating the basic patriarchal fallacy that women are closer to and more like nonhuman nature than men. They believe that women need to claim their equal humanity with male humans, their parallel capacity for rationality and leadership.[4] They too, like males, are separate from and called to rule over nature. But this solution to women's subordination ends with assimilating a few elite women into the male master class, without changing the basic hierarchies of the ruling class over dominated humans and nonhumans.

Most women remain subordinated in the home and in low-paid, menial jobs, even as a few elite women make it into the cabinets and boardrooms of the powerful. The same can be said of racial, ethnic men and women. A Colin Powell or a Condoleezza Rice may be able to enter the inner circle of the Bush administration by virtue of high achievement while being totally supportive of global American hegemony, but most black men and women are in the marginalized and impoverished sectors of American society. Such token inclusion of women, black or white, and racial, ethnic men, buttresses the claim that American society is completely inclusive and is open to talent from whatever group. The many who do not "make it" have no one to blame but themselves. This show of "equality" thus masks the reality of a system in which the super wealth and power of a few depends on the exploitation of the many.

Some ecofeminists do claim that there is some truth in the ideology that women are "closer to nature." They see this closeness as having been distorted by patriarchy to dominate both women and nature as inferior to male humans. But this distortion is rooted in an essential truth that women by virtue of their child-bearing functions are more attuned to the rhythms of nature, more in touch with their own bodies, more holistic. Women need to claim this affinity with nature and take the lead in creating a new earth-based spirituality and practice of care for the earth.[5]

Most ecofeminists, however, reject an essentializing of women as more in tune with nature by virtue of their female body and maternity. They see this concept of affinity between women and nature as a social construct that both naturalizes women and feminizes nonhuman nature, making them appear more "alike." At the same time by socially locating women in the sphere of bodily and material support for society, women may also suffer more due to the abuse of the natural world and hence also become more aware of this abuse. But this is a matter of their experience in their particular social location, not due to a different "nature" than males.

Moreover, such concerns would vary greatly by class and cultural location. An elite Western woman living within the technological comforts of affluent, urban society may be oblivious to the stripping of forests, and the poisoning of water, while a peasant woman who has to struggle for the livelihood of her family in immediate relation to these realities is acutely aware of them. Such awareness, of course, does not translate directly into mobilization for change. For that, one needs a conscious recognition of these connections and a critical analysis of the larger forces that are bringing them about, together with the rise of leadership that can translate this into organized resistance to dominant powers and efforts to shape alternatives to them.

One must also question the universality of the cultural ideology of culture over nature as male over female. Preurban people who depend primarily on hunting-gathering and small-scale agriculture often have very different patterns of thought. Often males are associated with either wild nature (the sphere of hunting) or the fields which men control, with women associated with the domestic realm. Men may see their activities as superior to those of women, but this is a matter of opinion, with women seeing their work as equal or better. A hierarchical sphere of male elites controlling culture and politics has not yet subsumed these earlier patterns that relate the whole society more directly to the fields and forests. But these earlier peoples have today been largely subordinated to patriarchal societies that identify themselves with a culture transcendent to nature and regard tribal and peasant peoples as inferior.[6]

Ecofeminist hope for an alternative society calls for a double conversion or transformation. Social hierarchies of men over women, white elites over subordinated classes and races, need to be transformed into egalitarian societies which recognize the fullness of humanity of each human person. But if greater racial and gender equality is not to be mere tokenism which does not change the deep hierarchies of wealth and power of the few over the many, there must be both a major restructuring of the relations of human groups to each other and a transformation of the relation between humans and the nonhuman world. Humans need to recognize that they are one species among others within the ecosystems of earth. Humans need to embed their systems of production, consumption, and waste within the ways that nature sustains itself in a way that recognizes their intimate partnership with nonhuman communities.[7]

In this chapter I will survey ecofeminist perspectives that are emerging from a number of religious and cultural contexts. I will begin with some examples from North American neo-pagan or earth-based spiritualities. I will then discuss some African perspectives on ecofeminism, followed with some examples from Latin America. I then focus on two major ecofeminist thinkers from North America, one a theologian, Catherine Keller, and another a historian of science, Carolyn Merchant. The chapter will conclude with some questions about the utility of this effort to interconnect the domination of women and of nature, social justice, and ecological health.

NORTH AMERICAN NEO-PAGANISM: WOMEN AND NATURE

In this section of the chapter I will look at two leading neo-pagan thinkers and practitioners, Starhawk, a Wiccan priestess, psychotherapist, and social activist, and Carol Christ. Starhawk (née Miriam Simos) is a Californian of Jewish background who was drawn into the neo-pagan spirituality movement in the 1970s.[8] In the 1980s she was increasingly involved in the anti-war movement and began to shape an understanding of neo-pagan ritual linked to and expressed in grassroots political action.

Starhawk roots her vision of an alternative society and relation to the natural world in a myth of an original matricentric society that preexisted patriarchy in human evolution. In this society the divine was understood as the immanent life force that animates all reality, linking all humans with one another and with the nonhuman world in one community of life which exists in a cycle of birth, growth, decay, death, and rebirth in new organic forms. In this society there was no hierarchy of men over women, masters over slaves, or humans over nature. This ecological egalitarian society was gradually subverted by the rise of patriarchy in the Neolithic and Bronze ages, but its essential vision has lived on in indigenous peoples' cultures throughout the world. Starhawk sees herself as recovering the shamanistic culture of prepatriarchal societies of the British Isles.[9]

In her ritual and therapeutic work Starhawk differentiates between three kinds of power: "power over," "power within," and "power with." Power over is the basic mode of power of patriarchal societies. It expresses the logic of domination by which some, mostly elite males, dominate women and subjugated classes and races, as well as the nonhuman world. This kind of power is fundamentally competitive. The more power one side has, the less the other side has. The wealthy and powerful gain their wealth and power by exploiting those they dominate, while forcing them to accept their impoverished and dominated position.

"Power within," by contrast, is a process by which dominated people shake off the control of others and their own internalization of the powerlessness and inferiority projected on to them, laying hold of their own innate power and goodness. "Power with" is the development of ways to share

power that do not negate others in order to affirm oneself, but can mutu-
ally affirm one another, while being able to acknowledge the special talents
of particular people. In these relations of mutual empowerment each person
flourishes by also promoting the flourishing of others.[10]

As a priestess and therapist Starhawk sees ritual as a group dynamics by
which people are freed from their need to dominate others, and learn to experience their own inner power and beauty and to affirm this power in one
another. As a social activist in the antiwar movement and global justice
movements, Starhawk has translated this small group ritual practice into practical guidelines for street protests against the police who defend the systems
of global power. She teaches the groups she works with how to maintain
their own calm in the face of repressive violence, defuse explosive situations,
and craft creative symbolic actions to communicate alternative visions.

In her 2002 volume, *Webs of Power: Notes from the Global Uprising,*[11]
Starhawk describes her involvement in direct action movements against the
World Trade Organization and the International Monetary Fund, starting
with the mass protests in Seattle in 1999. This involvement continues in the
street protests against these international organizations of globalization in
Prague in September 2000, Quebec in April 2001, and Genoa in July of that
year. Starhawk also reflects on her experiences as a participant in the World
Social Forum in Porto Alegre, Brazil, in January 2001.

Through her descriptions of her involvement as a trainer for these street
actions, especially in the second half of the book, she delineates her own understanding of creative transformative action and her vision of an alternative
society. This new society must be rooted in finding our just place in nature.
For Starhawk this interconnection of justice and ecology is based on her experience as a permaculture gardener. Permaculture gardening creates a deep
relationship with a particular area of land. One must observe it carefully, learn
its natural cycles and what grows there best. Gardening becomes truly a cultivation of the land based on holistic knowing of its own dynamics, rather
than an imposition of human demands disconnected with these realities. To
recreate the world from its present alienated state, we must put down roots
and become again "indigenous" to our chosen place of settlement.[12]

Democratic or "horizontal" organizing in the social justice movement,
for Starhawk, is parallel to permaculture gardening. One does not impose
power from outside the community in a top-down way, but nurtures power
within each person and the ability to share power with each other to en-
hance their mutual empowerment. Similarly in permaculture, one attunes
oneself to the seasons and patterns of the land, the interrelation of plants,
insects, and animals with each other to bring forth its best fruits, rather than
imposing on it monocultures of plants foreign to it.

Violent ways of treating the earth and violent ways of treating other humans are both inherently unstable. Neither form of violence nurtures the natural energies of those who are abused, and so both demand continual inputs of force to maintain themselves. The present global economy is based on deepening impoverishment of the vast majority of earth's people and the land for the excessive profits of the superrich, while also creating a shrinking middle class. The awareness of this inequity is growing with mass communication. The deprived and colonized people are becoming more critical and angry toward what is seen as a new empire led by the United States. The United States thus has become the major militarist, with a coerced cooperation of a few other nations to give its military aggression the fig leaf of a "coalition," although outside the consensus of the United Nations. Such an unjust and violent system is clearly headed for collapse.

Starhawk explores several scenarios for transformation. The present unjust system maintained by violence could drag on for an indefinite period. Or, like the Titanic, it could hit an unseen obstacle and suddenly collapse, creating great chaos for all peoples and the earth. There could be a fascist takeover by ruthless groups determined to continue the present patterns of domination or replace them with a similar pattern. There might also be a gradual transformation to a new society. Or there could be a sudden revolutionary uprising in which a militant group, representing the deprived people, could take over the reins of government and seek to refashion them. She sees deep problems with all these scenarios. The revolutionary option typically fashions the revolutionaries in the mold of the present power holders, in the very process of fighting to defeat them, and so they tend to reinstate a new system of domination, rather than really changing the model.[13]

The preferred way is the one of gradual change. But she sees the present power holders that control American militarism, global corporations, and the agencies of financial control, such as the WTO, as having mobilized to undermine and defeat the process of gradual reform, blocking efforts such as global climate treaties and laws for environmental protection.

Those like herself committed to world justice and ecological sustainability need to operate on two fronts. They must use public protest and communication media to delegitimize the present system. They must also shape alternatives that model the needed new society, starting in their own local communities. She suggests five principles of a sustainable economy: a shift to renewable energy, such as solar and wind energy; a return to human labor rather than reliance on machines; continual recycling of the waste side of production and consumption as fertilizer and materials for new growth and production; the cultivation of biological and cultural diversity and creativity, turning around the present trend toward monocultures; and, finally, effi- ciency, in the sense of doing more with less use of resources.[14]

She outlines nine keynotes for a new world society. These are: (1) the protection of the viability of life-sustaining systems of the planet presently under attack, applying the principles above; (2) rejecting the commodifica- tion of vital resources, such as water; (3) returning control of natural and hu- man resources to local control from global corporations; (4) protecting the land and cultural heritages of indigenous peoples; (5) establishing enterprises rooted in local communities and responsible to them; (6) creating opportu- nities to fulfill needs and dreams open to all human beings; (7) just com- pensation, security, and dignity to labor; (8) collective responsibility as the human community to assure that all members can meet their basic needs for life and growth; and (9) participatory democracy in which all members of the community have a voice in the decisions that affect their lives.[15]

For Starhawk, such principles of society and sustainable ecology de- mand a return of much of the control to local communities, turning around the trends toward more and more centralization of power in global institu- tions. This vision is not one simply to hope for in a distant future, but it de- fines a practice that must be lived now. Local communities must themselves seek to take back power and define their own relations to each other and to the land in a just, life-sustaining way. Global justice groups need to see them- selves as a network both of protest against the dominant system and mutual support for local community projects. We need to live the revolution now!

The second major neo-pagan thinker I discuss here is Carol Christ. Christ grew up in a Christian family of mixed denominational backgrounds and did her graduate work in theology at Yale. There she became increas- ingly alienated from Christianity as both sexist and anti-Semitic and was drawn into the Goddess spirituality movement, studying with Starhawk. Moving from religious studies to women's studies, she taught for a while at San José State College in California. But she experienced increasing burnout with the American academic rat race and began to journey to Greece to lead Goddess pilgrimages through visits to ancient settings. Fi- nally she moved to live in Greece permanently. In contrast to white Amer- icans, she found in Greece people deeply embedded in their local land with its roots back into prepatriarchal times. Even though their religion and cul- ture is patriarchal, many of their churches signal a cave or other holy site of Goddess worship. Many icons venerate Mary as the *Panagia* (All Holy) Mother linked with sacred trees.[16]

Christ sees the "fall into patriarchy" less as a sudden overthrow of ear- lier societies by horse-riding invaders and more as a gradual process of change from earlier gardening societies where women played a predominant role. A male takeover of land and its produce, slavery, and organized warfare shaped new societies based on domination of women, subjugated peoples, and the nonhuman world. Myths of the defeat and slaying of the Goddess supported this takeover. Goddess religion, for her, is an effort to resurrect the egalitarian harmony between humans, men and women, and nature of prepatriarchal times. What this was cannot be known exactly. So much of this work must be acknowledged as an imaginative effort in postmodern times that seeks to deconstruct the patterns of patriarchal religion and envision how its alienated hierarchical dualisms can be reintegrated in a life-giving communion.[17]

Christ seeks to avoid any essentializing of the female as "naturally" more in harmony with nature. One should not simply reverse patriarchal hierarchical dualisms, lifting up body, femaleness, and feelings as the superior side. Rather one has to bring together male and female, mind and body, heaven and earth, feeling and thinking, light and dark, the one and the many, transcendence and immanence in an interactive relationality.[18]

In her 2003 book, *She Who Changes: Re-imagining the Divine in the World*,[19] Christ seeks to define this thealogical stance through the lens of process theology, specifically the thought of Charles Hartshorne. Basic to this theological vision is a rejection of the "omnis" of patriarchal deity, omniscient, omnipotent, immutable, unchangeable goodness. These "omnis" make deity in the image of perfected patriarchal domination, controlling all, but in a one-sided unrelational way, guaranteeing to its followers infallible knowledge and immortality of the soul after death.[20]

Feminist process thought, by contrast, starts with the reality that all is finite and all is changing. Mutability, constant change in a cycle of birth, growth, decline, death, and renewal, is the basic pattern of life and maintenance of life. Humans are an integral part of this process of mutability, not outside it or able to escape from it into some static eternal world. This changing reality is not one of fragmented selves unrelated to each other, but a texture of interrelationship. There is no I without a Thou, no self without its reciprocal interaction with many other selves, human and nonhuman.[21]

Deity in feminist process thought is integral to this process, not outside it. But for Christ deity does not stand for all possible kinds of change, good or bad. Deity is the lure to goodness, to embodied love and life-giving relationality. Humans have free will to choose alienated, hostile relations, but this is against the primary thrust of reality that is toward harmonization of life in positive flourishing. Life is finite. Chance, as well as negative affect and denial of love, cause tragedy and suffering. There is no infallible knowledge, but only contextualized knowledge of where we need to go from where we are now, in particular situations.

No all-powerful deity assures us a good outcome. Indeed the forces of negativity caused by rejection of love and relationship are deeply embedded in the world systems since the rise of patriarchy. We can only respond to the positive lure of the divine within all reality by trying to fashion life-giving communities here and there as best we can. The fact that there is no infallible assurance of victory does not mean that there is not always abundant energy for creativity and transformation which we need to avail ourselves of in every moment and situation to deconstruct negative relations and fashion life-affirming ones. Christ ends the book with a series of prayers, by which she hopes to refashion the way we experience the divine in the world. She suggests we rise each day with the salutation to the rising sun: "As this day dawns in beauty, we pledge ourselves to repair the web."[22]

AFRICAN ECOFEMINISM

For North American neo-pagans the recovery of a prepatriarchal past reaches back into the distant mists of time, perhaps in the fifth or sixth millennium BCE in the ancient Near East. Whether such a time of equality and harmony between people with each other and with the land actually existed or is a modern projection is hotly debated. For Africans, the point of reference is a precolonial Africa that, while largely patriarchal, is often seen as more egalitarian, affording larger roles for women and having traditions of balance between humans and land. This past is much more recent, only a century ago, since Africa was divided up between the European powers only in the late nineteenth century. Remnants of that precolonial worldview are still present in village societies. Yet Africans look back to that precolonial past through a traumatic century of rapid appropriation of their land, marginalization of their people, and denigration of their traditional worldviews by Europeans. They often live today in violent regimes that prolong this trauma of impoverishment and exploitation in a global neocolonial system. This is the context in which African ecofeminists think about a more just and sustainable Africa.

Zimbawean ecofeminist scholar, Tumani Mutasa Nyajeka, in her essay "Shona Women and the Mutupo Principle," seeks to reclaim a worldview still present in her own experience of her culture.[23] The Shona people and their culture are a marriage of two traditions, one of which, the *Karanga*, arrived in the eighth century CE and the other, the *Mbire*, in the twelfth century CE. The *Karanga* saw all life as deriving from water, the Great Pool. The *Mbire* traced all life to the terrestrial region, summed up in the Great Monkey. Each people are divided into a plurality of subgroups, each with their *Mutupo* or totem animal. Aquatic peoples identify with such animals as the hippo, the crocodile, the eagle fish, and the water python. The terrestrial peoples identify with such animals as the antelope, pig, elephant, buffalo, lion, and monkey.

Each of these animal totems is seen as an intimate kin integral to one's communal identity. In Shona praise poetry, people are greeted according to their *Mutupo*. "Good morning, powerful, awesome one, Monkey" expresses a salutation of someone from the monkey clan. Assemblies of Shona people see each group dancing out their *Mutupo* identity as part of celebrating their gathering together and greeting each other. One's relation to one's *Mutupo* is one of veneration and respect. The totem animal is not to be killed, but protected. Each marriage is ideally a blending of the aquatic and terrestrial animals, thus harmonizing the two. Each clan also has particular trees or plants with which they are identified and which they protect. Thus the Shona worldview lacks the gap between human and nonhuman worlds of Western thought. Rather humans, animals, and plants are parts of one extended family.

Shona culture seeks to balance and interconnect humans and animals, aquatic and terrestrial, men and women, the old and the young, the dead and the living, earth and sky in mutual relation. Living in a fragile environment of frequent drought, Shona culture calls for penitence and petitions to the high God, *Mwari*, when rain fails. The community asks itself, "What have we done amiss that has caused this drought?" These traditions are evoked in a creative environmental movement in Zimbabwe that brings together indigenous and African Christian religious communities in the Association of African Earthkeeping Churches (AAEC).

Using the New Testament tradition of Creation as the Body of Christ in whom "all things hold together" (Col. 1:17), as well as Shona traditions that see the ancestors as becoming spirits that protect the land, causing drought when their laws are violated, the AAEC has developed tree-planting eucharists that are conducted in the outdoors. The assembled worshippers ask forgiveness of the spirits for their sins in abusing and deforesting the land. They then seek to reestablish communion with the land and its protecting spirits, fanning out to plant trees and care for watersheds. These churches also teach local communities how to preserve the vegetation cover on the land, clean water supplies, and engage in sustainable agriculture.[24]

Kenyan theologian Teresia Hinga, from the Gikuyu (or Kikuyu) people, also looks back to the traditional worldview of her people. For the

Agikuyu, *Ngai* (God, the Great Divider) is the source of the land and the whole created world. *Ngai* gave each people a portion of the land sufficient to maintain their life. This land is held collectively in usufruct under *Ngai* who remains its ultimate owner and Lord. Individual households are allotted the use of land, but it never becomes private property. One is responsible to God and to the community for one's use of land.[25]

When the European colonialists arrived, the Agikuyu people assumed that they too might have some share of the land according to their needs. But the Europeans had a totally different idea of land. They assumed that they should appropriate the land as their private property, displacing the people who had tilled and cared for it for generations. African people became landless or were turned into low-paid laborers on what had been their land. Their meager pay did not suffice for their maintenance, because they also had to pay heavy taxes to the colonial government out of these wages. What the colonial government perceived as "unused" land, often land understood by local people as pastoral areas, was appropriated as crown land, and the people were forbidden to use it.

The colonial government and its missionaries saw Kenyan people as savages and sought to wipe out their culture and replace it by a Westernized and Christian worldview. They brought in foreign crops for export, such as coffee and tea, to be grown in large plantations owned by Europeans, marginalizing the traditional food crops. Gikuyu society had included both men and women in decision-making councils, as well as joint agricultural work. But the colonial society legislated a strictly subordinate place for African women. This caused deep demoralization, impoverishment, loss of customs and patterns of community and of care for the land of indigenous tradition. This impoverishment and demoralization continues today, provoking violent conflicts under contemporary Kenyan governments that are corrupt and seek only their own short-term profits under a neocolonial relation to the West.

The major movement that has sought to counter this subjugation of women, the demoralization of rural people, and the deforestation and abuse of the land is the Green Belt Movement, founded by Kenyan feminist environmental activist Wangari Maathai in 1977.[26] Wangari Maathai began her work through the National Council of Women of Kenya when she was a member of the executive committee. Maathai had received her college and master's degrees in the United States and her doctorate in veterinary science in Nairobi. As a biological scientist she came to realize the severe problem being caused by deforestation and started a tree-planting movement that drew primarily upon the organizing energies of rural women. Starting with a tree nursery in her own backyard, she developed a movement that taught thousands of women how to develop their own tree nurseries. Over twenty million trees have been planted and some six thousand locally controlled tree nurseries developed in the first phase of this movement from 1977 to 1999.

Planting trees is only one aspect of the Kenyan Green Belt Movement. Equally important are food security, water harvesting, and civic advocacy in the face of land grabbing and violation of human rights by the powerful in league with outside corporations. Local people are taught sustainable agriculture with an emphasis on restoration of traditional food crops, such as yams, for direct consumption, rather than exotic cash crops for export, crops for which Kenyan farmers are often exploited without receiving the promised payments. Rural farmers, many of them women, learn how to grow trees near their homes to alleviate long walks for firewood, fencing, and building materials. They plant two trees for each tree felled, including fruit trees that provide food. The restoration of forest cover causes the return of animals and birds, protects and restores eroded soils, and cleans water sources. They also learn to conserve water through mulching, and they harvest rainwater through metal roofs that drain into storage tanks.[27]

Maathai sees her movement as rooted in a reclaiming of ancestral Kenyan values. This includes rediscovery of traditional knowledge of care for the land and communal solidarity with one another. The leaders of the movement model an ethic of fairness and honesty, in contrast to the corruption and dishonesty that has become rife in the way in which government deals with the people, thus restoring a sense of responsible relationships between people. People not only learn what caused impoverishment of the land and how to restore it, but are imbued with a vision of love for the land as an extension of themselves. They also see immediate benefits for their own survival, as well as long-term improvements of daily life. The image of women is elevated, as women show their ability to take leadership. Local communities, women as well as men, overcome demoralization and feel an empowerment to solve their own problems.

The Kenyan Green Belt Movement has developed training courses in how to develop such programs that have spread across Africa, with groups from more than fifteen African countries taking this training back to their own countries. Maathai has been highly praised and supported by many outside agencies in Europe and the United States. Unfortunately much of this work has been opposed by the Kenyan government. The president and other government leaders have viewed the movement as "subversive," undermining their ability to negotiate economic deals with outside corporations. Maathai has been vilified, imprisoned, and several times set upon and beaten by hired thugs. The verbal attack has often focused on seeking to discredit her as a "madwoman," insubordinate to male leadership, as a "frustrated divorcee" whose independence violates African tradition. One MP even said he would circumcise her if she set foot in his district (cut out her clitoris),[28] thus testifying graphically to the way a strong woman is seen as a threat to male virility. But her movement has survived and continued, due to its extraordinary success in mobilizing grassroots involvement of Kenyan people, mostly rural and female.

Maathai herself was raised in the Catholic tradition, the predominant form of Christianity in Kenya. She received her opportunities to study primarily through Catholic sponsorship. But she herself has developed a theology which is immanent and this-worldly. She speaks of God being in herself, in other people, and the earth. The Green Belt Movement seeks to restore the land and human community through an inner empowerment based on the presence of the divine in and through one another, not one that directs one's life to an otherworldly heaven.[29]

INDIAN ECOFEMINISM

In this section I discuss two leading Indian ecofeminists, Vandana Shiva, a Hindu in background, and Aruna Gnanadason, a Christian. Shiva was trained as a physicist, but abandoned her career in nuclear energy to become an environmental activist who writes and organizes against the Western systems of "development" which she sees as destroying the ecology and economy of India and causing destruction and impoverishment of humanity and the earth worldwide. She is director of the Research Foundation for Science, Technology and Natural Resource Policy in Dehradun, India, that seeks to propose nature-sustaining alternatives to the Western model of "development." She has written more than twenty books and spoken worldwide in the global citizens' movement against environmental destruction.

In her first major book, *Staying Alive: Women, Ecology and Development*, published in 1989, she enunciated the major lines of her ecofeminist critique and vision. She has continued to elaborate these views in her subsequent volumes, such as *The Violence of the Green Revolution: Third World Agriculture, Ecology and Politics* (1991), *Monocultures of the Mind: Biodiversity, Biotechnology and the Third World* (1993), *Biopiracy: The Plunder of Nature and Knowledge* (1997), and *Stolen Harvest: The Hijacking of the Global Food Supply* (1999). With Maria Mies, leading German feminist socialist, she wrote *Ecofeminism*, published in 1993.[30]

In her foundational volume, *Staying Alive*, Shiva delineated her critique against both the Western model of development and the Western concept of science in which she herself was trained. She speaks of both Western science and development as "projects of patriarchy."[31] Western developmentalism picks up in the post–World War II period where colonialism left off and so is a continuation of colonialism (neocolonialism). The British colonialists in India had stripped the forests for timber to build their ships and railroads and organized the land for expropriation into wealth that supported their empire. In the postcolonial period it becomes national elites of India who continue the same model of exploitation and plunder in the name of modernization and "development."

For Shiva this model of development is built on a false assumption that nature and women are mere passive objects that are unproductive in themselves. Both nature and human labor become productive only when taken into a system that uses them for profit within the dominant system of accumulation. This model of development is claimed to produce wealth for all, "lifting all boats." But it actually creates only a short-term extraction of wealth for a global elite, while impoverishing women, poor people, and nature itself, destroying the very base on which it is founded.

The destructive results of this model of development are not accidental, but are themselves rooted in the distorted epistemology of Western science. Drawing on Western feminist critics of science, such as Susan Harding, Evelyn Keller, and Carolyn Merchant,[32] Shiva defines Western science as based on an epistemology of male domination over women and nature. This epistemology abstracts the male knower into a transcendent space outside of nature and reduces nature itself to dead "matter" pushed and pulled by mechanical force. Western science thus "kills" nature, denying its possession of self-generating organic life. It also imagines nature as a dangerous female that must be tormented and forced to submit in the laboratory, even as witches were forced to submit to inquisitors in torture chambers.[33]

India, like other preindustrial countries, has been traditionally a rural society, based largely on subsistence agriculture in which women have played a predominant role. For Shiva, Indian rural women have been the base of a sustainable system of subsistence agriculture because they have understood the interconnections of the cycles of life in the land and animals that they have tended. Women's agricultural labor has linked together forests, water, animals, and fields in a system of continually renewed productivity. They have foraged in the forests for food, medicines, fodder for animals, fuels, and mulch for fields in ways that sustained, rather than destroyed, the forests themselves.

Women have tended the animals, feeding them from the fodder of forests and leftover leaves and stalks of the crops. They have harvested and prepared the food for the family and converted the animal dung into fuel and fertilizer. Through maintaining the forests and green cover on the fields and along waterways, they promoted the renewal of the groundwater. Through knowledge of properties of woods and plants, they provided clean water for their families. Thus women have been the sustainers of life in Indian rural agriculture.

Western science and developmentalism, by contrast, see this work of women as completely unproductive and the forests they tend as mere "wasteland" because they have not been incorporated into a system of commodities for profit in the market of international exchange. The British and later "developers" saw forests solely as timber mines whose trees were to be felled for ships and railroad ties, cleared for export agriculture, or replanted with rows of fast-growing but water-extracting trees for timber, such as eucalyptus, a species foreign to the Indian ecosystems. For them, the leaves and small branches of the trees, the small plants that sheltered under their branches, which for women are medicine, food, and fodder, were mere "waste" to be destroyed. Only the trunks of large trees were valuable, but only when felled, cut up, and sold.

Shiva also mounts a severe criticism against the Western-style imposition of agricultural development on India in the form of the "Green Revolution."[34] The revolution promised abundance for poor third world farmers through increased grain supply, but its actual effect has been a disaster. The basis of the green revolution has been the creation of hybrid seeds in Western laboratories that yield more and bigger grains per plant, but only when large quantities of chemical pesticides and water are added to them. These seeds are sterile. So farmers are unable to set aside some of the seeds for the next planting, but become dependent on the seed company for purchase of next year's seeds. The elimination of a diversity of plants for monocrops causes outbreaks of pests that are then dealt with through growing quantities of pesticides. The plants also grow much less leaves, so fodder for animals is lost. Only rich farmers with tractors can afford this mode of agriculture, so smaller farmers are bypassed and lose their land.

The long-term result of the promotion of this style of corporate agriculture is disaster for most Indian rural people. Women are eliminated from agriculture and with them their roles as the maintainers of sustainable soils, forests, and food for humans and animals. Petroleum-based fertilizers, pesticides, and fuel for tractors poison the soils and waters, and the water table itself is depleted through overuse for irrigation. Rivers and wells dry up, and regions that had sufficient water suffer water famine for humans, animals, and agriculture. Farmers must buy their seeds, fertilizers, pesticides, and fuel and sell their harvest to companies who charge them high prices and pay them low wages. The result is impoverishment of the people and the land. Yet this disastrous model continues to be promoted by Western global corporations, development banks, and national elites as the epitome of "modernization."

Western development banks and national elites then see the solution to water famine as the creation of big dams. These dams displace large numbers of local people who have lived in valleys that are to become dams. These people are never compensated or adequately resettled. But big dams themselves never supply water adequately to most of India's farmers who had traditionally maintained an adequate water supply through sustainable use of rivers, springs, and wells. The stripping of forests also causes drought, as well as cataclysmic floods during monsoon weather that course down denuded hillsides, sweeping away both villages and topsoil.[35]

Shiva's solution to this disaster of modernization and development is to turn back to traditional sustainable agriculture. There needs to be a recovery of the ecological knowledge of how forests, water, plants, animals, and humans are maintained in a renewable system of interaction with nature, a partnership that based itself on nature's own cycles of renewal. Women and tribal people are the privileged repositories of this ecological knowledge. Thus instead of seeing them as ignorant, primitive, passive, and unproductive, one must learn from them how to maintain genuine life within nature.

The Western model of knowledge and economic value has proven to be delusory. We must shift to a different understanding of knowledge and economic value. The epistemological model we need is not one of dominating mind over passive body, but how to think within nature's own interrelationships. The economic system that produces true value that maintains life is not one that destroys nature, but one that cooperates with it and fits human life within its cycles of self-maintenance.

Shiva turns to traditional Hindu cosmology to express the worldview that is needed for the recovery of ecological knowledge and life-sustaining practice. She speaks of this as the recovery of the "Feminine Principle," not in the Western sense of a dichotomizing of masculinity and femininity as binaries of aggressive activity and dormant passivity, but as a dynamic interaction of creative energy, female *Shakti*, together with male form (*Purusha*), which together produce nature (*Prakriti*). In Hinduism, both *Shakti*, activating energy, and *Prakriti* (nature) have been understood as feminine and even as Goddesses. Shiva thus suggests that traditional Hindu culture, both in its high philosophy and in its popular spirituality, has understood and venerated women as the active principle for the maintenance of life.[36]

To reclaim the Feminine Principle is thus, for Shiva, a reclaiming of human interdependency with and immersion in the organic vitality of the natural world. Shiva argues that this veneration of the Feminine Principle as self-creative nature is not a gender ideology that makes women different from or better than men. Rather it is a rejection of the Western gender ideology that defined males by a masculinity of disconnection from the body, women, and nature, violent domination over it, and a distortion of women and nature into passive objects of this violence. Men need to overcome their alienation and violence, and women their passivity and acceptance of denigration. Both men and women must see themselves as active participants in nurturing life in partnership with nature's own vitality.

Some Indian ecofeminists have been critical of Shiva for her use of this Indian tradition of *Shakti* and *Prakriti* as feminine cosmological principles for ecological life. They see her as ignoring the negative aspects of this feminine cosmology as world negating and its use to subordinate women to male control.[37] Some critics also see her as ignoring the caste structure intrinsic to Hinduism that has traditionally marginalized tribal people and *Dalits* (untouchables).[38] Shiva often seems to sound as if patriarchy was invented in the seventeenth century and imported entirely from the West, rather than having been a part of Hindu society for millennia.

These are valid criticisms, but Shiva is not claiming to be a scholar of traditional Hinduism. Rather she is using popular symbols in Indian culture to honor rural women as the base of knowledge and practice of a sustainable subsistence economy. She also wishes to point to a vision of nature itself as vital and dynamic, not as dead matter to be dominated by knowers disconnected from it. Perhaps it is not accidental that in her subsequent books she had ceased to speak of a feminine cosmological principle, of *Shakti* and *Prakriti*. But she has grown even more devastating in her critique of the model of development coming from Western neocolonialism that is impoverishing rural people in India and throughout the world. She sees rural women and tribal people as centers of resistance to this model of development and preservers of ecological knowledge of sustainable life. This is a precious resource for an alternative that we all, men and women, east and west, urban and rural people, need to relearn if we are to survive on the planet earth.

The second Indian ecofeminist to be discussed here is Aruna Gnanadason, who was a leader of the Indian feminist movement for many years. From that work she moved into leadership in the Christian churches and became the head of the All India Council of Christian Women. In 1991 she was called to become the head of the women's desk of the program unit of Justice, Peace and Integrity of Creation of the World Council of Churches in Geneva, Switzerland, of which she presently is the coordinator. She has a keen interest in introducing ecofeminism as a lens for the World Council to see its justice, peace, and creation work, both socially and theologically. In November 2003 she completed a Doctor of Ministry thesis on Indian Ecofeminism for the San Francisco Theological Seminary, titled "Creator God, in your Grace, Transform the Earth: An Ecofeminist Ethic of Resistance, Prudence and Care."[39]

In this thesis Gnanadason details the history of ecocide and impoverishment of the Indian people and land during the years of British colonialism, followed by independent governments that have adopted the neoliberal model of industrialism and integration into global capitalism. She also draws on the stories of resistance and struggles for alternative ways of survival among Dalit and Adivasi or indigenous women, as well as national and global networks of women. She focuses on two defining themes from Indian tradition. One of these is what she calls an "ethic of prudence." By this she means traditional methods among Dalit and Adivasi people of using natural resources carefully, not overharvesting, but taking only as much as can be renewed from forests and natural growth, holding certain areas of forests and pools of water as sacred. She also seeks to reclaim the theme of "motherhood" as an ethic of care, citing the way that indigenous women and men refer to the earth as mother who sustains and selflessly serves us, her children.

Gnanadason recognizes the ambiguity of the theme of motherhood in a patriarchal society, such as India, in which the maternal ethic of care has been exploited to make women "long-suffering" victims of service to their men and children, without any rights to self-development. But she also seeks to liberate this theme of maternal care from its subjugation and exploitation and to vindicate its potential to express resistance to exploitation of the family and the earth and militant struggle to survive against all odds.

Gnanadason concludes the thesis by developing an ecofeminist theology of grace. Her choice of this theme is in intentional preparation for the Ninth Assembly of the World Council of Churches to be held in Porto Alegre, Brazil, in February 2006. The theme for this conference will be "Creator God, in your grace, transform the world." Gnanadason has some concerns that this assembly might see a backing away from the strong commitment to a theology of creation and to a critique of corporate globalization taken in some circles in the World Council of Churches. The Council is divided between some groups that believe that there is no alternative to the present world system of globalization, and that the only possibility is to reform the Bretton Woods institutions to make them more democratic and accountable, and those who feel that these institutions cannot be significantly democratized, and that the focus should be on supporting alternative forms of sustainable communities.

Through the publication of her thesis Gnanadason wishes to contribute to the thinking on ecofeminism and alternatives to globalization both within the WCC and within ecofeminist networks in India and internationally. By focusing her own theological work on an ecofeminist reading of the doctrine of grace, she wishes to go beyond a merely individual and anthropocentric reading of grace as God's redemptive activity toward fallen humans. Grace needs to be read within God's continuing action of sustaining and renewing the creation. Transforming grace is not just about individual humans. It is about human community within and interdependent with communities of "otherkind." Economic justice and ecological sustainability are two aspects of one process of creating renewable communities in resistance to and as alternatives to the present system of corporate developmentalism.

LATIN AMERICAN ECOFEMINISM

In this section I will focus on the thought of the leading ecofeminist theologian in Latin America, Ivone Gebara. I will also discuss the work of *Conspirando*, which calls itself a "journal of ecofeminism, spirituality and theology." This journal has been published four times a year since 1992 and networks ecofeminist writers across Latin America. I will then detail some stories of Latin American feminists who describe their personal spiritual journeys toward an ecofeminist worldview in the book *Lluvia para Florecer: Entrevistas sobre el ecofeminismo en América Latina* (*Rain for Flourishing: Interviews on Ecofeminism in Latin America*) conducted by the editor of *Conspirando*, Mary Judith Ress.

Ivone Gebara is a Brazilian and a member of the Sisters of Notre Dame. For sixteen years she taught theology and philosophy to seminarians and lay ministers at the Theology Institute in Recife, Brazil. Since this institute closed with the accession of a more conservative bishop, she has continued to live in a poor neighborhood in Recife, and travels and lectures worldwide. In her book, *Intuitiones Ecofeministas* (*Ecofeminist Intuitions*), Gebara talks about how she came to adopt an ecofeminist perspective.[40]

Although Gebara acknowledges the criticism of some Latin American feminists that ecofeminism continues the stereotyping of women as "closer to nature," she believes that her own viewpoint has nothing to do with such essentialist anthropology. Rather it springs from her concrete experience in her impoverished neighborhood. There she observes that poor women are the ones who primarily have to cope with the problems of air pollution, poverty, poor quality of food, lack of clean drinking water. This creates health problems for themselves and their children for which they are primarily responsible.[41]

Gebara speaks of doing her theology "between noise and garbage." The noise is that of a crowded neighborhood with machinery, trucks, and cars that lack mufflers, but also the shouts and music of the people as they find ways to survive each day. The garbage is the waste of society disproportionately discarded where the poor live, with little organized clean-up. To do one's theology amid noise and garbage is to do it in daily awareness of the oppression of the poor and the degradation of their environment. It is also to do theology inspired by the vitality of the poor who manage somehow to keep going and even sometimes to celebrate despite these challenges.[42]

Gebara sees her ecofeminist theology as a third stage of feminist theological work in Latin America. In the first stage in the 1970s a new feminist movement was arising in Latin America and feminist theologies were being translated from Germany and North America. Stimulated by these influences, Latin American women theologians realized that "we are oppressed as historical subjects. We discovered our oppression in the Bible, in theology, in our churches." The response was to look for liberating female role models in the Bible, Jesus' women disciples, biblical matriarchs and prophetesses. In the second phase they began to question the dominance of masculine theological symbols and to search for feminine symbols for God, such as Wisdom.[43]

For Gebara both of these phases are still expressions of a "patriarchal feminism," a feminism which has not deeply examined the androcentric model of theology, of God and the cosmos, but are simply seeking to include women in it. Gebara sees ecofeminism as moving to a new and more radical stage of feminism. This stage calls for a deconstruction of patriarchal thinking, with its hierarchical structure and methodology of thought. Ecofeminism seeks to dismantle the whole paradigm of male over female, mind over body, heaven over earth, transcendent over immanent, the male God outside of and ruling over the created world, and to imagine an alternative to it.

Changing the patriarchal paradigm for an ecofeminist one starts with epistemology, with transforming the way one thinks. Patriarchal epistemology bases itself on eternal unchangeable "truths" that are the presuppositions for knowing what truly "is." In the Platonic-Aristotelian epistemology that shaped Catholic Christianity, this means eternal ideas that exist a priori, of which physical things are pale and partial expressions. Catholicism added to this the hierarchy of revelation over reason. Revealed ideas come directly from God and thus are unchangeable and unquestionable, compared to ideas derived from reason.

Gebara, by contrast, wishes to start with experience, especially the embodied experiences of women in daily life. Experiences cannot be translated into thought finally and definitively. They are always in context, in a particular network of relationships. This interdependence and contextuality include not only other humans, but the nonhuman world, ultimately the whole body of the cosmos in which we are embedded in our particular location. Theological ideas are not exempt from this questioning from the point of view of embodied, contextual experience. In addressing ideas, such as God as Trinity, she asks, "to what experience is this idea related?" What in our embodied daily life is the basis for thinking about reality as trinitarian and hence ultimately of God as Trinity?[44]

Such an effort to dismantle patriarchal epistemology for ecofeminist thinking includes the nature of the human person. How do we move from a patriarchal to an ecofeminist understanding of the self? Patriarchal theology and philosophy start with a disembodied self that is presumed to exist prior to all relationships. In Platonic thought this actually means individual souls that preexisted in the heavens and only later were incarnated in bodies. The body is seen primarily as an impediment to the soul to be controlled, not an integral part of the self. The ideal self is the autonomous self, the self that has extricated itself from all dependencies on others and stands outside and independent of relationships as a "free subject." In this view of the human only elite men are fully selves; women and subjugated people are by definition dependent. Such a view, of course, depends on making invisible this whole structure of support on which the apparent male freedom is itself "dependent."

This notion of autonomy and independence is translated into corporate realities, autonomous nations, and global corporations. Such corporations dominate and control all else, turning them into things and making invisible their dependency on them. Claiming to be a law unto themselves, they assume they can trample on local societies and intervene in their lives whenever they are seen to be a threat to their "way of life." Obviously not all nations can behave in this way, but only nations that claim hegemonic power, and finally only one nation, the Number One who has a right to rule over all others.[45]

An ecofeminist understanding of the human person, by contrast, starts with the person in a network of relationships. The person does not exist first

and then assume relationships, but the person is constituted in and by relationships. One does not seek to extricate oneself from relationships in order to become "autonomous." Such autonomy is a delusion based on denial
of the others on whom one depends. Rather one seeks to become ever
more deeply aware of the interconnections on which one's own life depends, ultimately the network of relations of the whole cosmos. One seeks
to shape those relations in ways that are more life giving and reciprocal, to
respect the integrity of the other beings to whom one is related, even as one
is respected by them and respects oneself. To be is to be related; shaping the
quality of those relations is the critical ethical task.[46]

This reflection on the network of relationality which reaches from the
most intimate relation with one's own body-self, to interpersonal relations,
to intergroup relations to each other and humans to earth culminates finally
in recognizing our interrelations with and dependency on the whole cosmos. It is on this understanding of interrelationality that Gebara bases her
reflection on the meaning of God as Trinity. For Gebara, God as Trinity is
not a revelation from on high which one imposes on people as eternal and
unchangeable truth outside of and incomprehensible to daily experience.
Rather the idea of God as Trinity is itself an extrapolation from our daily
experience of interrelationships.

For Gebara, the Trinity is a way of expressing the dynamics of life as
interrelational creativity. Creativity by its nature ramifies into diversity while
at the same time interconnecting in community, leading to new diversification. This process of dialectical diversification and intercommunion can be
seen on every level of reality. Gebara starts with the development of the cosmos itself, following Brian Swimme and Thomas Berry's account in *The
Universe Story*.[47] Starting with one concentrated nucleus of energy the universe explodes into expanding diversity. Then part of this diversity is destroyed as new stages of creativity develop. The whole unfolds as a process
of ongoing interconnectivity.

The same pattern is repeated on the level of planet earth. The biosphere
unfolds in increasing diversity of species, allowing phases of extinction and
new development of diversification in a process of cocreation and interconnection. Humans also divide into many races and cultures. They develop new
stages of interconnection and communication as they shape an increasingly
unified community of human life on earth. So also interpersonal society and
finally the person herself exist in a dynamic of diversification and interdependency.[48] This story of trinitarian dialectics as the process of creation of
life on earth raises the issue of good and evil. If whatever develops is part of
a natural process, from whence come systems of violence and oppression?

Gebara insists that there is good and evil in natural life itself. Natural life exists in a dynamic tension of life and death, creativity and vulnerability. Death is an integral part of life, not foreign to it, as traditional Christian cosmology had claimed. But the very vulnerability and fragility of life provide the impulse for possible distortion of this dialectical process. Each person in its species context seeks to protect and expand its own life against others that compete with it. Nature limits the extent to which some species can expand at the expense of others. When some exceed their life support niche by destroying others on whom they depend, this precipitates the collapse of the dominant group.[49]

But humans have developed an ability to stand out somewhat from these limits. They have been able to organize their own species power in relation to land and animals to monopolize means of life. This takes place in the context of some humans seizing power and organizing relations to other humans so these subjugated people do the brute labor. Those in power extract this into means of wealth, dominating power and leisure for themselves at the expense of others, while claiming to represent the well-being of "all."

This pattern of construction of systems of exploitative power of some humans over others and over the nonhuman world has been endlessly repeated through human history, since the rise of plow agriculture, warfare, slavery, and social hierarchy in early human "civilizations." These systems of exploitative distortion are always based on denying the interconnection of the powerful with the powerless, men with women, ruling class with slaves, workers, and peasants. Those on top imagine themselves as "autonomous" and naturally superior, while the inferiority of those they rule over demands their subjugation. Thus the systems of exploitation "naturalize" themselves by shaping ideologies that pretend that these systems simply represent the "order of creation" and the will of God or the gods.

We are now living in the nadir of this system of distortion that has grown increasingly centralized worldwide, while impoverishing the majority of humans and the earth more and more. Yet this system continues to claim that the privations it imposes on others are necessary for all to eventually prosper and attain comfort and leisure equivalent to the affluent. If the poor but "tighten their belts" a bit more, the wealth generated at the top will "trickle down" and "lift all boats." But this is a fallacious ideology belied by reality. This system of distortion, violence, impoverishment, and oppression is immoral or "unnatural" evil, built on the denial of interconnection of all beings with one another.

For Gebara there is no original paradise of blessedness without finitude or death at the beginning of human history, nor is it possible to construct a paradise of deathless goodness in some future millennium. Rather humans need to accept our limits, our fragility, our texture of joy and sorrow within finite life. What we can and must do is to dismantle the systems of distortion that allow some few humans to flourish inordinately at the expense of most other humans and the earth. We must shape egalitarian societies where joys and sorrows, flourishing within fragile limitations, are shared more equally and more justly between humans and between humans and the other earth beings with whom we share this planet. This is the very real but limited utopia which Gebara allows herself, recognizing that within our lives today we can expect only momentary glimpses of this more justly shared life in interconnected mutuality.[50]

Gebara does not write simply as an isolated individual. Her writings and workshops have helped create a network of women and men throughout Latin America that identify with her perspective. A major source of the promotion of ecofeminist theology, spirituality, and practice is the journal *Con-spirando*. This journal, edited in Chile, but with contributors from all over Latin America, as well as translations of articles from North America, Europe, and Asia, defines itself as working from an ecofeminist perspective. In its years of publication since 1992 it has covered such topics as the worldviews of Latin American indigenous women, the understandings of the body, of violence, of Mary and Jesus, art and mysticism, work, human rights, social transformation, the different ages of women in the life cycle, birth and death, and women's history. These topics are always covered from a variety of perspectives and with the focus on experience, not abstract theory.[51]

In the book, *Lluvia para Florecer* (*Rain for Flourishing*),[52] Mary Judith Ress interviewed twelve Latin American feminists on their own intellectual and spiritual journeys toward an ecofeminist perspective. I will mention only four of these interviews by way of example. The first woman interviewed is Agamedilza Sales de Oliveira, a Brazilian born in Amazonas in 1950. Sales de Oliveira remembers the religion of her childhood as very nurturing, like her family itself. God the Father, Mary, and Jesus made up a cozy family trinity that was immediately and lovingly present. This friendly religiosity was abruptly broken when she was sent to a German Dominican school in a distant city that taught her to see God as a punishing dictator.

Sales de Oliveira is grateful for the good education she received in this school, but, after her own marriage, she was determined not to subjugate her own children to this alienating experience. She moved with them to the city where they could get a good education. Feeling lonely, she began to do biblical studies from a liberation perspective. But she became aware of the lack of any women's stories in this tradition. She began to search for women's stories in the Bible and also began to be influenced by the women's movement in Latin America. Always she sought to rediscover the nurturing feminine presence of the divine of her childhood. Through the influence of Ivone Gebara's work, she was able to shape a new vision of the divine as the creative power of the universe. She founded a feminist group, "Maria Sem Vergonha" (Mary without guilt), as a way to explore rituals and creative reflections on this ecofeminist understanding of the divine.[53]

The second woman interviewed is Marcia Moya, born in 1965 in Ecuador. Moya grew up in a large and lively family with several brothers and a father who valued education for all his children. But she also learned to be a strong woman to hold her own in this relation with her brothers and father. She was trained as a dentist, but also began to work with prostitutes in the city. The sufferings of these women caused her to experience a crisis of faith. What kind of God exists that would allow such inhumanity? This led her to theological studies through the perspective of liberation theology, but in a way that situated this reflection in the context of women, blacks, and indigenous people. She also came to claim her own indigenous roots as a "mestiza" (of mixed European and indigenous ancestry). An ecofeminist perspective has allowed her to integrate these different aspects of her thought and experience by seeing the divine as the underlying process of the universe that relates women and men, the diversity of cultures, humans, and nature in an interconnected world.[54]

Coca Trillini is an Argentinian born in Buenos Aires in 1951. She grew up in a middle-class family of Basque roots with a tradition of women as educators. She began to do literacy work and biblical catechetics with poor rural people. But eventually encountered a crisis of faith as she realized the marginalization of women and of herself as a women in the church and society. An encounter with Ivone Gebara in a workshop allowed her to go beyond the patriarchal God and to imagine a feminine and pantheistic sense of divinity as divine Wisdom that underlies the universe and interrelates all things. "We are a circle within a circle without beginning or end" expresses her ecofeminist view of the divine as the cosmic energy that underlies and sustains all life.[55]

These three women all grew up and remain marginally identified as Catholics. The fourth women interviewed, Sandra Duarte, comes from a Methodist family from São Paulo, Brazil. Born in 1966, Duarte early began to explore mythology about Goddesses. At the same time she became very interested in the indigenous people of Brazil, working with a poor, indigenous community near São Paulo. Her studies in the United States led her to write a master's thesis influenced by the work of feminist anthropologist

Marija Gimbutas on the theme "In the beginning God was a woman." But this work led her to be rejected for ordination in the Methodist church.

This rejection caused Duarte to concentrate more strictly on academic work, while also continuing her relation with the indigenous people. She wrote a doctoral thesis on ecofeminism, seeking particularly to critique an "essentialism" which would identify women as "closer to nature." She is presently an instructor in philosophy and religious studies at the Methodist University in São Paulo. Since writing her thesis she has come to see the complexity of the relation of women and nature, since women are socially constructed as "closer to nature," as well as free to redefine themselves. She admits to a spirituality that resonates with the sacrality of the universe, while being suspicious of any quick identification of the women's "nature" with the natural world.[56]

These four interviews and the additional eight stories contained in this volume give the reader graphic experiences of the diverse contexts in which these Latin American women undertake their spiritual journeys. The particular time when they were born, their distinct national cultures, religions, class and family contexts, each set them in different beginning points. Yet all seem to move through a similar, though not identical, path of development, starting with a quest for education, immersion in theological and biblical studies, often with a liberation perspective, work with poor people at the grass roots, moments of crisis as they realize their exclusion as women that leads to the gradual transformation of their worldview from a patriarchal to an ecofeminist understanding. They grow toward an ecofeminist perspective as the answer to a quest for a more adequate worldview that encompasses their own experiences of the wholeness of life.

NORTH AMERICAN ECOFEMINISM: CATHERINE KELLER AND CAROLYN MERCHANT

I have chosen to conclude my analysis of ecofeminisms with two significant thinkers, one a Christian theologian, Catherine Keller, and the other a secular historian of science, Carolyn Merchant. Catherine Keller wrote her first book, *From a Broken Web: Separation, Sexism and Self*, on the pivotal theme of the definition of self in Western theology, psychology, and philosophy.[57] She identified a dualism of two kinds of self, the male self whose goal is separation and autonomy and the female self or rather no-self, which both supports and serves as the scapegoat for the separative male self. Her proposal is a transformative integration of these dualistic selves, self-in-relation, which is neither false autonomy nor self-sacrificial support for the selfhood of another bought at women's expense. In her exploration of process theology she recognizes that this complexity of self-in-relation is not simply about humans, but defines the matrix of individuation and interconnection of the universe.

From this exploration of self as separation and relationship, Keller moved to a study of "end-time" thinking in Christianity, piquantly entitled *Apocalypse, Now and Then: A Feminist Guide to the End of the World.*[58] Apocalyptic thinking is in us and all around us, constituting "a multi-dimensional, culture-pervading spectrum of ideological assumptions, group identities, subjective responses and . . . historical habits."[59] Projections of archetypal females encompass the apocalyptic dualisms, the Whore of Babylon, to be annihilated, and the Woman Clothed with the Sun who flees into the wilderness to birth the messianic humanity, sheltered from the devouring Dragon. Not just reactionary fundamentalism, but revolutionary visions readily employ the idiom of apocalyptic. Feminist, liberation, black, and ecological theologies imagine messianic comings that dismantle the systems of evil and install a redeemed world in our midst.

Keller declares that we cannot completely extricate ourselves from apocalyptic "end-time" thinking. But she hopes to "sublate" it into pneumatology (the doctrine of the Holy Spirit), "into a dis/closive play of hope as a shifting luminosity at the edge of the present."[60] By this she seems to mean an insurgent hope that continually arises in the midst of defeats and disappointments, surrendering the clarity of absolute good against absolute evil, of decisive triumphs of the first over the second. Such insurgent hope reroots its vision of the future in cosmology. Hope finds its capacity to sustain itself, not by the endless leaps into an alternative that never comes, but by whatever grounds us in the depths of the Now, the Creator Spirit of the beginnings which makes newness ever again possible. In so doing it allows a marriage of eschatology and ecology, renewal, not as rejection of bodies and nature, but as their springtime new greening that again and again makes possible the overcoming of drought and death.[61]

Keller's third book turns to the ambiguous relation toward those cosmological "beginnings" in formless, watery darkness which Christian thought declares to have been abolished by the authoritative "fiat" of God's Word though which the "world" was created. This book is entitled *Face of the Deep: A Theology of Becoming.*[62] The priestly writer of Genesis, in common with ancient Mediterranean thought generally, assumed that the Creator God is an artisan who shaped the creation from preexisting "matter."[63] This preexisting "stuff" which God shaped into the cosmos is "without form and void" as "darkness on the face of the deep." The Spirit of God is described as "moving on the face of the waters" (Gen 1:2).

This watery formlessness which God shaped by dividing light from darkness, the waters above from the waters below, the dry land from the sea, has been seen as a survival in Hebrew thought of the ancient myth of Tiamat, conquered and dismembered by the hero god Marduk who shapes the cosmos from her dead body.[64] Yet God's work of shaping the cosmos from the body of the primal monster appears incomplete in the Hebrew Scripture. Leviathan, the sea monster, continues to appear as God's adversary whom God must defeat, although at other times it is simply one of God's creatures in whom God rejoices.[65]

Keller asks whether the description of the New Jerusalem in the Christian book of Revelation might not represent the imagined final triumph of the Creator God over primal chaos. In this vision of the ultimate future it is said that "the sea was no more" (Rev. 21:1) and "night shall be no more" (Rev. 22:5). In this final victory of God the dry triumphs over the wet, light over darkness, abolishing its opposites.

By the end of the second century early Christianity became uncomfortable with this tradition of primal chaos and watery depths that God shapes into the cosmos. The church fathers invented the doctrine of *creatio ex nihilo* (creation from nothing) to abolish these preexisting conditions to which God responds. Such limits on God were seen as threatening divine omnipotence. God cannot be a mere artisan interacting with realities he did not create. Rather he brings forth the universe "from nothing," perhaps, as Augustine surmised, first creating the primary matter that he then shapes into the cosmos.[66]

Yet the primal chaos negated as "nothing" shows an alarming tendency to return as demonic monsters, often female gendered, to be again and again abolished, as if God's victory over his opposite is endlessly incomplete. Watery chaos and darkness assume the face of evil, of an antidivine "nonbeing" from which humanity itself is rescued by God in creation as the first act of redemption.[67] Modern Christian exegesis of Genesis has come to recognize the error of the *ex nihilo*, but has retained the Christian ambivalence toward the watery chaos, seen as limiting the omnipotence of God. Christian theology, Keller declares, has been compulsively "tehomophobic" (fearful of darkness and disorder).[68]

Keller, by contrast, seeks to radically question and revise the Christian theology of creation by embracing, rather than abolishing, primal chaos. In shaping a theology of Becoming that finds a third space between Being and Nothingness, she also questions all of those claims of omnipotence that shape the "dominology" of church and state, the powerful over the powerless, men over women, white over black, which have been justified by the myth of divine victory over watery darkness. For Keller, a theology of Becoming that allows space for creative interaction between Creator God(s) and chaotic matrices of possibilities is a sociospiritual practice. By shaping a theology of Becoming, we can embrace rather than suppress plurality and difference.

The trinitarian theology of Becoming interconnects *tehom* (chaos), *elohim* (God/s), and the *ruach elohim* (breath of God).[69] It allows *tehom* and *elohim* to be interacting capacities through which what *is* materializes in ever new and creative forms, without absolutes of the beginning or of the end. It is in that creative space where new possibilities materialize that the *ruach elohim*, the vibrating breath of God, hovers over the watery deep, calling and empowering us to begin and begin again.

The final ecofeminist thinker I mention here is Carolyn Merchant, a historian of science at the University of California at Berkeley, whose 1980 book, *The Death of Nature: Women, Ecology and the Scientific Revolution*,[70] has been formative for most of the writers discussed in this chapter. Merchant opens her book with the dramatic declaration, "The world we have lost was organic."[71] In this work she details the organic view of nature that the medieval world inherited from Mediterranean antiquity. In this worldview nature was typically imaged as female, as virgin or nurturing mother, or as witch, as disorderly, demonic woman. The whole universe was seen as organic and alive. The *anima mundi* (world soul), imaged as a woman, animated the universe. In Plato's *Timaeus*, human souls were themselves part of the residue of the world soul which the creator first put in the heavens and then had the planetary gods incarnate into bodies.[72]

In the seventeenth century, with the rise of Cartesian philosophy and Newtonian science, this model of the world as organism was converted into a view of the world as mechanism. The clock and other such machinery became the image of the world. Metaphors based on the persecution of women as witches were taken into scientific thought by writers such as Francis Bacon. Nature was described as needing to be "unveiled," stripped of her concealing clothing, dragged by her hair into the laboratory, "vexed" (tortured), and forced to "yield her secrets."[73] Despite these personalized metaphors, nature came to be seen as a mechanical order composed of tiny hard dead balls of matter (atoms) which are pushed or pulled by external mechanic force. All intelligence, soul, or life was taken out of the material world and lodged in a transcendent mind (God) manifest in the human (white Western male) mind. This intellect knows reality from outside, objectively, in a value-free and context-free fashion,[74] based on mathematics. Scientific knowledge was identified with power to control nature. The fallen humanity was seen as having lost dominion over nature. Both humans and nature thereby fell into disorder. Through scientific knowledge dominion is being restored to humanity and nature, and humanity thereby redeemed.

Although the mechanical model came to dominate and still dominates scientific thinking, organic thinking by no means disappeared from European thought. It remained a counterview asserted by alternative philosophical traditions, such as Neoplatonism and romanticism, as well as by artists and poets. Merchant sees an organic holistic view of nature being reclaimed in ecology. She calls for the redevelopment of "communities based on the integration of human and natural ecosystems." This "may be crucial if people and nature are to survive."[75]

Merchant's 2003 book, *Reinventing Eden: The Fate of Nature in Western Culture*,[76] picks up these themes from a different perspective. In this volume Merchant sees Western cultures shaped by two opposing narratives, both aimed at the "recovery" of Eden, the primal paradise of the biblical narrative where humans, male and female, nature and God were in harmony. One narrative, which has dominated Western thought since the seventeenth century, secularizes the Christian story of redemption through Christ that pointed to a transcendent heaven as the ultimate place of redemption. In the secular progressive redemption story paradise is reestablished on earth.

Based on Bacon's view, human dominion over nature, given by God at the beginning, was seen as impaired by the Fall. Disorder and savagery have reigned since this early collapse. But science and technology are restoring human dominion and thus transforming primitive disorderly nature into civilization. This task of civilizing nature is the "white man's burden." The white Western male is subduing the whole world, first Europe and then the colonized areas of the Americas, Asia, and Africa and elevating them to this higher order. Women, Africans, the indigenous peoples of the Americas are also to be subdued, domesticated, cleared out of the way, or transported as slaves as the work force for civilization, although denied its full benefits.

Merchant sees the North American shopping mall as the ultimate image of this reinvented Eden.[77] Surrounded by a concrete desert of parking lots, the shopping mall presents an artificially constructed total world of commodified pleasure. Shops and restaurants line the walkways that are set in artificial gardens with waterfalls, flowers, and trees, even with modeled animals and birds and live fish. Some shopping malls are designed to be places where the entire family can sojourn for one or more days, with hotels, swimming pools, beaches with mechanized waves, child care centers, and amusement parks. Needless to say banks are often present, and sometimes churches, medical clinics, and psychological counseling centers.

Against this narrative of recreating Eden as a fabricated world freed from natural constraints is what Merchant calls the "declensionist" narrative. This narrative has been adopted by some feminists, ecologists, and ecofeminists. This narrative looks back to an original Eden that subsisted in human history for hundreds of thousands of years before the rise of plow agriculture, urbanization, slavery, and war sometime in the eighth to fifth millennium BCE in the ancient Near East. All these ills are often spoken of collectively as "patriarchy," the rise of societies dominated by a male elite who subjugated women, turned the majority of humans into slaves, serfs, or low-paid workers and redefined all these humans, as well as nature, as property.[78]

These systems of patriarchy or elite male domination are seen as being further developed in Western colonialism and modern scientific technology and economics. These patterns of domination are leading to impoverishment of most humans and the natural world and rapidly producing a crisis that threatens survival on earth. Thus ecologists and ecofeminists call for an urgent revolutionary transformation of the world order that has been shaped by a "5000-year" process of domination, and the recreation of "Eden," as small self-governing communities that integrate democratic relations and economies of natural renewal. This is what David Korten, leading critic of the neoliberal corporate global economy, has called in his new work, "The End of Empire and the Step to Earth Community."[79]

Merchant concludes her book, *Reinventing Eden*, with a call for a partnership ethic. This ethic she sees as integrating the narratives of both progress and decline but in a new way. The basis for this ethic of partnership draws upon new scientific and philosophical developments of quantum mechanics and chaos and complexity theory that have come to recognize that nature is not passive or mechanical, much less composed of "dead" matter. Rather nature is alive, holistic, and interconnected. Nature has its own self-organizing patterns of life. Humans need to connect with nature, not as dead objects to be exploited, but rather as active subjects with which they must learn to partner.[80]

Merchant sums up her partnership ethic in the following way: "A partnership ethic holds that the greatest good for the human and nonhuman communities is in their mutual living interdependence."[81] A partnership ethics is based on five precepts: (1) Equity between the human and nonhuman communities. (2) Moral consideration for both humans and other species. (3) Respect for cultural diversity and biodiversity. (4) Inclusion of women, minorities, and nonhuman nature in ethical accountability. (5) Ecologically sound management consistent with continued health of both the human and nonhuman communities.[82]

Merchant's partnership ethic envisions replacing litigation between polluting corporations and environmental groups with a process of negotiation and cooperation. Partnership would focus particularly on local and regional work together. Present at the table must be not only corporations, businesses, and government agencies, but also representatives of ethnic minorities, indigenous people, African Americans, members of poorer communities, and women of all groups, as well as environmentalists who can speak for the interests of rivers, wetlands, forests, animals, and other nonhuman participants.

Negotiation between these spokespersons would seek to find a balance between human and nonhuman interests in a way that would both be life enhancing for nature and provide for the basic means of life for the whole human community, not simply the interests of the rich and powerful at the expenses of most humans and nature, as is presently the case. Merchant seeks a hopeful way forward beyond conflict and destruction to a renewal of community where the best interests of all are taken into account in concrete expressions of reconciling mutuality.

CONCLUSION

This survey of ecofeminist theologies and ethical theories from North America, including neo-pagans, a Christian theologian, and a historian of science, to Indians, Africans, and Latin Americans, reveals a remarkable level of commonality. Most of them share a critique of Western epistemology based on the isolated knower outside of and unrelated to the reality that is known, whose knowledge is a means of control over others. Most of them question a model of the self based on the isolated individual disconnected from relationships that ignores the actual support services that other humans and nature are providing to create this privileged appearance of the "autonomous" self.

They also reject a view of nature as "dead matter" to be dominated, in favor of an understanding of nature as living beings in dynamic communities of life. They call for democratic relationships between humans, men and women, ethnic groups, and those presently divided by class and culture. They seek a new sense of partnership between humans and nature. The keynotes of interrelationship, interdependency, and mutuality echo across all these perspectives, calling for a renewed sense of how humans should relate to one another and with the natural world.

What accounts for this remarkable commonality across diverse cultures and contexts? For one thing, this reflects the global level of communication that is now possible and that links thought worlds readily with one another. Vandana Shiva and Ivone Gebara both testify to the importance of reading Carolyn Merchant's book, *The Death of Nature,* early in the formation of their own thought. Vandana Shiva's work, in turn, is widely read among Western ecofeminists and critics of the global economy. Ivone Gebara's work, both as published writing and as workshops, is widely circulated in Latin America and was the compelling moment for many Latin American feminists to turn to an ecofeminist cosmology in their journey of personal spirituality. Her books are also on the reading lists of many North Americans and Western Europeans interested in a theology linked to ecology and feminism.

All this circulation of ecofeminist ideas across cultures, of course, would have little effect if it did not resonate with deep conflicts, struggles, and changes of consciousness that are happening worldwide. The destructive impact of a pattern of "dominology," based on top-down epistemology and a concept of the self and its relation to other humans and nature, is widely seen as the root of the evils of sexism, racism, and imperialism, with its ongoing expressions in neocolonial exploitation of third world societies and their natural resources. Groups of people around the world are struggling to change these patterns. Similar ideas of the needed alternatives are emerging in many contexts and linking up with one another.

It is widely assumed that there is a need to refound local community, in democratic face-to-face relations with the variety of people, men and women, across classes and ethnic groups, living in that community. There is a need for renewed regional communities to redevelop their relation to the land, agriculture, and water in a sustainable way, based on democratic decision-making that takes all parties, including nonhuman nature, into consideration. This also means withdrawing from the centralized systems of control that have been forged by colonialism and neocolonialism. By banding together in communities of accountability, it is hoped that this system of domination can be undermined and perhaps overthrown altogether for new ways of networking local communities across regions and across the globe.

Visions of humans in interrelation with one another and with nature express this longing for an alternative way of situating people in relation to society and the world. To see nature itself as a living matrix of interconnection provides the cosmological basis for this alternative vision of relationship. This common ecofeminist theology or worldview shares some of the following characteristics. There is a rejection of a splitting of the divine from the earth and its communities of life to project "God" as a personified entity located in some supercelestial realm outside the universe and ruling over it. The concept of God is deconstructed. The divine is understood as a matrix of life-giving energy that is in, through, and under all things. To use the language of Paul in the Book of Acts, God is the "one in whom we live, and move and have our being" (17:28).

This is not pantheist in the sense of reducing life-giving energy to what "is," for what exists now is dominated by the superstructures of oppressive power, the transnational corporations, the Pentagon, and the World Trade Organization. Rather we need to think of this life-giving matrix as pan-en-theist, or transcendently immanent. It both sustains the constant renewal of the natural cycles of life and also empowers us to struggle against the hierarchies of dominance and to create renewed relations of mutual affirmation.

This divine energy for life and renewal of life is not male, female, or anthropomorphic in any literal or exclusive sense. It can be imagined in many ways that celebrate our diverse bodies and spirits. What is excluded are metaphors that reinforce gender stereotypes and relations of dominance. It can be called "divine Wisdom," the font of life that wells up to create and recreate anew all living things in what Thomas Berry calls "ecozoic"[83] community. Holy Wisdom calls us into life-giving community across many strands of tradition, culture, and history, and also empowers us to stand shoulder to shoulder against the systems of economic, military, and ecological violence that are threatening the very fabric of planetary life.

NOTES

1. See Carol J. Adams, ed. *Ecofeminism and the Sacred* (New York: Continuum, 1994), xi.

2. Plato, *Timaeus,* 49–50. See also Rosemary Ruether, *Gaia and God: An Ecofeminist Theology of Earth Healing* (New York: HarperCollins, 1992), 22–24.

3. See Val Plumwood, *Feminism and the Mastery of Nature* (New York: Routledge, 1993), 104–40.

4. On the essentialist debate about ecofeminism, see, for example, Mary Mellor, *Feminism and Ecology* (New York: New York University Press, 1997), 44–70; also Stephanie Lahar, "Ecofeminist Theory and Grassroots Politics," in Karen J. Warren, *Ecological Feminist Philosophies* (Bloomington: Indiana University Press, 1996), 11–12.

5. Mellor speaks of this view as "affinity ecofeminism," 56–58, 75–77. The complexity of this "affinity" can be seen in an essay such as that by Charlene Spretnak, "Earthbody and Personal Body as Sacred," in Adams, ed. *Ecofeminism and the Sacred*, 261–80.

6. See discussion of the relativity of culture-nature hierarchies and their inapplicability to tribal and peasant peoples in Heather Eaton and Lois Ann Lorentzen,

Ecofeminism and Globalization: Exploring Culture, Context and Religion, (Lanham, Md.: Rowman & Littlefield, 2003), especially chapters 3 and 4, 41–71.

7. For an effort to imagine an ecofeminist society, see Ruether, *Gaia and God*, 258–68.

8. Starhawk's first major book was *The Spiral Dance: A Rebirth of the Ancient Religion of the Great Goddess* (San Francisco: HarperSanFrancisco, 1979; 2nd edition, 1989).

9. See her comments in the 1989 edition of *The Spiral Dance*, 16–17; also her book, *Truth or Dare: Encounters with Power, Authority and Mystery* (San Francisco: Harper and Row, 1987), 18–19.

10. See her *Dreaming in the Dark: Magic, Sex and Politics* (Boston: Beacon, 1982), 1–15; also *Truth or Dare*, 8–19.

11. *Webs of Power: Notes from the Global Uprising* (Gabriola Island, B.C.: New Society Publishers, 2002).

12. Ibid., 160–68.

13. Ibid., 251–55.

14. Ibid., 244–45.

15. Ibid., 237–41.

16. See her *Rebirth of the Goddess: Finding Meaning in Feminist Spirituality* (New York: Routledge, 1997), 50–60.

17. Ibid., 62–67, 98–104, 158–59, 170–76.

18. Ibid., 109–12.

19. *She Who Changes: Re-imagining the Divine in the World* (New York: Macmillan Palgrave, 2003).

20. Ibid., 25–44.

21. Ibid., 45–92.

22. Ibid., 240.

23. In Rosemary Radford Ruether, ed. *Women Healing Earth: Third World Women on Ecology, Feminism and Religion* (Maryknoll, N.Y.: Orbis Books, 1996), 135–42.

24. See Marthinus L. Daneel, "African Independent Churches Face the Challenge of Environmental Ethics," in David Hallman, ed. *Ecotheology: Voices from South and North* (Maryknoll, N.Y.: Orbis, 1994), 248–63; also Daneel, "Earthkeeping Churches at the African Grassroots," in Rosemary Ruether and Dieter Hessel, eds. *Christianity and Ecology* (Cambridge, Mass.: Harvard University Press, 2000), 531–52.

25. See her "The Gikuyu Theology of Land and Environmental Justice," in Ruether, *Women Healing Earth*, 171–84.

26. Wangari Maathai tells the history of this movement in her book, *The Green Belt Movement: Sharing the Approach and the Experience* (New York: Lantern Books, 2003).

27. Ibid., 32–52.

28. See Priscilla Sears, "Wangari Maathai, You Strike the Woman...," In *Context: A Quarterly of Human Sustainable Culture* (Spring 1991), available at www.context.org/ICLIB/IC28/Sears.htm. Also Katy Salmon, "Forest Profile: Wangari Maathai," in *People and Planet* (August 1, 2000), available at www.peopleandplanet.net/doc.php?id=39.

29. Priscilla Sears, "Wangai Maathai."

30. *Staying Alive* was published originally in Delhi, India by Kali for Women. *The Violence of the Green Revolution* appeared with The Other India. *Monocultures of the Mind* was published in the West by Zed Press and *Biopiracy* and *Stolen Harvests* by South End Press of Boston. *Ecofeminism* appeared with several world presses, including Zed Press.

31. See *Staying Alive*, 1 and 15.

32. Susan Harding, *The Science Question in Feminism* (Ithaca, N.Y.: Cornell University Press, 1986; Evelyn F. Keller, *Reflections on Gender and Science* (New Haven, Conn.: Yale University Press, 1985); and Carolyn Merchant, *The Death of Nature: Women, Ecology and the Scientific Revolution* (New York: Harper and Row, 1980).

33. She cites for this theme the oft-cited book by Brian Easlea, *Science and Sexual Oppression: Pariarchy's Confrontation with Women and Nature* (London: Weidenfeld and Nicholson, 1981).

34. See her chapter on "Women in the Food Chain" in *Staying Alive*, 96–178. Also her book *The Violence of the Green Revolution*.

35. See "Women and Vanishing Waters" in *Staying Alive*, 179–219; also her book, *Water Wars: Privatization, Pollution and Profit* (Boston: South End Press, 2002).

36. *Staying Alive*, 38–54.

37. See the critique of these themes in Hinduism in chapter 2 of this book.

38. This critique was made by Aruna Gnanadason in a conversation at a World Council of Churches consultation on ecofeminism in Geneva in July 2003.

39. Gnanadason received the D. Min. in May 2004; the thesis is available through the San Francisco Theological Seminary in San Raphel, California. Gnanadason plans to publish the thesis.

40. *Intuitiones Ecofeministas* (Madrid, Spain: Editorial Trotto, 2000).

41. Ibid., 22–24.

42. Ivone Gebara, "A Cry for Life from Latin America," in *Spirituality of the Third World: A Cry for Life*, K. C. Abraham and Bernadette Mbuy-beya, eds. (Maryknoll, N.Y.: Orbis Press, 1994), 109–18.

43. "Ecofeminism and Panentheism," interview by Mary Judy Ress, *Creation Spirituality* (November–December 1993), 9–11.

44. Ivone Gebara, *Longing for Running Water: Ecofeminism and Liberation* (Minneapolis: Fortress Press, 1999), 25–65. Also Rosemary Ruether, *Women Healing Earth*, 13–23.

45. *Longing for Running Water*, 71–76.

46. Ibid., 82–92.

47. Brian Swimme and Thomas Berry, *The Universe Story: From the Primordial Flaring Forth to the Ecozoic Era—A Celebration of the Unfolding of the Cosmos* (San Francisco: HarperCollins, 1992).

48. See note 42 above.

49. See her reflections on "The Trinity and the Problem of Evil," Rosemary Ruether, *Women Healing Earth*, 19–22.

50. See particularly her chapter on "Women's Experience of Salvation," in *Out of the Depths: Women's Experience of Evil and Salvation* (Minneapolis: Fortress Press, 2002), 109–44.

51. Published by the Colectivo Editorial, Malaquias Concha 043, Casilla 371-11, Correo Ñuñoa, Santiago, Chile. The *Con-spirando* story is also told in Mary Judy Ress's D.Min. thesis completed for graduation from the San Francisco Theological Seminary in May 2002: *Without a Vision, the People Perish* (published by *Con-spirando*, Santiago, Chile, 2003). For an overview of the *Con-spirando* story, see her essay, "The *Con-spirando* Women's Collective: Globalization from Below," in Eaton and Lorentzen, *Ecofeminism and Globalization*, 147–61.

52. Mary Judy Ress, *Without a Vision, the People Perish*.

53. *Lluvia para Florecer: Entrevistas sobre Ecofeminismo en América Latina* (Santiago, Chile: Con-spirando Collective, 2003), 37–50.

54. Ibid., 51–70.

55. Ibid., 71–87.

56. Ibid., 89–107.

57. *From a Broken Web: Separation, Sexism and Self* (Boston: Beacon, 1986).

58. *Apocalypse, Now and Then: A Feminist Guide to the End of the World* (Boston: Beacon, 1996).

59. Ibid., xi.

60. Ibid., 276.

61. See also her essay, "Talk about the Weather," in Adams, ed. *Ecofeminism and the Sacred*, 30–49.

62. *Face of the Deep: A Theology of Becoming* (London: Routledge, 2003).

63. See Plato's *Timaeus*, 49, for his view of preexisting matter.

64. Keller, *Face of the Deep*, 28–31.

65. Job 40:15–41:34. Other references to Leviathan in Hebrew Scripture are Psalm 74:14, Isaiah 30:7 and 51:9, and Ezekiel 29:3 and 32:2.

66. On Augustine's development of this doctrine, see Keller, *Face of the Deep*, 65–83.

67. See particularly her account of Barth's demonizing of primal chaos, ibid., 84–99.

68. Ibid., 25–40; also her essay, "No More Sea: The Lost Chaos of the Eschaton," in *Christianity and Ecology: Seeking the Wellbeing of Earth and Humans*, Dieter Hessel and Rosemary Ruether, eds. (Cambridge, Mass.: Harvard University Press, 2000), 183–99.

69. *Face of the Deep*, 213–28.

70. *The Death of Nature: Women, Ecology and the Scientific Revolution* (San Francisco: Harper and Row, 1980).

71. Ibid., 1.

72. See Plato, *Timaeus*, 42, where human souls were shaped from the substance of the world soul.

73. For Bacon's sexual imagery, see Merchant, *Death of Nature*, 168–72.

74. Ibid., 290.

75. Ibid., 295.

76. *Reinventing Eden: The Fate of Nature in Western Culture* (New York: Routledge, 2003).

77. Ibid., 167–70.

78. Ibid., 26–36.

79. David Korten, lecture, Call to Action Conference, Milwaukee, Wisconsin, November 7–8, 2003.

80. Merchant, *Reinventing Eden*, 205–20.

81. Ibid., 223.

82. Ibid., 224.

83. Thomas Berry and Brian Swimme, *The Universe Story*, 240–61.

4

ALTERNATIVES TO CORPORATE
GLOBALIZATION: IS A DIFFERENT
WORLD POSSIBLE?

In this chapter I address the key question of this volume: Is another world
possible? Can we create a different world system from that being ham-
mered in place by the transnational corporations, the World Bank, the International Monetary Fund, the World Trade Organization, and the politi-
cians representing the wealthy elites? Can a different way of relating human
beings to each other and to the earth emerge that would manifest equity
and sustainable community? Perhaps the way we think is the heart of the
problem. As Subcomandante Marcos, leader of the military wing of the Zapatista Liberation Army in Chiapas, Mexico, has said, "The problem is not
why the global economy is inevitable, but why almost everyone agrees that
it is."[1]

In this chapter I sketch myriad ways that groups of people all over the
world in every social sector, from former development officers and economists for the World Bank to landless peasants, are protesting the present corporate global system and seeking alternative ways of relating to each other
and to the earth outside its stranglehold. In the first section of this chapter
I point to three movements that initiated the challenge to the dominant system and began to imagine alternatives to it: the 1994 Zapatista uprising in
Chiapas, Mexico; the anti-WTO protests that began in Seattle, Washington
at the end of November 1999 and have continued since that time; and the
World Social Forum where NGOs from every social sector from all over the
world gather to imagine and discuss alternatives to corporate globalization.

I go on to discuss a number of other protests against the dominant system, such as the farmers of Karnataka, India, who burned the genetically altered seeds planted by Monsanto and the student-led antisweatshop actions
in the United States. I point to a number of efforts to create alternatives to
the present system of production and trade, such as community-supported

agriculture, fair trade coffee, and cooperatives. I then move to the efforts of theoreticians to imagine a different way of organizing aid and trade and how to dismantle the present financial institutions and curb the global corporations, while rebuilding democratic accountability in local communities. The chapter will close with a critique of the economic and religious ideologies that justify the present system and outline a different way of thinking about human life on earth.

INITIATING THE STRUGGLE: THE ZAPATISTA REBELLION

On January 1, 1994, the day NAFTA (North American Free Trade Agreement) was scheduled to go into effect, 3,000 masked, mostly indigenous, men and women with makeshift weapons seized the former capital city of the Mexican state of Chiapas, San Cristóbal de las Casas, as well as the town halls of six other municipalities and numerous ranches. They burned the judicial and police records of these towns and proclaimed their rejection of the ruling Mexican state party, the PRI (Party of the Institutional Revolution) that had blatantly stolen the election in 1988 when the leader of an alternative party, Cuauhtemoc Cardenas, of the PRD (Party of the Democratic Revolution), was clearly winning the popular vote. This insurgent army took the name of the leader of the 1910 revolution, Emiliano Zapata, calling themselves the Zapatista National Liberation Army (EZNL).

Within twenty-four hours the Mexican government sent 12,000 soldiers into the region and bombed numerous indigenous communities, killing at least 145 local people. But, to the surprise of the government, huge demonstrations took place in Mexico City and elsewhere in Mexico, calling for an end of military repression and demanding a negotiated solution. A cease-fire was declared on January 12. Peace talks began January 21 under the aegis of the Catholic diocese, led by its bishop, Don Samuel Ruiz Garcia, a liberation theologian who had for fifteen years pursued a pastoral policy of empowering local indigenous communities. Manuel Camacho Solis, former mayor of Mexico City, a man respected for his integrity, was chosen to represent the government, while Subcomandante Marcos and Zapatista military and civil leaders spoke for the Zapatistas. (In the Zapatista democratic communal system, the civic leaders of the communities are the comandantes to whom the military wing is accountable. Marcos, as the head of the military wing, is subcomandante, i.e., under the civil leaders.)[2]

Although the Zapatistas maintained the cease-fire thereafter, claiming only the right of self-defense of the indigenous communities against armed violence from private armies of the landlords, the Mexican government rapidly militarized the region, seeking to undermine the Zapatistas by a combination of military repression and bribery. Meanwhile the Zapatistas maintained their communication with Mexican civil society and sympathizers throughout the world. They issued a series of proclamations that not only denounced the perfidy of the government, but began to sketch a different philosophy of social change from the Latin American guerrilla movements that sought to seize control of the central government. It is these proclamations that have earned the Zapatistas, and their spokesman, Marcos, the name of being the first "postmodern" revolution of the twenty-first century.[3]

The Zapatista program enunciated eleven demands of the oppressed peasantry and indigenous people: land, work, housing, food, health care, education, independence, freedom, democracy, justice, and peace, to which they later added two more, information and culture.[4] But they also spoke in terms that the government found puzzling, calling for "dignity" for the indigenous people and for the rights of women. Women should not be forced to marry against their will, should not be raped and abused in their families and in the larger society, should be able to choose if and when to have children and to hold any leadership position. Justice and democracy, in the Zapatista view, begin at home. These demands for dignity and women's rights the government negotiators proclaimed "incomprehensible" and "irrelevant."[5]

The Zapatistas began to shape an alternative vision of power. The centralized one-party state that had ruled Mexico for seventy years must be reshaped, not by seizing power at the top, but rather by withdrawing from centralized power, creating democratic space in every local community and social sector. This strategy, they claimed, is not a fragmentation of the larger Mexican society into separate regions, but recognition of local differences within a larger whole. Mexico as a nation must embrace genuine diversity and equality of all communities, rather than seeking to create one society by suppressing difference. The great diversity of indigenous peoples, with their many cultures, traditions, and languages, must become genuinely citizens of Mexico for the first time, by being accepted as equals in their differences, rather than erasing their differences through assimilation into the culture of the Spanish conqueror. Against this historic trend of conquest and assimilation since the sixteenth century, the Zapatistas declared that "in the world that we want many worlds fit. The nation which we are building is one where all communities and languages fit."[6]

The Zapatista protest was not only against the one-party state built by the PRI, but also against the sell-out of the Mexican people and its resources to the global system of corporate control under NAFTA. President

Salinas had anticipated this sell-out of Mexico to corporate globalization by rescinding one of the most central victories of the 1910 revolution, namely the commitment to land reform that distributed *ejidos* or inalienable land grants to the local peasantry. Such land grants were central to the hopes of indigenous people for land. When Salinas erased this guarantee from the Mexican constitution in 1992 it was the signal that the hopes of the masses were being sold out so that a few wealthy Mexicans could profit from the system of corporate domination.[7] The promises of NAFTA that Mexico would thereby join the "first world" and could expect a great increase in jobs and rising prosperity for all were a delusion. The indigenous people had no doubts that for them the NAFTA agreement signified death.

In his most detailed critique of the system of corporate globalization which is impoverishing Mexico, Subcomandante Marcos called it the beginning of a fourth world war. This fourth world war follows the end of the third world war, the cold war of the 1960s to 1980s, in which the socialist sector of nations was defeated and socialism discredited as an alternative to capitalism. The defeat of socialism unleashed the fourth world war in which capitalism seeks to extend its hegemony over the whole world, subordinating national governments and their leaders to being simply branch managers of global corporations. Not only national governments but also national markets are being dismantled for this global "order," which in reality is chaos for most people. The lies of the capitalist ideology that promised democracy and freedom, equality and fraternity are discarded, and all that remains is the rule of the rich over the rest of humanity.

Marcos analyzed this economic system as six big pieces of a puzzle that are prevented from coalescing into one by a seventh piece made up of many pieces that refuses to fit with the others. The six pieces of the puzzle are (1) the concentration of wealth in the hands of a few while the majority are impoverished; (2) globalization of exploitation, expelling more and more people from productive employment, while those who have jobs work longer hours in worsening conditions for lower wages; (3) the uprooting of political and economic refugees who wander the world looking for survival; (4) the globalization of financial power and organized crime as one; (5) the militarization of government whose only remaining role is violent repression of dissent; and (6) the fragmentation of nations into smaller and more powerless entities, as global economic power tightens its grip on the world.

The seventh piece of the puzzle that prevents these six from coalescing into one unified world domination is the proliferation of "pockets of resistance," such as that represented by the Zapatistas. People from all sectors of society, "women, children, old people, young people, indigenous people, ecological militants, homosexuals, lesbians, HIV activists, workers, and all those who upset the ordered progress of the new world system."[8] It is out of these many pockets of resistance that reject the dominant system that Marcos stakes his hopes for building a different world, "a world in which there is room for many worlds."[9]

SEATTLE TO CANCÚN: POPULAR PROTEST AGAINST THE WTO

Corporate leaders and their political and media supporters were caught by surprise when more than 50,000 people gathered in Seattle on November 30, 1999, to protest the Millennial Summit of the World Trade Organization. This summit was designed to bring together trade ministers from around the world for a new "round" of market-opening negotiations. The highly organized protests that assembled in the Seattle streets did not, of course, arise spontaneously. They were the fruit of a decade of struggle against free trade agreements that had proved to be inimical to the interests of farmers, workers, human rights, and food and environmental safety.

In the early 1990s labor unions and environmentalists had battled the passage of NAFTA and lost, but in a way that left a restive grass roots that saw their concerns sold out by political bribery. In 1997 we witnessed the battle to deny President Clinton "fast track" rights to negotiate WTO trade rules, while 1998 awakened an international struggle against the passage of the Multinational Agreement on Investment (MAI), secretly negotiated in Paris by representatives of the twenty-eight wealthiest nations.[10] Although victories were won in both these struggles, corporate accountability advocates were horrified by a series of WTO rulings from 1995 to 1999 that beat back national laws to protect the environment and human rights. Laws protecting dolphins and sea turtles from destruction by wide net fishing, that banned toxic chemicals added to gasoline, and that restricted imports from countries of oppressive dictatorships, such as Burma, were being ruled as "impediments to trade" by unelected judges representing corporate interests in secret courts from which the public was excluded.[11]

When the World Trade Organization announced its plans in January 1999 to hold its Summit in Seattle at the end of November, a vast network of groups began to make plans to bring a major protest to the streets and to close down the meeting. The call went out across the country and the world to "come to Seattle." Nonviolent training groups, such as the Ruckus Society, swung into action to teach people skills in nonviolent street protest. The

AFL-CIO planned a major march representing the opposition of labor. New coalitions that brought labor and environmental concerns together, such as the Alliance for Sustainable Jobs and Environment, summoned their troops. The organizers planned four days of protests, each with a different emphasis: environment, agriculture, human rights, and labor.

But even the organizers were surprised by the large numbers of people from many sectors of society that showed up. Labor representatives, not just from the United States, but from one hundred other countries, were present. French farmers seasoned by protests against McDonald's, environmental groups from many countries, students who had organized against sweatshops, medics prepared to help people injured by beatings and gas, communication groups, who set up an Independent Media Center to support freelance reporters, all arrived. A coalition of activists versed in nonviolent direct action set up a "convergence center" where protestors could get food and training and could formulate their plans. Protestors were organized into affinity groups of ten to thirty people for flexible response in the midst of action. The participants were asked to commit themselves to certain guidelines for duration of the Seattle actions: to refrain from violence, physical or verbal, to carry no weapons, and to not bring illegal drugs or alcohol.[12]

The first day of the protest was stunningly successful. The street blockades prevented the opening ceremony of the Summit at the Paramount Theatre from taking place. The police, outnumbered and outmaneuvered by the protestors, soon resorted to force, with volleys of pepper spray, tear gas, and rubber bullets. Soon they were bludgeoning nonviolent protestors and using brutal methods in mass arrests. A large downtown area was cordoned off as a "non-protest" zone in which even peaceful distribution of flyers was forbidden. A state of emergency was declared with reinforcements from the Washington State National Guard. Tear gas and pepper spray hit passersby and shoppers. Some people simply trying to leave their offices to go home were gassed and beaten. The police riot was aided by about 100 members of a "Black Block" group that did not adhere to the nonviolent guidelines, but came determined to smash the windows of corporate businesses, such as Starbucks, Nike, and Banana Republic. The police effort to portray the protestors as violent was picked up by some of the corporate media, but the excesses of the police were also widely reported.[13]

The conflict in the streets was soon reflected in dissension within the meeting. European Union delegates rejected the U.S. efforts to impose MAI-like investment rules, enforce trade in genetically altered foods, and disallow farm subsidies. Third world delegates complained about the failure of rich countries to lower their tariffs on imports, while they were forced to do so by WTO rules. The secrecy of WTO rulings and failure to allow advocates for labor, environment, and human rights to be heard were criticized. Delegates from eight Latin American countries announced they would not sign and others followed suit. Late in the evening on the fourth day the official meeting was adjourned without having successfully negotiated any agreements. The delegates headed for the airports without even issuing a final communique.[14]

The next two years saw efforts to repeat the successes of Seattle in street protests at other high level meetings of corporate powers: the meeting of the International Monetary Fund and World Bank in Washington, D.C., from April 16 to 18, 2000, the IMF and WB annual meeting in Prague in September 2000, the Summit of the Americas to discuss the extending of NAFTA to all of North and South America in the Free Trade Agreement of the Americas (FTAA) in Quebec City in April 2001, and the meeting of the G-8 nations (the organization of the wealthiest nations: the United States, Canada, Britain, France, Germany, Italy, Japan, and Russia) in Genoa, Italy, July 20–22, 2001.

These efforts were met by increasing police violence, including preemptive strikes at the protestors. In Washington, D.C., the police barricaded off a sixty-block area of downtown Washington, which the protestors could not enter. Before the protests could even begin, the police raided the convergence center and shut it down, arresting 600 people doing preparations there and confiscating puppets and medical supplies. Copy centers were closed down so leaflets could not be reproduced. U.S. marshals and National Guard supplemented the police and were given orders to shoot to kill.[15]

The protests in Prague brought together groups more ready for property damage and street fighting, but the police were also ready with preemptory strikes, mass arrests, and beatings in jail. The protests in Quebec were met by an armed city that constructed a four-kilometer, nine-foot fence around the area of the city where delegates gathered, where any protest, including speech or distribution of literature, was forbidden. The most extreme police brutality took place at the Genoa meeting. There it appeared a "Black Block" group that engaged in property damage was actually functioning as provocateurs in collaboration with the police. This group was allowed to pass, while nonviolent protestors were savagely beaten. The police even broke into a building at night and beat many protestors as they lay sleeping. Beating and torture continued in jails, where the arrested were forced to chant allegiance to Mussolini. Evidently memories of Italian fascism still lingered in the Italian Carabinieri, with the connivance of the right-wing prime minister, Silvio Berlusconi.[16]

Renewed protests were planned for the end of September 2001 at the IMF and WB meeting in Washington, D.C., but these were cancelled in light of the September 11 attacks on the World Trade Center in New York and the Pentagon. The militarization of the Washington streets in response to the attack, as well as general shock, made protests at that time inappropriate. However, these protests were renewed when these institutions met in Washington in 2002. But clearly it was time to reassess the usefulness of street protests and how to make opposition to the WTO more effective in the light of the police response that increasingly blurred the line between police containment of legal protest and a militarized war against those seen as "terrorists" and national enemies.

A significant example of the new stage of protest took place at the fifth Ministerial Meeting of the WTO in Cancún, Mexico, September 10–14, 2003. Some 10,000 protesters showed up outside the meeting, coming from Mexico and all over the world. These demonstrators included a global federation of farmers, Via Campesina. On the first day of the meeting the plight of farmers due to WTO agricultural policies was dramatically illustrated when a Korean farmer, Lee Kyung Hae, climbed on the fence intended to keep the protesters out of the meeting area and stabbed himself, dying the next day. Unintentionally illustrating his gesture, some farmers carried placards reading, "WTO kills farmers."[17]

But in the Cancún meeting the primary resistance was mounted from within the assembly, while the groups outside worked primarily as their supporters. The agenda constructed entirely by the wealthy countries, especially the United States and the European Economic Union, continued to allow these countries to impose heavy tariffs on developing nations' imports, while maintaining subsidies on their own production. The developing nations demanded that these policies be adjusted to fairer trade conditions for poorer countries. But the United States and EU refused to budge, while at the same time trying to introduce new issues having to do with investment, trade facilitation, competition policy, and government procurement. All of these four new issues were designed to favor wealthy transnational corporations wishing to dismantle regulations by governments of poorer nations.

But the developing nations were now better organized to resist this pressure. A group of twenty-one (G-21) nations, representing more middle-sized developing economies, such as Brazil, India, China, Colombia, and Costa Rica, refused to consider these additional issues until the tariffs and subsidies were dealt with. The developing nations had brought with them NGO leaders and trade experts to advise them on the implications of the agreements. They had also constructed ties between each other over the previous couple of years that allowed them to stand together firmly against the G-8 nations. When these wealthy nations refused to modify their position, a larger coalition of some ninety developing and poor nations (including forty African nations and thirty least developed nations) rejected the draft Ministerial Text that had been presented to them. The WTO meeting broke down without an agreement on Sunday afternoon, September 14.[18]

For the first time since the late 1970s, when the United States moved to break up coalitions of nonaligned nations, a global coalition of poorer and developing nations was emerging to resist the policies of the wealthy governments and transnational corporations. This was a cause for celebration among the opponents of corporate globalization. But it also left open the possibility that the wealthy nations and corporations might abandon the WTO altogether as their agent of control over world resources, moving instead to direct bilateral agreements with nations where they could pressure them in a more isolated way.[19] In this struggle, clearly neither side can remain static. Even a small victory of the critics of corporate globalization causes the wealthy to adapt to new strategies of control, forcing their opponents to find new strategies of opposition.

THE WORLD SOCIAL FORUM

The World Social Forum is a gathering of NGOs, groups, and individuals from around the world to discuss alternatives to the system of corporate globalization and to network together. The WSF met for the first time January 25–30, 2001 in Porto Alegre, Brazil. Some 20,000 people attended, with 4,700 delegates of organizations from 117 countries. The conferences, seminars, and workshops were organized around the four themes of "production of wealth and social reproduction," "access to wealth and sustainability," "asserting civil societies and the public realm," and "political power and ethics in the new society."

The next two meetings also took place in Porto Alegre in January 2002 and January 2003. The second gathering brought together more than 50,000 people with 12,274 delegates of organizations from 123 countries and the third gathered more than 100,000 with 20,000 delegates from 123 countries. In addition 25,000 young people took part in the youth camp. The themes of the third gathering were "democratic, sustainable development," "principles and values, human rights, diversity and equality," "media, culture and alternatives to commodification," "political power, civil society and democracy," and "democratic world order, combating militarism and promoting peace."[20]

In 2004 the WSF met in Mumbai, India where more than 100,000 gathered from 130 countries. This change of venue reflected the desire to affirm this gathering as fully international, not centered in Brazil. Participants pledged to build a more powerful united global movement against the Bush administration's policies of militarism and aggression. These commitments included: (1) mass demonstrations around the world on March 20, 2004 on the anniversary of the U.S. attack on Iraq in 2003; (2) a heightened campaign led by Mayors for Peace representing 560 cities to abolish nuclear weapons; and (3) a campaign led by leaders from the Caribbean and the Asian–Pacific region to remove 702 U.S. military bases around the world. Although the participants in the forum committed themselves to the continuance of the forum as a framework for debate, they also believed it was time to build a movement.[21]

The World Social Forum is also generating many more regional and thematic gatherings. In 2002 and 2003 fora on "the neoliberal model in crisis" were held in Buenos Aires, Argentina. A Palestinian forum discussed "negotiated conflict solution" in Ramallah, Palestine. A forum held in Colombia discussed "democracy, human rights, war and drug trafficking." There were also regional forums in Europe, Asia, Africa, and Latin America. The World Social Forum was originally organized by a Brazilian Organizing Committee. After the first forum in 2001 it was decided to set up an international council to define its strategic directions and mobilize support. A Charter of Principles was drafted to give the forum a permanent framework and process.[22]

This Charter of Principles, adopted in São Paulo, Brazil, on April 9, 2001, defined what the World Social Forum wishes to be and what it does not wish to become. What it wishes to be is "an open meeting place for reflective thinking, democratic debate of ideas, formulation of proposals, free exchange of experiences and interlinking for effective action by groups and movements of civil society opposed to neoliberalism and to domination of the world by capital and any form of imperialism, committed to building a planetary society directed toward fruitful relations among humankind and between it and the earth." It wishes to become an ongoing world process committed to building "democratic international systems and institutions at the service of social justice, equality and the sovereignty of peoples."

The World Social Forum does not want to become itself an institution, political party, or representative organization. It does not take votes or decisions as a body. It does not seek to monopolize the debate on alternatives or become a locus of power to be disputed by participants. This does not prevent organizations or groups of organizations that participate in its meetings from deliberating on declarations or actions they may decide to do and from circulating social decisions. The forum itself wishes to remain a venue for such debate and networking, rather than becoming a governing body over such activities. It wishes to remain open to the widest diversity of activities and ways of engagement, as well as the diversity of genders, ethnicities, cultures, generations, and physical capacities. Political parties as such and military organizations are excluded from the forum, and government leaders and members of legislatures may participate only as individuals.

How successful is the forum in continuing to be this framework for open debate and networking? Peter Waterman, a journalist attending the 2003 forum, saw the forum as having limitations and problems.[23] Its huge size itself made it difficult to maintain openness, transparency, and accountability. Women and gender issues were inadequately represented, and indigenous and poor people found it difficult to attend. The built-in biases of a world in which richer people have the advantage in being able to travel, attend meetings, read, and debate meant that the majority present were middle-class white males. The youth camp put young people in their own group, rather than having their voices present throughout.

The forum also deals inadequately with communication. It relies too much on the spoken and written word and big demonstrations, without exploring other ways of communicating. Its website is out of date and does not give a full enough coverage of what is happening. But for all such limitations, it is still one of the major ways today in which people can address the key issues of global society, exchange ideas with thinkers and activists from all over the world, and network for action. By committing itself to avoid becoming itself an oligarchy or power broker, it builds in flexibility and capacity to generate its own internal critics who can propose new approaches and dimensions of the struggle to affirm its central article of faith: "another world is possible."

DIRECT ACTION CAMPAIGNS AGAINST GLOBALIZATION

As the criticism of privatization and corporate buy-up of basic human resources grew, a number of direct action campaigns against these practices developed all over the world. Here are only a few examples of some of these actions. One such case is the campaign against genetically engineered seeds mounted by the Karnataka (India) State Farmers Association, an organization which networks ten million farmers in the state of Karnataka. In late November 1998 this Farmers Association issued a letter to the Monsanto Corporation announcing their intention to go to three sites where Monsanto was growing Bt cotton (with DNA from the soil microbe Bacillius thuringiensis to produce proteins poisonous to the bollworm pest), where they would uproot and burn these genetically engineered plants.

This action, called Operation Cremation Monsanto, was publicly announced in advance and the farmers association promised to cover any losses to the owners of the fields (not to Monsanto). This action was to be only the beginning of a continual campaign by farmers, not only in Karnataka, but in other Indian states, Maharastra, Gujurat, and Madhya Pradesh. In addition to burning the plants, the farmers announced several other goals of their campaign, to stop genetic engineering, reject patents on life, and bury the WTO. By not only burning test fields, but also squatting in Monsanto and other biotech corporate offices, the farmers vowed to drive Monsanto, Novartis, Pioneer, and other such corporations out of India.[24]

This action has been repeated in several other countries. José Bové, a militant French farmer, who dismantled a McDonald's restaurant in his town of Millau, led farmers in Brazil on an expedition to burn test fields of genetically engineered soy plants. Bové had organized farmers in France and then in Europe in the 1980s. In the 1990s this became an international network of farmers against corporate farming called the Via Campesina that has regional networks in every continent.[25]

Direct action campaigns have also been mounted against the privatization of water and electricity. This privatization has been forced on countries by the World Bank that made such sales of public utilities a requirement for granting loans. For example, in 1998 the World Bank informed the Bolivian government that it would not guarantee a US$25 million loan to refinance water services in the Bolivian city of Cochabamba unless the city sold its water utility to a private corporation. In response the government of Bolivia forced the sale of the Cochabama water utility to Aguas del Tunari, a recently formed subsidiary of the giant multinational corporation Bechtel. The World Bank demanded full cost water pricing and told the Bolivian government that loan money could not be used to subsidize water for the poor.

In 2000, as the new privatized water system was put in place, water rates in Cochabama quickly rose by 35 percent. Poor people found that they had to spend more on water than on food, often as much as 20 percent of their monthly income. Tens of thousands of people took to the street in protest, shutting down the city for four days. The Coalition in Defense of Water and

Life (Coordiadora de Defense de Aqua y la Vida) sprang up to coordinate the protest. Bolivian President Hugo Banzer put the country under martial law, but also announced that the government would break the contract with Bechtel. Bechtel's subsidiary, Aguas del Tunari, departed from Bolivia.

The Bolivian government then handed over the running of the water services to the former workers at the local water company. The community promptly elected a new board of directors and developed alternative guide-lines. These mandated that the company must be run efficiently and with-out corruption, be fair to its workers, and reorganize in cooperation with local neighborhoods to assure that water was provided to all, especially the poorest. This community-controlled system continues to run Cochabamba water, even though Bechtel has brought a suit against the Bolivian govern-ment under WTO rules to complain of loss of profits due to the breaking of the contract.[26]

It is not only water utilities in third world countries that are the object of takeovers by huge transnational water corporations. These companies have also been eyeing water utilities in the developed world, particularly in the United States where most people get their water from publicly owned com-panies. In 2002 the huge German company, RWE AG, which had already purchased the British-based Thames Water, sought to acquire CalAmerican Water, which provided water to many California areas. But the small town of Montara, with only 4,900 people, saw that this would lead to both higher water prices and lack of local accountability. Montara prevailed upon the California Public Utility Commission that regulates utilities either to prevent the sale or to allow local communities to buy out their own water systems. The residents of Montara then passed an $11 million bond measure to pur-chase its own water system and put it under community control. Montara's success has become an example for many other U.S. communities who want to keep or return their water systems to community ownership.[27]

The new postapartheid South Africa has also seen militant organizing against the privatization of water and electrical utilities. In the apartheid era, utilities were publicly owned but primarily serviced whites. Blacks mostly got along without water and electricity, cooking, heating, and lighting their homes with paraffin, coal, or wood. After the end of apartheid the African National Congress government promised electricity and water for all, but in fact bought into a privatization scheme for development that quickly put such services out of the reach of the poorer blacks. In the Johannesburg-Soweto area the Electricity Supply Commission (ESKOM), developed to service whites, was privatized. Even though the black townships were now included in the electrical grid, the costs soared almost 50 percent, often costing as much as 35 percent of the monthly income of poorer households. Many households had their electricity cut off because of inability to pay the bills.

In 2000 the Soweto Electricity Crisis Committee was formed and quickly expanded to more than twenty branches with 7000 members. The Committee is run democratically, with each local council deciding on its own actions. The representatives of each local committee meet weekly and overall leadership is elected yearly. In 2001 the Committee developed the Khanyisa (light) Campaign in which teams taught people how to reconnect their electricity to the grid. More than 3000 households were reconnected, and prepay meters attached to the households were taken out and dumped at the major's office. What had been seen as a covert and illegal act was converted into an act of defiance. The campaign took thousands to the streets. Groups went to the city councillors' homes to disconnect their electricity. This campaign culminated in a trip to the mayor's house in the Kensington suburb in which his electricity and water were disconnected and garbage dumped in his swimming pool. Although 87 people were arrested, they were eventually cleared (by March 2003).

These militant actions were backed up by the creation of a wider network of organizations called the Anti-privatization Forum which has demanded that electricity and water not only be extended to every household, even the poorest in the rural areas, but that a flat monthly rate that people could afford be charged for the service. In South Africa the militant tactics that brought down apartheid are being retooled to oppose corporate privatization schemes that exacerbate the gap between the rich (mostly white) and the poor (mostly black) that is the legacy of the racist system.[28]

One of the most militant and long-standing protests against corporate development schemes that impoverish the poor and undermine environmental health has been the struggle against megadams in India, one of the favorite projects of both the World Bank and the Indian government for several decades. Since independence in 1950 some 3,300 dams have been built on India's rivers, causing great suffering by displacement of people, as well as environmental damage. In the 1980s a vast scheme for the development of 2 megadams, 30 large dams, and 135 medium-sized dams was projected along the Narmada River that runs for 800 miles westward from the Maikal hills to the Arabian Sea where it empties some 200 miles north of Mumbai (Bombay).

In the mid-1980s protests developed against the displacement of people who were not being provided with the promised relocation on comparable land. But it soon became apparent that it was impossible to provide these many thousands of displaced villagers with comparable land. Most of these local villagers would receive no benefit from the dams. Irrigation waters and electricity would go primarily to big cane farmers, urban areas, and even tourist water parks. Moreover water could be provided to many more people at a fraction of the price of the dams by traditional methods of water harvesting through small tanks and methods of recharging wells.[29] With this evidence, the protest movement moved from the issue of resettlement of the displaced people to opposing the dams altogether. The Save Narmada Movement (Narmada Bachao Andolan or NBA) was founded in 1989 and has been the major coordinator of the protest movement.

From that time to the present the Save Narmada Movement has conducted continual nonviolent protests against the construction of the dams, undertaking long treks along the river, occupation of sites to be flooded, including people willing to stay even when their villages became submerged, fasts, and blocking of trucks delivering construction materials. In 1993 the World Bank finally withdrew funding and support for the dam project. But the Indian government has continued its commitment to the dams, beating, teargassing, and arresting opponents. This repression has only caused the resistance to grow, and to become a popular cause for the mobilization of masses of Indians across the social spectrum to the corporate globalization of Indian resources. Even though the movement's petition to the Indian Supreme Court to stop the dams, based on careful assessment of their social and ecological impacts, was turned down in 2000, the resistance continues into the twenty-first century.[30]

Dams are not only being opposed in third world countries, such as India, but there is increasing skepticism about the usefulness of dams in the United States. The United States has built many dams in its history. Some 75,000 dams are listed on the Army Corps of Engineers National Inventory of Dams, which includes only dams over six feet tall. These dams eventually silt up, and also prevent the flow of water that supports local plant and fish life. In Wisconsin alone there are 3,800 dams. But many of these dams are in poor repair and are no longer needed for their original purposes. Consequently there is a movement to decommission dams, restoring rivers to their original free flow. In Wisconsin alone some 108 dams have been removed since 1955, 57 of them since 1990. People along these rivers are rediscovering the beauty of these waters, plants, and wildlife.[31]

THE GLOBAL STRUGGLE FOR WORKER JUSTICE

These protest movements are not only about impeding exploitative practices that harm humans and the environment. They also envision alternatives:

healthy food grown organically, community-run utilities that are affordable and responsible to local consumers, and renewable ways of harvesting water that serve the needs of the poor. Today there is a new emphasis on struggle for justice for farmers and issues of agriculture and environment. But there is also a resurgence of concern for worker justice. The workers' movements in the developed world appeared to have won the rights to unionize, to be paid a living wage, to work in safe conditions, and to receive pensions and health insurance sixty years ago. But all these gains are now under jeopardy in the global economy and are losing ground in the developed world as well, especially in the United States.

The vast majority of factories located in Asia, Africa, and Latin America that produce clothes, shoes, electronic equipment, toys, and other such goods for the global market operate under sweatshop conditions. But even in the United States many factories that produce clothes or process meat, as well as jobs such as hotel cleaning, are sweatshops, often employing immigrant workers.[32] What is a sweatshop? A sweatshop is any workplace where any or all of these conditions prevail: workers receive less than a living wage, are forced to work long hours (ten to twelve hours a day) without overtime pay, work in unsafe conditions, are harassed on the job, physically and verbally abused, and are prevented from organizing unions and bargaining for better conditions.

Such conditions prevail in most of the factories that are producing not just for local markets, but, above all, in those that contract for global corporations, such as Wal-Mart, J.C. Penney, and Banana Republic, and big logos, such as Nike, Gap, and Disney. For example, in Indonesia the average Nike shoe worker receives $1.25 per day for a ten- to twelve-hour shift. In Vietnam women working nine- to ten-hour shifts earn as little as six cents an hour making promotional toys, such as Disney characters for McDonald's. In El Salvador workers are paid about sixty cents an hour and work for up to seventy hours a week. In Honduras pay averages about forty-three cents an hour for up to fourteen-hour shifts, with sometimes mandatory twenty-four-hour shifts.[33] Such miserable wages contrast with the enormous profits made by these companies. While a Nike worker in Asia makes less than $2 a day, Nike CEO Phil Knight owns stock worth $4.5 billion and Nike's 1999 revenues were $9 billion.[34]

The workers in most factories are young people, in some cases children under ten. Carpet factories in Egypt, Pakistan, and other Middle East countries, especially exploit children as young as four years of age. They work ten-hour days and make an average of $5 a week.[35] In most garment factories there is a preference for young women between seventeen and twenty-six who are seen as docile and easily exploitable. The long hours and toxic conditions of many such factories burn these women out young. By their late twenties many have respiratory problems and are seen as no longer employable. Physical and verbal abuse, such as slapping and throwing material in the women's faces, as well as sexual abuse, are rampant in these factories. The poor pay also means that the women cannot afford adequate food, especially since they are usually supporting children, parents, and siblings. Unsafe water, polluted air, and poor housing available to such women contribute to their chronic health problems. In some cases, such as the Mexican border city of Juarez, young women *maquiladora* (factory) workers have been systematically targeted for rape and murder. In recent years thousands of such young women workers have been found murdered, their bodies often mutilated, in cases that remain unsolved.[36]

Efforts to organize against the sweatshops had begun among labor rights activists, such as Charles Kernaghan of the National Labor Committee, in the mid-1990s, but had received little attention from government or the media. But the campaign took off when the organizers began to target popular logos, such as Nike. Kathie Lee Gifford, entrepreneur of a popular line of clothes sold through Wal-Mart, inadvertently sparked this new media attention by tearfully denouncing and threatening to sue Kernaghan on her popular TV show, *Live with Regis and Kathie Lee*, for suggesting that she exploited children. Kernaghan had reported to a congressional committee that workers as young as thirteen worked twelve-hour shifts, up to seventy-five hours a week, for thirty-one cents an hour making apparel for Wal-Mart with the Kathie Lee Gifford label.[37] As a result of this incident the U.S. media began to pay attention to the issue.

The antisweatshop campaign moved to a higher level of intensity in the late 1990s as students in U.S. universities began to link sweatshop conditions with the production of caps, sweatshirts, and other paraphernalia that bore university logos. In the summer of 1997 student interns with the AFL-CIO and UNITE (United Needle and Textile Union) began to research the conditions under which the campus apparel was made and to press their universities to insist that manufacturers adhere to a code of conduct. By 1998 the student movement became more fully organized with a national leadership and regional representatives under the umbrella organization, United Students against Sweatshops (USAS).[38]

Many universities sought to derail the issue by joining President Clinton's initiative, the Fair Labor Association (FLA), partnered with big corporations, such as Kathie Lee Gifford and Nike, that called for only voluntary monitoring by the corporations themselves and no promise of a living wage for the workers. The students rejected this solution and insisted on organizing an alternative to the FLA, called the Workers Rights Consortium (WRC). Student activism exploded on dozens of campuses in the winter of 1999, with sit-ins in campus offices, fasts, marches, and other direct action tactics. At the University of California at Berkeley, students held a fashion show in which they modeled different apparel, announcing the conditions under which each one was made.[39]

A number of universities were persuaded to leave the FLA and join the WRC. By 2002 112 universities had signed on to the WRC as the basis for contracts for campus apparel. Unlike the FLA, the WRC created a framework by which the workers themselves could organize and voice their grievances. Corporations had to disclose where their apparel was made and to allow unions to help workers organize. Fact-finding committees of student and union activists made trips to factories where the apparel was made and interviewed workers directly to reveal the conditions of the workplace. Thus the student movement against sweatshops moved rapidly from a consumer boycott that asked for voluntary codes of conduct from corporations to direct efforts to empower the workers themselves to organize and better their own conditions.

A major victory for this strategy was won in 2001 when workers in a Korean-owned plant called Kuk Dong in Atlixco, Mexico, who made collegiate gear for Reebok and Nike, went on strike. The plant owners fired five leaders and called in the police who beat the 300 workers occupying the factory. The WRC sent a fact-finding delegation to document the repression. The police brutality was also widely reported in the media. The WRC demanded that Reebok and Nike put pressure on their subcontracting factory to rehire the fired workers, improve wages, and allow the workers to organize a union. Students set up protests and rallies on campuses throughout the United States. They demanded that university administrators put pressure on Reebok and Nike to make the Kuk Dong management accept these conditions. On September 18, 2001, the Kuk Dong management conceded. The workers, under their own independent union, SITE-MEX, signed a collective bargaining agreement with the management. This is one of the first successful efforts to organize an independent union in Mexico for *maquiladora* workers. [40]

The antisweatshop movement thus signals a new stage of union organizing. Labor unions in the United States and other countries developed in national contexts. They have generally been protectionist toward jobs for workers in their own countries, with little concern for workers elsewhere. But in a global economy, in which corporations can move to any country at will to exploit the lowest labor costs, where there is little provision for environmental protection, labor organizing must also become global. Local union struggles need to network together across borders to insist on decent wages and working conditions for workers throughout the world. The WRC signaled the beginning of such cross-border organizing on behalf of worker justice.

Wages need to be linked, not to minimum wages in each country (which are often below poverty level, including in the United States[41]), but to a living wage in the context of each local economy. Agreed upon standards for maximum hours (i.e., no more than forty-eight hours a week for full wages), decent working conditions, respect for workers' health and dignity, health benefits and pensions, need to be pressed by international bodies representing workers of the world. Only when such global standards are recognized and enforced will it no longer be possible for corporations to engage in a "race to the bottom" by exploiting low-waged and unprotected labor pools.[42]

ALTERNATIVE AGRICULTURE MOVEMENTS

The nineteenth- and twentieth-century Left concentrated on organizing workers (the industrial proletariat) and was less concerned with peasant farmers. Peasants were seen as reactionary and lacking the capacity for revolutionary consciousness.[43] However the corporate globalization of agribusiness, which threatens the survival of small local sustainable agriculture worldwide, has sparked international networks of farmers that are challenging WTO policies and seeking to create alternative agricultural methods and trade policies. One of the most significant of these movements is the Movimento dos Trabalhadores Rurais Sem Terra (Landless Rural Workers Movement) in Brazil.

In Brazil about 40,000 large ranchers, about 1 percent of the proprietors, own 46 percent of the land in *fazendas* (ranches) of more than 5,000 acres each, much of it unused. About 12 million peasants either have no land or work a small piece of land that may or may not belong to them. A third of these, 4 million peasants and their families, are landless, working as sharecroppers or tenant farmers.[44] The Brazilian constitution declares that unused land can be expropriated and distributed to needy farmers. But in practice the government has done little land reform.[45]

In 1975 the Catholic Church set up a Pastoral Commission on Land that helped to educate many landless farmers about their rights and to train leaders. Some peasant groups began to organize and occupy land in the late 1970s and early 1980s. In 1984 this movement was organized nationally. The *Sem Terra* movement deliberately remains autonomous of either political parties or the church. It also avoids centralization, focusing on local groups that develop encampments. Each encampment is typically organized into fifteen or twenty committees to solve particular problems of daily life. Together these committees make up a self-governing community. The local encampments, in turn, send representatives to regional and state-level meetings where fifteen to twenty-one people are elected to steering committees for these areas. Every five years there is a nationwide congress that draws delegates from the whole country and elects the national leaders. In 2000, 11,750 delegates attended the national congress. The national executive committee consists of twenty-one people, 40 percent of whom are women (through their own merits, not because an allotment of places are saved for women).[46]

The movement is largely self-financed, with local encampments raising their own funds, with some help from the churches, labor unions, and international solidarity groups, but not in a way that allows the movement to be dependent on outside funders. Every encampment contributes 2 percent of its profits to the national organization. If they lack the funds to do that, they contribute to the larger organization through volunteer labor.[47]

By 2002 some 350,000 families had taken over land through the movement, with 250,000 of them having won land titles, while some 80,000 continue to camp on land and demand official recognition of land titles. Encampments are organizing by getting together groups of landless farmer families willing to engage in this effort, preferably several thousand, who plan for several months and develop their leadership committees. The group then moves onto unoccupied land in the middle of the night and quickly begins to set up tents, then builds housing, and sets up schools, water, and electrical infrastructure. They are often met by the police representing the government and landowners. The bigger the group the less easy it is for the police to drive them off the land by force. The lawyers of the movement also arrive to defend the constitutional rights of the squatters to the land.

Each encampment runs itself in a participatory democratic fashion. They have learned and practice sustainable agriculture. They have created more than sixty food cooperatives and develop small agricultural industries. Rejecting genetically modified seeds, they produce organic seeds for their own use and for sale for other farmers. They are also working with smaller *assentamentos rurbanos* (settlements on the edge of urban areas) where groups take over smaller plots of land and do intensive farming, such as fruits or vegetable growing or chicken-raising, combined with local agroindustrial work.

Education is a major priority of the movement. More than 1,000 primary schools from first to fourth grades, and fifty schools from fifth to eighth grades, working with 95,000 children, have been built in the settlements. Roughly 2,800 teachers work with these schools. Some universities are committed to work with the movement to train 700 teachers a year. An Itinerant School has been developed to go wherever there are encampments. The movement has also developed its own curriculum to reflect its needs and worldview, although the government still refuses to recognize these schools and their curriculum. Near São Paulo they have built the National Florestan Fernandes School to train leadership cadres.[48]

The Sem Terra movement is a major participant in the worldwide Via Campesina, an international network of farmers' movements that has groups in eighty-seven countries. The Via Campesina works to remove international agricultural policy entirely from the World Trade Organization and from the control of transnational corporations and to defend alternative production and trade policies. Central to the movement is the demand for food sovereignty for each country and local region. They see their struggle, not as a conflict between North and South, but one between two different models of production. The one favored by agribusiness, the WTO, the United States, and the EU stresses large industrial agriculture for export, using pesticides and GM (genetically modified) seeds, and promoting low agricultural prices in their own countries, supplemented by direct payments to farmers. The agricultural surpluses are then exported to poor countries. The result of this export dumping of low-priced food is the destruction of local agriculture that cannot compete with the cheap imports.

The Via Campesina champions a renewal of local production by small farmers for local markets, rejecting GM seeds and using environmentally sustainable methods of water use, fertilizer, and composting. Via Campesina demands that local and national governments restore policies of protection of local agriculture. They must aid farmers to have access to land, seeds, water, and credit, assist in local production and marketing, and tax imports to prevent dumping. Policies of control of production are needed to avoid surpluses. International agreements should regulate supply and guarantee fair internal prices based on the costs of production by the farmer, so the farmer can make an adequate living through his/her work.

Export and international trade in food should be limited primarily to a few products grown only in certain regions, but with fair prices based on farmers' cost of production. But each country and region should prioritize diversified production for local and regional markets, so each country is, as much as possible, self-sustaining in basic food production. The peoples of the world are thus guaranteed an adequate and healthy food supply they either produce themselves or can buy at prices they can afford.[49]

Several agricultural alternatives are also developing in the United States that allow socially aware producers and consumers to partly opt out of the dominant food production and distribution system. One of these is community-supported agriculture, a movement that came to the United States from Japan and England. Community-supported agriculture (CSA) connects farmers directly with consumers in their area. Small farms of 20–200 acres, generally run by organic or biodynamic farming methods, grow a large variety of crops for the growing season, or year-round in mild-weather areas, such as California. By intercropping or crop rotation, using natural fertilizers and pesticides, such farms avoid the toxic effects of the dominant agricultural methods in the United States.

Community-supported agriculture is based on direct subscriptions by members who pay the farm on a yearly basis and receive a box of fresh seasonal foods delivered within days of its actual harvesting. There are presently about 1,000 CSA farms in the United States, most of them concentrated in the upper Midwestern, New England, and Pacific Coast states. The farmers going into such farming are generally younger than the average U.S. farmer, highly educated, and socially aware. Nearly 40 percent are women.[50]

CSA farms also sell wholesale to nearby restaurants, as well as in local farmer's markets and roadside stands. Such farms are able to guarantee an equitable living for farmers, as well as healthy organic food to consumers with whom they have a direct relationship. Many such farms also offer food based on work shares to low-income people and provide for agricultural interns and festivals to create relationships with the community. There is a minimum of waste of food because long-term storage and distant transportation are eliminated.

One highly successful example of CSA is Full Belly Farm in Guinda, California, north of San Francisco. Full Belly Farm was begin in 1984, with a partnership of four men and women, and maintains thirty-five year-round employees. Full Belly Farm grows over eighty different crops, including a great variety of vegetables, fruits, and nuts. It is a 200-acre certified organic farm using sustainable practices since its inception. The farm has a flock of chickens, a herd of sheep, and several cows, and uses the animals for fertilizer and soil renewal. It also uses cover crops that fix nitrogen and provide organic matter for the soil, as well as planting habitat for beneficial insects and wildlife.

Full Belly Farm sells to restaurants and farmer's markets, as well to 650 subscriber members who receive a box of seasonal fresh produce weekly that is delivered to pick-up places in their neighborhoods. Full Belly is proud of providing a living wage to its year-round employees, as well as help on medical insurance and housing. The result is a highly stable work force that has been with the farm for many years. Full Belly also has study interns, and provides many community activities, such as educational tours, school groups, and an annual Harvest Festival designed to acquaint the public with the process of growing food in a sustainable manner.[51]

Another scheme to link consumers directly to producers, eliminating middlemen and providing farmers with a living wage, is fair trade coffee. Free trade policies and the entry of new coffee producers, such as the Vietnamese, into coffee production for export have glutted the world coffee markets, pushing prices to the farmers well below the costs of production. The result is the devastation of many coffee farms in Central and Latin America. Fair trade coffee creates a direct relation with a group of coffee farmers and a distributor who contracts with consumers, thus allowing the farmers to gain a sufficient price for their coffee to cover costs of production and make an adequate living. Farmers also grow their coffee in an organic sustainable way.

Church organizations and other institutions concerned about justice contract in bulk to buy fair trade coffee from a group of farmers. There have also been efforts to encourage independent grocery stores and coffee bars to offer fair trade coffee. One example of such a relationship between church institutions and fair trade coffee is the Our Sister Parish network. Our Sister Parish works directly with Finca Emilia in El Salvador. Finca Emilia coffee is planted in the shade of fruit trees and taller trees to provide protection and prevent erosion. The farmers use organic methods, fertilizing with the residue of the coffee cherry, not with chemical fertilizer. Adequate pay for the coffee has allowed the local farming community to expand a sewing cooperative, install solar panels in village housing, design rainwater collection systems for drinking water, and develop cultural and educational programs. The relationship between Finca Emilia and Our Sister Parish has allowed the coffee farmers to triple their income, compared to the prices offered by the dominant coffee distributors.[52]

Community-supported agriculture and fair trade coffee are, at this time, small niche markets for a socially critical minority of consumers that do not threaten the dominant agribusiness system. They need to be accompanied with intentional educational outreach designed to help the consumers of these alternatives understand the larger context of the unsustainable and exploitative nature of the dominant systems. Such movements need to link up with global networks, such as Via Campesina, to be part of a world effort to restrain the trade policies of international agribusiness and the WTO. Unjust "free trade" needs to be changed to fair trade for all products worldwide. This will demand an overhaul of the whole system of agricultural production along the lines envisioned by Via Campesina.

WOMEN IN THE STRUGGLE AGAINST CORPORATE GLOBALIZATION

As we detailed in chapter 1 of this volume, globalization undermines the daily means of survival for families. It cuts basic services to health, education, and transportation to the poorest, subsidies for food, and assistance for local farmers. Women typically respond by redoubling their work, adding labor in the informal economy to increased gardening, raising small animals, and spending longer hours to fetch water and gather wood. But this very redoubled labor of women to bridge the gap of survival needs for their families impels women to new critical consciousness, both about the global structures that are causing this impoverishment of daily life and about their own capacities as women. With the aid of movements of resistance in their societies and international NGOs, women begin to name global systems, such as the WTO, Structural Adjustment, and neoliberal economics. Their new creativity forces men in their families or in social movements to change their relationship to women and recognize their leadership skills and vital importance.

This expanded role of women is recognized in many of the movements we have mentioned in this chapter. João Pedro Stedile, one of the founders and leaders of the Sem Terra movement in Brazil, acknowledges the vital importance of women to their struggle.

> As far as gender goes, because our form of struggle involves whole families, there has been a break with the traditional model of men-only farmers' movements. This is not to say that there's not still a strong macho culture among men in the countryside—on the contrary. But the way our movement is organized means the women are bound to play a role. In an encampment there are as many women as men—and even more children. In general women are very active in the committees set up to solve everyday problems, but they're much less represented at higher levels—which is where the influence of machismo comes in. A male comrade will often object to his partner traveling so much, or going to meetings in the capital. Family life imposes restrictions that impede women's broader participation at the state and national level. All

the same, even though we haven't adopted a quota system, 40 percent of the 21 comrades on the national executive committee are women.[53]

Chittaroopa Palit, leader of the Save Narmada movement against the damming of the Narmada River, acknowledges her own feminist ecological consciousness as vital to her involvement in this struggle. She also details the central importance of peasant and tribal women to the continued resistance.

> The leading role of women in these actions—they braved hot summers and monsoons, kept vigil in the darkest of nights, suffering violent police beatings and brutal arrests—electrified the surrounding areas and put enormous pressure on the Madhya Pradesh government.[54]

This militancy of tribal women she attributes to their closeness to the land and survival needs of daily life. A separate women's organization within the Save Naramada movement, the *Narmada Shakti Dal* (*Shakti* signifies female cosmic power), was set up in 1998. Peasant women were two-thirds of those on dam barricades and were also important in the core decision-making group. Sustaining the long struggle was only possible because of the participation of women. "They proved far more radical and militant than the men, and capable of more imaginative protests."

Peasant women's distance from the market and its economic mentality meant that "they never saw the land and the river—which they worshipped as a mother—as commodities that that could be sold for cash." Even though the government began to raise the level of compensation for the families, women led in refusing to take these funds. They would not allow their land to be swapped for money. Also, according to Palit, women's relative exclusion from the political system meant "they had not been colonized by mainstream party ideology—they hadn't been deluded into construing their own destruction as 'development.' Nor did the power of the state leave them cynical or demoralized. Their imaginative approach kept opening unexpected forms of struggle."

When thousands were arrested at a dam site in January 2000 and taken to jail, the women refused to leave the prison until their questions had been answered about the actual costs and effects of damming the site. The wardens fled, while the women stayed in the prison demanding answers to their questions about the exact costs of the electricity from the dam, compared to existing power sources, and the extent of waterlogging of the region that the dam would cause. The result was a heightened critical consciousness about the dam, even among those who had at first supported it.[55]

The long revolutionary struggles in El Salvador, Nicaragua, and Guatemala from the 1970s to the 1990s also resulted in a new militancy of women and willingness to organize their own movements to meet the needs of daily life. In Nicaragua the Sandinista government in the 1980s encouraged credit and services cooperatives and also agricultural cooperatives. In the credit and services cooperatives small farmers keep their own properties, but band together to buy seed, fertilizer, and equipment and apply for loans. In the agricultural cooperatives the small farmers pool their land, tools, and livestock and share work and profits communally.

During the Samoza dictatorship, put in place and subsidized by the U.S. government from 1936 to 1979, a huge gap had opened between rich and poor. 1 percent of the population controlled over 50 percent of the land, with 30 percent of the arable land owned by the Somoza family alone. Much of this land was unused. With the Sandinista revolution, much of the unused land was confiscated to distribute to small farmers, preferably in cooperatives, although the Sandinistas intentionally did not touch land that was being farmed efficiently by its owners.[56]

The United States attacked the Sandinista revolution through a murderous Contra War, embargo, and denial of international trade and credit. Exhausted by the war, the Nicaraguans voted out the Sandinista presidency in 1990, expecting to receive relief from the embargo and the opening up of U.S. aid. But the result was a draconian implementation of Structural Adjustment policies imposed through the IMF. Public spending for health, education, and public services was severely cut, import tariffs and quotas to protect the Nicaraguan economy were eliminated, and state-run businesses, utilities, and schools privatized. The popular literacy and health centers were closed down, and the costs of meeting these needs became much more expensive. By 1994 70 percent of the Nicaraguans were living in poverty. Nicaragua became the poorest Central American and Caribbean country with the exception of Haiti.

Although much of the public spending for social needs was cut, many small farmers clung to the land they received from the Sandinista government. The feminist movement and its network of women's centers refused to close, but continued without government aid. They became key institutions for spreading critical consciousness and skill training to women, as well as education on reproductive and general health. Freed from the limitations of the Sandinista male leadership (which supported women's political and economic empowerment, but was ambivalent about issues such as reproductive rights and family violence),[57] feminist consciousness expanded in the 1990s. Many women responded to the economic crisis by banding together in producer and credit cooperatives.

Two women-organized credit and service cooperatives are the Association of Rural Women Workers of Chinandega (AMOC) and the Multiple Services Cooperative of Masaya. AMOC was founded in 1995. It serves four municipalities with over a thousand farmers. It provides small loans to buy cattle, chickens, and other agricultural needs for small farmers. They receive the funds from a variety of NGOs and charge 6 percent interest on the loans. This interest mainly goes to pay for the AMOC administration itself. The women have three years to repay, and if they cannot fully repay in that time, there is a system of loaning cows to a jointly owned project which sells the milk to pay off the loans, after which time the cows can be reclaimed. The money becomes revolving funds that are recycled into new loans as the old ones are repaid. Women learn the skills of administration and organic farming, obtain land titles, and gain self-confidence through this process.[58]

The Multiple Services Cooperative was also founded in 1995. It too receives funds through NGOs and loans to small farmers and craftswomen to raise sheep, chickens, pigs, cattle, basic grains, and medicinal plants, as well as to create craft businesses for cornhusk flowers, painting, embroidery, and cultural programs, such as theater. Women defend their land and get land titles; they learn organic methods of farming to avoid toxic fertilizers and pesticides. Capacitation programs include self-esteem and reproductive health workshops. Multiple Services is linked to the National Federation of Cooperatives, as well as to the international peasant organic farmers network, Campesino a Campesino.[59]

Although many of these women leaders were former Sandinista militants, they avoid ties to that or other parties, all of whom are seen on the national level as unhelpful to grassroots needs. They are also consciously ecumenical, bringing together Evangelicals and Catholics, without claiming any official religious identity. The official Catholic Church of Nicaragua, closely tied to the neoliberal policies of the post-Sandinista governments, has been of little help to the poor, although both Protestant and Catholic groups sympathetic to liberation thought have been helpful over the years. For example, Maryknoll nuns live in small groups in many areas of Nicaragua and help peasant women start small cooperatives for chicken-raising, natural medicines, and the like. The chicken-raising cooperatives have worked by organizing a small group of women to receive a starter group of chicks. They promise to raise them and pass on a proportion to a second group of women and so on, thus creating a self-expanding process.[60]

Some women's groups band together to address a great range of community needs. For example, UPAVIM (Unidas para vivir mejor, United for a Better Life) was founded by the Esperanza Community on the outskirts of Guatemala City by a group of peasants uprooted from their villages by the military. They settled in what had been a garbage dump, clearing the land and using scrap metal and wood to build their houses. On tags attached to the handicrafts sold by UPAVIM, their work is described in the following way: "By working together these women have developed a community medical clinic, a dental clinic, a scholarship and tutoring program, a day care center with Montessori trained teachers, and a crafts project that generates income for individual women and for these community programs. Moreover they have maintained a spirit of Hope which many in similar circumstances have lost long ago, By purchasing this product you support the entire community."[61] Liberation-oriented nuns and priests have also been helpers in developing this organization of women in Esperanza, although UPAVIM is independent of official church ties.[62]

Although the success of such cooperatives is owed to the enormous energy and creativity of these women, they also could not have gotten off the ground without some help from outside. They need starter funds, skill training, and technical aid from international NGOs, such as the Norwegian group NORAD, the British group OXFAM, and many others, including church-sponsored groups. But these international NGOs and aid groups function in a totally different way from the global financial institutions. They are typically small and with modest funds, run by people who are both critical of the dominant system and in solidarity with the local people. Their aid workers live simply in the local communities, working directly with the people. They avoid creating dependency or ongoing debts, but empower the people to become self-sufficient. Starter loans become revolving funds, managed by local leaders and continually recycled within the community. The way such NGOs work provides a model for an entirely different kind of globalization, a globalization that creates a network of mutual aid.

With the help of such international alliances, leaders of local women's cooperatives can show up at global meetings, such as the NGO meeting at the United Nations' women's conference in Beijing, China in 1995. Here leaders of women's alternative movements from every country of the world were present. North-South conflict, so prominent at early UN Women's meetings, had virtually disappeared. Rather the women from all over the world quickly gravitated to workshops with other women of similar interests. Women interested in microbanking plans, health clinics, reproductive rights, agricultural cooperatives, popular education, alternative theater, and many other projects gathered to exchange information and to network together.[63] The women then carried back to their local communities not only fresh ideas and information, but a whole set of contacts around the world on which they could draw for support. When local governments come down on them in repressive actions, they can communicate with a network of supporters around the world to protest and come to their aid. E-mail communication becomes vital for maintaining such global networking of local groups.

One example of such first world–third world empowerment that avoids creating ties of dependency is the CFFC-CDD network (Catholics for a Free Choice, based in Washington, D.C., and Católicas por el Derecho a Decidir, in Bolivia, Brazil, Mexico, Columbia, Chile, and Argentina). CFFC and the Latin American CCDs are a network of mostly Catholic women who critique the dominant sexual ethics of the Catholic church, and lobby for legalization of abortion, accessible family planning, sexual education, and reproductive health. Highly effective in raising funds for these issues with major donors, CFFC has helped the Latin American CCDs organize with starter funds, but also through education in fundraising to become self-sufficient. Through their journal *Conscience*, and its independent Spanish counterpart *Conciencia*, this movement not only deconstructs patriarchal sexual oppression of women, but presents a vibrant vision of how healthy sexuality and just human relationships might be imagined.[64]

Religious inspiration motivates women to resist and to create alternatives. Generally this does not flow from the dominant institutional expressions of the religion, but from small alternative networks that are often critical of the dominant tradition, yet also envision a liberating rereading of it. Thus, in the examples of movements in South America, members of religious orders inspired by liberation theology helped create cooperatives. Women inspired by feminist rereading of Catholicism created the CFFC-CDD networks. In India popular spirituality that venerates the river as divine mother strengthens the resolve of women not to sell their land and water.

The engaged Buddhist movement based in Thailand sponsored a conference in Bangkok in December 1997 entitled "Alternatives to Consumerism." Under this rubric representatives of numerous local projects throughout Asia gathered to share their visions. One group of women from Sri Lanka shared their project. They had organized the mothers throughout most of the island to resist buying bottled drinks from transnational companies, such as Coca-Cola. Instead the women were taught how to create healthy fruit drinks from local resources. Training and recipes for the locally produced beverages included information on global corporations and why they need to be resisted.[65] In the conclusion to this volume I will return to this question of how religion can best contribute to these struggles for alternatives to corporate globalization.

REIMAGINING AN ALTERNATIVE GLOBAL SOCIETY

The various projects of resistance and survival mentioned in this chapter could easily be dismissed as lacking the power and scope to really challenge the dominant corporate and financial institutions that are causing the havoc to which they are responding. They could be seen as simply arising in small spaces not yet fully under the control of these dominant institutions, spaces that these institutions themselves are rapidly seeking to close off through their control of resources and police power. Discarded populations that do not have, or wish to accept, employment in the exploitative sweatshops created by the corporations invent small subsistence farming or handicrafts businesses outside the system, but do not challenge its global power.

Even though the anti-corporate globalization movement is far from having the power to undo this system, it is essential to begin to imagine how these dominant institutions might be dismantled, or at least curbed, so that the spaces for alternatives can grow and become bases for recreated societies. Three major global institutions, which presently constitute the dominant system of world power, need to be reformed, paralyzed, diminished, and ultimately dismantled to open space for different ways of organizing human life. These are the transnational corporations, the Bretton Woods institutions (the IMF, World Bank, and the WTO), and the American military. Clearly neither the space of this book nor my expertise are sufficient for a full account of how to diminish and dismantle these global institutions. Rather, I will only point briefly to the paths that might be taken and some resources for thinking about how to do that.

David Korten has done some of the most extensive work on the construction of transnational corporations and how to dismantle them. This work is found in his two major books, *When Corporations Rule the World* and *The Post-Corporate World: Life After Capitalism.*[66] The major steps to curbing and dismantling the limited-liability-for-profit public corporation, in Korten's view, are the following. First, the legal basis for such corporations must be changed. The legal fiction of the corporation as a "person" who has permanent rights to exist, but without liability for the harm it causes to individuals or communities, must be altered. Rather corporations need to be chartered for limited renewable terms and in such a way as to be liable for the harm they may cause.

Second, corporations need to be excluded from political participation as funders of political candidates and parties. This funding from corporations has turned modern democracies increasingly into plutocracies, resulting in most candidates being tools of the corporations. Political campaigns need to be publicly funded without monies from corporations or large donors. Third, corporate welfare needs to be eliminated. Tax breaks and corporate subsidies need to be abolished. Rather, corporations' profits need to be taxed to reflect the actual amount of their wealth, thereby providing the tax base needed for public community needs.

Fourth, financial speculation needs to be made unprofitable.[67] By taxing each financial transaction, global manipulation of the stock market for quick profits would be largely shut down and investment could be directed toward its proper goal, actually building or renewing productive factories. Fifth, production should be organized primarily on a local basis and with boards of directors that reflect the stakeholders from all sectors of the community, thus reembedding economic institutions in communities to which they are responsible.

Reforming or dismantling the Bretton Woods institutions represents the second challenge vital to allowing a different, more just, and environmentally healthy world to emerge. Much debate has gone into the question of whether these institutions should be reformed or decommissioned altogether.[68] In my view this debate does not present actual alternative options. Rather reform and dismantling are part of a continuous process. Since these institutions, as they presently exist, are almost entirely at the service of global corporations, any effort to reform them to more equitably serve impoverished sectors of the population and to protect the environment will result in their eventual dismantlement.

These institutions have proven very facile in adopting the rhetoric of alleviating poverty and protecting the environment, but their proposals for doing so have followed the same neoliberal policies to serve the same corporate interests. Thus any effort to reform them so that they actually adopt policies that would protect the environment and serve impoverished populations would result in their being no longer useful to the corporate interests they presently serve. As we have seen in the aftermath of the WTO meeting in Cancún, if there is any real reform of the WTO the corporate powers are likely to abandon it to find other ways to serve their interests, ways which the global justice movement would also need resist.

Probably these institutions are incapable of deep reform and should be decommissioned.[69] Alternative institutions should be put in their place. Rural banks that manage revolving funds for small loans would be more helpful to the sort of small farmers presently being served by credit and service cooperatives of the kind we saw in Nicaragua.[70] International NGOs with small funds from their countries, of the kind represented by the Norwegian NORAD, could be helpful funders of such rural banks. The United

Nations, as the basis for a democratic framework of world government, needs to be rebuilt to provide the agencies for trade rules that would genuinely serve local economies, without making them hostage to global corporations.

The International Forum on Globalization (IFG) had suggested several major regulatory institutions under the United Nations that need to be built or renewed to create a more just global framework for trade rules.[71] These include strengthening UNCTAD (United Nations Conference on Trade and Development) as the rule-making body for trade and creating a UN Insolvency Court to settle debt claims. Such a court should have balanced representation of debtor and creditor countries. Private debts should remain private and not be converted to public debt. "Odious" debts (i.e., debts contracted by autocrats without democratic consensus which did not benefit the public and which have already been paid many times under present rules of interest taking) should be repudiated. There should be systematic a plan for debt relief, and no further debts allowed.

The IFG also suggests several other UN institutions that need to be developed. These would include a UN Finance Organization to keep a database on international accounts (not to be a lending institution) and facilitate negotiation to correct trade imbalances. For short-term emergency foreign exchange loans there should be regional monetary funds accountable to member countries of their region. No country should be allowed to be a voting member of more than one regional fund.

A UN Trade Disputes Court should be developed to mediate trade disputes between countries, although the main strategy for trade should be to encourage primarily internal local and national markets in each country. There can be regional trade, but there should be a sharp reduction in global trade between regions, limited to a few products that can be grown or produced only in a few regions. Global trade in goods, with its long transportation chains, is both highly polluting and largely unnecessary for the necessities of human life.

Finally, a UN Organization for Corporate Accountability should be developed primarily to support national initiatives on corporate accountability on the lines envisioned by David Korten. This would provide information and advisory services on monopolistic practices of particular corporations, monitor pricing practices and publicize unfair competitive practices, keep records of direct and indirect subsidies and the public costs of substandard wages and working conditions, discharge of harmful wastes, and other externalized costs. A uniform code of standards for corporations operating in more than one country would be developed to help governments shape local laws regulating corporations in their countries. International guidelines should be developed for national legislation to limit or prohibit corporate contributions to political parties and candidates and spending on advertising and public relations campaigns related to legislation on public issues.

A third and most fraught area of global power concerns the U.S. military. So far neither the critics of corporate power nor those of the global financial institutions have addressed this issue.[72] It has only been recently recognized the extent to which the U.S. military is functioning as an arm of U.S. corporations at the service of a total military-political-economic scheme of American world imperialism. The struggles against global corporations, against the Bretton Woods institutions, and against the global reach of the U.S. military are finally one interconnected struggle.

There are three interconnected strategies for curbing the global reach of the U.S. military. One is the strengthening of the United Nations capacity to refuse to sanction and to condemn invasions of the kind mounted by the U.S. in Iraq in March 2003. The beginning of such resistance was seen in the UN refusal to sanction the Iraqi invasion, but it needs to be strengthened and the guidelines for UN sanctioning of "peacekeeping" operations clearly laid out. Secondly, regional networks need to be strengthened that can mount campaigns to remove American military bases from around the world. The campaign to remove U.S. military bases from the Philippines is an example of such a campaign, but they need to become much more widespread. The need for and purposes of such U.S. military bases in other countries need to be challenged throughout the world. [73]

Finally the American people must become critical of a military budget that gives more than 50 percent of its resources to a huge military system. This budget is presently twice the size of the U.S. military budget at the height of the Cold War and constitutes almost 50 percent of the military expenditures of the whole world.[74] This budget dwarfs the military budgets of the other seven of the G-8 nations put together, not to mention the military budgets of the nations of the rest of the world. The American people are finding their own infrastructures for educational, health, and public services deeply undermined by a government primarily invested in the military for international power adventures.

There must be a concerted national campaign to challenge the legitimacy of such an imperialist military at the expense of the welfare of most U.S. citizens. The U.S. military should be cut back, perhaps by half. This will involve a national discussion of what is legitimate national defense and what are imperial adventures. Ultimately the need for large national militaries itself should be questioned. One should ask whether global security would not be best served with each country abolishing its military for national police, with the United Nations providing the basis for an international peacekeeping force, contributed to and controlled equitably by all member nations, not under the control of one nation or group of nations.

By limiting, curbing, and dismantling these institutions of dominating power, space is opened up to create more locally accountable, democratically governed, and environmentally sustainable forms of human society. The International Forum on Globalization has suggested ten guiding principles for such healthy social institutions. The first such guideline is participatory democracy. Democracy should not be identified with the sort of national elections that today function primarily as public displays of competition between rival representatives of the wealthy corporate elite. Democracy needs to be rooted in local town councils that represent those who bear the costs of the decisions that are being made. Regional and national representation needs to arise from and be rooted in local democracy.

A second key principle of healthy societies is subsidiarity. This principle means focusing production, consumption, and trade primarily on local communities. Again this means locating the decision making about the reproduction and exchange of the means of daily life primarily on the level of the people directly affected. Higher levels of organization, regional, national, and international, need to be auxiliary to the local as the primary place of decision making and understood to serve those local communities. The structure of the Sem Terra movement, where governance is located in the committees of the local communities and regional and national councils arise from and serve these local communities, is an example of such a system of subsidiarity.

A third principle is ecological sustainability. Economic activity needs to meet the needs of the people today, without compromising the ability of future generations to meet their needs, and without diminishing the viability of the planet's natural support systems. A great deal is presently known about how to do that, for example, how to farm through organic fertilizers and natural pesticides that rebuild soils and replenish water, rather than exhausting them. All waste needs to be recycled. Manufacture should be primarily based on reuse of materials, rather than new "virgin" materials. Energy and materials should come from renewable resources and should not exceed the rates of their regeneration.

A fourth principle is respect for the "commons" which should be shared as a community heritage. This commons includes three categories.

First it means forests, land, air, water, and fisheries on which all depend. Second, it means culture and knowledge that are collective creations of the human species. Third, it includes public services on behalf of the whole community to meet basic needs, such as public health, education, libraries, safety, and social security. None of these areas of the commons should be privatized as for-profit businesses, but they need to remain under public ownership and control.

A fifth principle is diversity, both biological and cultural. Diversity is today recognized as key for the vitality and creativity of living systems. But the corporate global system is reducing both biological and cultural diversity to a dangerous homogenization. The diversity of nonhuman species needs to be defended, as well as the cultural diversity of the many languages, cultures, and ethnic traditions evolved by the variety of peoples of human history.

A sixth principle is human rights. This means the recognition of the full and equal humanity of groups of people traditionally discriminated against, women, nonwhite people, indigenous people. But this should not be limited to civil and political rights. It needs to be extended to the areas of social, economic, and cultural rights. The right to an education, to health, adequate livelihood, and cultivation of distinct cultures are part of human rights.

Human rights moves on to the seventh principle, the right to an adequate livelihood. This includes the right to work, to have a free choice of employment, to just and safe working conditions, and to protection against unemployment. The right to unionize and bargain for just wages and working conditions is also part of this right to work. Those unable to work or work fully need to be guaranteed access to basic needs.

The eighth principle is one of food security and safety. Every person should have access to sufficient food, and this food should be safe from toxic additives. This means food sovereignty of each nation and region of the sort envisioned by the Via Campesina, including the organic production and local distribution of most food. Equity is the ninth principle. This means every society needs to overcome extreme gaps between rich and poor, men and women, ethnic groups, different jobs, and the handicapped. All people need to have access to equivalent means of life and access to culture. Differences of wealth should be kept within limits. The final or tenth principle is the "precautionary principle." This means that when any activity or product has potential harm, it should be restricted or banned, even if all the evidence is not yet in about the extent of its harmfulness. It should be allowed only when it is fully certified as safe for humans and the environment.

RETHINKING THE IDEOLOGIES OF CORPORATE
AND MILITARY DOMINANCE

As we have seen in the section of chapter 1 on dominating ideologies, the global systems of dominance—the transnational corporations, the Bretton Woods institutions, and the U.S. military—depend on justifying ideologies that make them appear unquestionable. These ideologies pervade all the media of communication and socialization: schools, print, television and radio media, and even churches. The pervasive control of all social institutions by these ideologies make them appear to be natural, normal, and the will of God. Any questioning or dissent from them then is made to appear crazy, heretical, subversive, and socially dangerous. In the United States, the term "terrorist" is rapidly becoming the omnibus word for labeling any dissent from these dominant ideologies. Once labeled a "terrorist," one becomes an "enemy combatant," even if you are a U.S. citizen, and can be arrested and imprisoned without legal rights.[75]

These dominant ideologies need to be intellectually refuted, alternatives to them proposed, and their hegemonic control over social communication dismantled to make space for discussion of alternatives. I suggest two areas where such ideological critique needs to take place, although this is not an exhaustive list.

One of these is the neoliberal economic ideology that presently controls official economics, both in its teaching in universities and academic publishing and its practice in political and economic institutions. The second is the ideology of messianic nationalism that dictates the vision of American world empire.

The restriction of economics to "purely" mathematical models, based solely on the calculations of individual self-interest to expand profits, needs to be overcome. Economics needs to be reintegrated with social and environmental ethics and a vision of human and planetary life as self-generating organisms in community. The values of justice between humans, particularly in relation to marginalized peoples, such as women and poorer classes and races, and economic sustainability, need to become normative for economic calculations, not cut off as irrelevant "externalities," as is presently the case. Although there are feminist and ecological economists that have begun such work, much more needs to be done to make such social justice and ecological economics available in mainstream economic teaching, publishing, and practice.[76]

The second major type of ideology that needs to be challenged is American messianic nationalism that feeds its imperial military passions. This ideology is generally discredited or simply incredible for most peoples of the world. So the major work on dismantling it needs to be done by American Christians to whom it seeks to appeal and to justify itself as "Christian." American messianic nationalism, as we have seen in chapter 1 of this book, is based on a belief that the United States is uniquely an elect nation chosen by God to impose its ways of life on the rest of the world by coercive economic means, and finally by military force. Nations who pursue other ways of economic development and social and political organization than "free market capitalism" can be regarded as enemies, not only of the United States, but of God. To repress such alternatives is a divine crusade to which the United States is uniquely called.

From the point of view of normative Christian tradition, there are four basic heresies involved in this American messianic nationalism. They have to do with the nature of God, of the relation of God to nations, the nature of evil, and how evil is overcome or at least lessened in human affairs. I will briefly unpack these false theological claims.[77] (1) "God chooses one nation above other nations." In Christian tradition God is a God of all nations. "In Christ there is neither Jew nor Greek" (Gal 3:21). Christianity confirmed a development within universalist Judaism that God is the creator of the whole world, loves all peoples and nations equally, and chooses no one nation above or to the exclusion of others.

(2) "The United States is God's uniquely chosen nation to express God's will on earth." Since God is the God of all peoples and loves all peoples equally, God cannot be seen as choosing the United States for a unique mission over other peoples. The concept of "election" cannot be nationalized in Christianity. Every person and people needs to grapple with their responsibilities before God, but this cannot be construed as setting any individual or people above others as uniquely "chosen" to do God's will.

(3) "Evil is socially located in the enemies of the United States." In Christian teaching all humans are created in the image of God and all have a potential for good. Yet all have sinned and fallen short of the will of God. Evil exists particularly in the way humans violate their relation to one another. To usurp power and wealth in the hands of one person or group, depriving others of bare existence, is the basis of evil on earth. To defend such injustice as divinely given is blasphemy, attributing evil to the will of God. Every person and nation must struggle with how they have helped construct systems of evil that are impoverishing the earth and how they have blasphemously defended such evil as good and divinely given. Although all are responsible for some evil, it is the task of the United States and its people to ask how they in particular are contributing to it and helping to perpetuate it.

(4) "Evil can be overcome by external coercive force, ultimately by military force." Coercive force has a limited role to restrain criminal activity within and between national communities, but governments need to use their legal sanctions primarily to encourage justice and fair treatment of all. Coercive force can never be construed theologically as "overcoming evil." Evil can only be overcome by conversion, which takes place in the hearts of persons in community. Those who monopolize wealth and power and use them to harm others must be changed inwardly to recognize their evildoing. This change is an expression of divine grace, that is, the positive power of life and renewal of life inherent in reality, that opens us up to compassion for others and recognition of our wrongdoing in harming them.

American Christians, in dialogue with other religious traditions, especially with Jews and Muslims, need to come together through local, regional, and national networks and church bodies, as well as through world church bodies, such as the World Council of Churches, to repudiate these false theological claims. Only in this way can Americans hope to reestablish their country as a nation among other nations that, together with other peoples of the world, might actually lessen the evils of military violence, social injustice, and environmental degradation and create a more peaceful, just, and sustainable future for humanity.

NOTES

1. Subcomandante Marcos, "Don't Forget Ideas Are also Weapons," originally appeared in *Le Monde Diplomatique*, 2000; translated into English, Harry Forster, reprinted, *The Zapatista Reader*, ed. Tom Hayden (New York: Thunder's Mouth Press/Nation Books, 2002), 313.

2. For a definition of this relationship see the speech of Comandante Esther at the Congress of the Union, Mexico City, March 2001, in Hayden, *Zapatista Reader*, 196.

3. See Daniel Nugent, "Northern Intellectuals and the EZLN," originally published in *Monthly Review*, July 1995, reprinted in *Zapatista Reader*, 352–63.

4. See the list of demands in the First Declaration from the Lacondón Jungle, January 1, 1994 and the addition of the words "information and culture" in the Fourth Declaration, January 1996, in *Zapatista Reader*, 220, 248.

5. On the women's struggle within the Zapatista movement see Guilomar Rovira, *Women of Maize: Indigenous Women and the Zapatista Rebellion*, Anna Keene, trans. (London: Latin American Bureau, 2000); also Elena Poniatowska, "Women Battle for Respect Inch by Inch," *Los Angeles Times*, September 8, 1997, reprinted in *Zapatista Reader*, 55–57.

6. From the Fourth Declaration from the Lacóndon Jungle, January 1996, in *Zapatista Reader*, 250.

7. See George A. Collier, *Basta! Land and the Zapatista Rebellion in Chiapas* (Oakland, Calif.: Food First, 1994), 85–87.

8. Marcos' essay, "The Fourth World War has begun," originally appeared in *Le Monde Diplomatique*, September 1997; see *Zapatista Reader*, 270–78, especially 282.

9. Ibid., 284.

10. For an account of these struggles against NAFTA, Fast Track, and MAI, see Kevin Danaher and Jason Mark, *Insurrection: Citizen Challenges to Corporate Power* (New York: Routledge, 2003), 229–60. The Canadian struggle against MAI is detailed in Maude Barlow and Tony Clarke, *The Multilateral Agreement on Investment and the Threat to American Freedom* (Toronto: Stoddard Publishing, 1998).

11. On these WTO rulings see Danaher and Mark, *Insurrection*, 268–77. These rulings are also discussed in greater detail in Lori Wallach and Michelle Sforza, *Whose Trade Organization? Corporate Globalization and the Erosion of Democracy* (Washington, D.C.: Public Citizen, 1999). This book was summarized in a pamphlet, edited by Wallach, Sforza, and Ralph Nader, *The WTO: Five Years of Reasons to Resist Corporate Globalization* (New York: Seven Stories Press, 1999). The WTO subversion of the laws to protect dolphins is told in Danaher and Mark, *Insurrection*, 111–36, while the ruling undermining the protection of turtles is found in Peter Fugazzotto and Todd Steiner, *Slain by Trade: The Attack of the World Trade Organization on Sea Turtles and the U.S. Endangered Species Act* (San Francisco: Sea Turtles Restoration Project, 1998).

12. On the nonviolent direct action training and guidelines, see Starhawk, *Webs of Power: Notes From the Global Uprising* (Gabriola Island, B.C.: New Society Publishers, 2002), 17.

13. For a detailed first-person account of the police violence, see Alexander Cockburn, Jeffrey St. Clair, and Allan Sekula, *Five Days that Shook the World: Seattle and Beyond* (London: Verso, 2000), 13–52.

14. Danaher and Mark, *Insurrection*, 277–88.

15. On the April 16 Washington demonstrations, see Cockburn, St. Clair, and Sekula, *Five Days*, 70–86; also Starhawk, *Webs of Power*, 35–48.

16. For an eyewitness account of these events, see Starhawk, ibid., 49–115.

17. See Mary Durran, "Development and Peace at the WTO in Cancun," *Catholic New Times*, October 19, 2003, p. 9.

18. Ibid., also Rick Rowden, "WTO talks collapse in Cancun," September 16, 2003, ActionAid, webexclusive.

19. On the possibility that the wealthy nations and corporations might abandon the WTO if they no longer control it, see George Monbiot, "The Worst of Times," *The Guardian*, September 2, 2003; also Anil Netto, "Poorer Nations Celebrate Trade Talks Failure," *Asia Times online*, September 20, 2003, www.atimes.com/atimes/Global_Economy/EI20Dj01.html.

20. www.forumsocialmundial.org, "Background: Events of 2001, 2002, and 2003," September 29, 2003.

21. Susan Webb, "When Bush Comes to Shove, Resist," *People's Weekly World*, January 31, 2004, www.pww.org/article/articlereview/4700/1/200.

22. "World Social Forum Charter of Principles," August 6, 2002: www.forum-socialmundial.org.

23. Peter Waterman, "The World Social Forum: The Secret of Fire." 6/18/2003, www.opendemocracy.net/articles/ViewPopUpArticle.jsp?id=6&articleId=1293.

24. See "We will Reduce Your Fields to Ashes: An Open Letter from Indian Farmers," in *Rethinking Globalization: Teaching for Justice in an Unjust World*, Bill Bigelow and Bob Peterson, eds. (Milwaukee: Rethinking Schools Press, 2002), 228–29.

25. See interview with Bové in *A Movement of Movements: Is Another World Really Possible?* Tom Mertes, ed. (London: Verso, 2003), 137–51. For Via Campesina, see www.Viacampesina.org.

26. Maude Barlow and Tony Clare, *Blue Gold: The Fight to Stop the Corporate Theft of the World's Water* (New York: The New Press, 2002), 154–56, 185–87. Also Jim Schultz, "Bolivia's Water War Victory," *Earth Island Journal* (Autumn 2000).

27. See Carolyn McConnell, "Tap Water Takeover," in *Yes!: A Journal of Positive Futures* (Winter 2004), 16–17.

28. On the development of the Soweto Electricity Crisis Committee and the Anti-Privatization Forum, see an interview with a leading organizer, Trevor Ngwane, in *Movement of Movements*, 111–34.

29. See Vandana Shiva, *Water Wars: Privatization, Pollution and Profit* (2002). Reprinted in *Yes!* (Winter 2004): 30–34.

30. See interview with one of the major organizers, Chittaroopa Palit, in *Movement of Movements*, 71–93.

31. See Elizabeth Grossman, "A Canoe in Singing Waters," in *Yes!* (Winter 2004), 26–29.

32. On sweatshop conditions in the United States, see Joann Lim, "Sweatshops are Us," and Helen Zia, "Made in the U.S.A.," in Bigelow and Peterson, *Rethinking Globalization*, 162–69.

33. *Rethinking Globalization*, 158–59.

34. Ibid., 151.

35. Ibid., 158–59, 200; See also the story of Iqbal Masih, who was sent to work in a carpet factory at age four. When he was eleven he was able to break free and to speak against the exploitative conditions for the Bonded Labor Liberation Front. He was assassinated at thirteen. Ibid., 206–7.

36. Between 1993 and May 2002, more than 450 women in Juarez have disappeared and 284 found murdered. See petition to End Violence against Women in Juarez, www.petitiononline.com/JUAREZ/petition.html.

37. This occurred on May 1, 1996. Transcript from ABC *Prime Time Live*, May 22, 1996. See also *Insurrection*, Danaher and Mark, 65–66.

38. For an interview with USAS organizer Bhumika Muchhala on the history of the USAS, see *Movement of Movements*, 192–201.

39. Ibid., 98.

40. Ibid., 104–5.

41. In 1998 the minimum wage in the United States was $5.15. If a worker worked full time (i.e., forty hours a week, fifty weeks a year) at this rate s/he would make $10,300—79.2 percent of the official poverty level for a family of three ($13,003).

42. For ongoing antisweatshop campaigns, see Maquiladora Health and Safety Network (www.igc.org/mhssn), Sweatshop Watch (www.sweatshopwatch.org), and the antisweatshop campaigns organized by Global Exchange (www.globalexchange.org).

43. See David Mitrary, *Marx against the Peasant: A Study in Social Dogmatism* (London: Weidenfeld and Nicolson, 1951).

44. See interview with Joâo Pedro Stedile, *Movement of Movements*, 32.

45. Ibid., 23, 24.

46. Ibid., 25–27, 31.

47. Ibid., 28–30.

48. Ibid., 29–30; also www.mstbrazil.org/education.html.

49. Ibid., 42–44; also www.viscampesina.org.

50. See Daniel Lass, G. W. Stevenson, John Hendrickson, and Kathy Ruhf, "CSA across the Nation: Findings from the 1999 Survey," October, 2003, Center for Integrated Agricultural Systems, College of Agricultural and Life Sciences, University of Wisconsin at Madison, Madison, Wisconsin.

51. See www.fullbellyfarm.com; www.newfarm.org; www.localharvest.org.

52. See www.oursisterparish.org.

53. Stedile interview, *Movement of Movements*, 31.

54. *Movement of Movements*, 81.

55. Ibid., 84–85.

56. See Denis Lynn Daly Heyek, *Surviving Globalization in Three Latin American Communities* (Orchard Park, N.Y.: Broadview Press, 2002), 205–12.

57. See Rosemary Ruether, "The Art of Survival: Feminism in Nicaragua," *Sojourners* (July 1993), 18–23.

58. Interview with María del Rosario Flores Neira, founder and president of AMOC, op. cit., Heyek, *Surviving Globalization*, 223–33.

59. Interview with Olfania Medina, founder of the Multiple Services Cooperative, ibid., 241–52.

60. Personal experience with Maryknoll Sisters in various locations in Nicaragua in the late 1980s and 1990s.

61. From a tag attached to a bag acquired from the UPAVIM project.

62. This comes from personal experience, having visited the Esperanza community several times in the 1980s and 1990s, bringing seminary study groups to visit and donating medical supplies to the clinic.

63. Personal experience of the 1995 United Nations conference on women, Beijing, China.

64. See www.conscience-magazine.org and www.catolicasporelderechodedecidir.org

65. This account comes from personal participation in the Alternatives to Consumerism conference in Bangkok and the follow-up conference on local projects. See Rosemary Ruether, "They Meet to Overcome Consumerist Evils," *National Catholic Reporter* (January 30, 1998).

66. For the first book see note 17, chapter 1. The second is published by Berrett-Koehler, San Francisco, 1999.

67. One proposal to tax and so make financial speculation unprofitable is the Tobin tax. See James Tobin, "A Tax on International Currency Transactions," UNDP, *Human Development Report 1994* (New York: Oxford University Press, 1994), 70. See also the Tobin Tax Initiative, available at www.ceedweb.org/iirp.

68. See the discussion and proposals in the "50 Years Is Enough" network: www.50years.org.

69. This view is an emerging consensus found in David Korten's work, the International Forum on Globalization and in Walden Bello's network, Focus on the Global South. See Focus on the Global South Work Plan for 2003–2005, available at http://focusweb.org.

70. One of the suggestions made by Maria del Rosario Flores Neira, president of AMOC, is that her credit and savings cooperative needs to be supplemented by rural cooperative banks to replace the urban banks that refuse to fund small farmers and businesses: *Surviving Globalization*, 228.

71. "From Bretton Woods to Alternatives," in *Alternatives to Economic Globalization*, editors of the International Forum on Globalization (San Francisco: Berrett-Koehler, 2002), 228–38.

72. Seymour Melman did an excellent critique of the American military system. Unfortunately his work has not been updated. See his *Pentagon Capitalism: The Political Economy of War* (New York: McGraw-Hill, 1970) and *The Permanent War Economy* (New York: Simon and Schuster, 1985).

73. The proposal to dismantle all U.S. military bases was one of the decisions at the 2004 World Social Forum in Mombai.

74. For current American military expenses compared to the rest of the world see the websites of the Center for Defense Information, www.cdi.org, and the War Resisters League, www.warresister.org.

75. As an example of the effort to outlaw public dissent, see the proposal of the Republican National Committee to the Federal Election Commission to issue rules that would shut down any groups that would seek to communicate with the public in any way critical of President Bush or members of Congress: www.fec.gov/press/press2004/20040312rulemaking.html.

76. See Frances R. Wooley, "The Feminist Challenge to Neoclassical Economics," in *Gender and Economics*, ed. Jane Humphries (Aldershot: England: Edward Elgard Publishing, 1995).

77. This challenge has been developed more extensively by Rosemary Ruether, in "Christians Must Challenge American Messianic Nationalism: A Call to the Churches," available on the PSR (Pacific School of Religion) website, www.psr.edu.

CONCLUSION

In chapter 2 of this volume on "The Greening of World Religions" we saw a variety of efforts to apply the ecological potential of different religions to care for the earth. The Jain tradition is one source of inspiration for the program on environmental ethics at Schumacher College in Devon, England. Buddhism is interpreted by engaged Buddhist thinker Sulak Sivaraska in Thailand as an ecological liberation worldview, inspiring campaigns against deforestation. Trees are ordained to confirm their sacredness and prevent them from being cut down. Buddhist ashrams and monastic communities in Thailand and also in the United States, in retreat centers such as Green Gulch Zen Center and Spirit Rock mediation center, are shaped to express an integrated ecological spirituality.

Jews also are applying Judaism to environmental spirituality and ethics. Arthur Waskow of the Shalom Center in Philadelphia has inspired a generation of American Jews to renew traditional observances, such as resting on the Sabbath and keeping kosher, applying them to contemporary issues of injustice, workaholic lifestyle, toxic farming, and exploitative farm labor. Islamic environmentalists seek to integrate care for the earth and the animals into Shari'a, or Islamic law. The World Council of Churches has integrated "integrity of creation" into its mandates for peace and justice as one of the three guiding principles of its work.

Ecofeminist spirituality provides inspiration for direct action against corporate globalism and also for permaculture gardening for pagan priestess and psychotherapist Starhawk in Northern California. In Zimbabwe Christianity and Shona religious traditions are combined in earth-keeping churches that plant trees and care for watersheds. Wangari Maathai leads women in massive projects of tree planting and water conservation through a combined inspiration of Christianity and Kenyan indigenous religion. Vandana Shiva in India takes the Hindu religious theme of Shakti as key for resistance to Western developmentalism. Faith in Shakti also inspires the women of the antidam movement to resist dam building projects on the Narmada River. Aruna Gnanadason integrates Indian tradition and a Christian theology of grace to promote an ecofeminist theology as the base for her work in "peace, justice and integrity of Creation" at the World Council of Churches.

In Latin America the ecofeminist theology and spirituality of Ivone Gebara inspire communities of women all over the continent to apply this vision to their daily life. Programs, such as *Capacitar*,[1] seek to overcome the mind-body split of traditional Christian culture. Techniques of body work help women to recover their bodies as the basis of their spiritual vitality, not an enemy of it, as in traditional ascetic spirituality. In the United States historian of science Carolyn Merchant constructs a "partnership ethic" to bring humans and nature together in joint decision making about sustainable environments. Although not identifying with any particular religious tradition, Merchant draws from the broad streams of Western culture to envision this partnership relationship between humans and nature in holistic interconnection.

How can this application of different world religions to ecological sustainability and resistance to exploitation be expanded? How can environmental work in different world religions be brought more into partnership with one another? One creative way to try to do that has been pioneered by the Interreligious Sustainability Project of Metropolitan Chicago. This project was put together by a partnership between the Center for Neighborhood Technology and several theological schools in Chicago area, especially the Lutheran School of Theology and Meadville-Lombard theological school of the Unitarian-Universalist tradition. Theologians and environmental activists together charted the environmental issues of the greater Chicago area. They produced a map showing the concentrations of population and environmental pollution and the relationship of these factors to health problems. A study guide was prepared which analyzed these interconnections and proposed various programs of actions.

This study guide then became the tool for a neighborhood-by-neighborhood organizing program. Organizers based at the Center for Neighborhood technology went to each neighborhood, locating the religious congregations across all traditions, Christian, Jewish, Buddhist, Muslim, Sikh, that might be willing to band together, study the program guide together in a joint adult education process, and then come up with projects of environmental care for their neighborhood. These projects might be anything from improving the waste disposal process to restoring green spaces in their neighborhood. Each neighborhood group engages in this study and develops their project as an expression of an interfaith religious vision and also comes to see themselves as members of a bioregional community of communities of the greater Chicago area.[2]

The ancient religious forms of monastic life are also providing the basis for building new communities of ecojustice spirituality. We have seen examples of this in Buddhist ashrams and retreat centers in Thailand and the United States. Catholic religious communities, especially women religious, are also adapting monastic life to ecological spirituality and practice. One such group is Sisters of Earth, a network of Catholic women's religious orders seeking to live an ecological lifestyle as an expression of their faith and mission. Sisters of Earth was founded in 1993 by three Sisters of St. Joseph who put out a call to other religious women for an organizing gathering of those interested in earth spirituality. Fifty people came. Sisters of Earth was launched as a networking group with a yearly newsletter and a meeting every two years. The network now has several hundred members, including a small male group, Brothers of Earth.[3]

Sisters and Brothers of Earth have been particularly inspired by the work of priest and "ecologian" Thomas Berry who pioneered a vision of ecological spirituality. Berry believes that the patterns of religious culture and daily life that have defined humanity since the agricultural revolution are in crisis. An ecological revolution is necessary to convert humanity into a new relationship with nature if the human species is to survive. Berry calls this the "great work" of our generation.[4]

For practical advice on how to make an ecological transformation of their way of life, Sisters of Earth turned particularly to mentors such as Al Fritsch, founder of Science in the Public Interest in Appalachia.[5] Fritsch's Center does environmental sustainability inventories for institutions, including those of religious orders. From the mid-1980s Fritsch carried out more than sixty such inventories for motherhouses of religious orders in the United States. Since religious orders have roots in a preindustrial agricultural world and typically have land on which many produced their own food in an earlier generation, such motherhouses still include a considerable amount of land.

Fritsch's environmental audits include energy use, food use, land use, the physical plant, transportation, waste management, water use, and wildlife. The audit of energy use includes both conservation of present sources of energy and recommendations on how to convert to renewable sources of energy, becoming partially self-sufficient in energy use. He recommends such options as solar, wind, biomass, and hydro energy, solar drying and cooking, the use of greenhouses, passive solar space and water heating, and hydroelectric units. The audit points out ways to increase self-reliance in food and reduction in the costs of food from production to preparation. He examines land use to promote more self-sufficiency, such as edible landscaping, aquaculture, multiple land use, wildlife refuges, as well as the aesthetic and spiritual aspects of relation to the land.

Fritsch examines the physical condition of the buildings and their use patterns to suggest more efficient use of present structures, ways of heating and cooling more efficiently, as well as alternative sources of energy. He examines the transportation practices of the community, both public and private, to recommend better efficiency and lessened environmental damage. Waste disposal is assessed to recommend methods of recycling and composting, including composting toilets. Water use includes management of wetlands, conservation, and better use. Relation to wildlife flora and fauna is assessed to suggest improved habitat protection. This inventory gives the community a comprehensive map of what they are presently doing and how they can convert to greater ecological sustainability.

Women religious orders began to apply principles of ecological sustainability to their lands and buildings in the early 1980s. The Grail, a lay women's movement that came to the United States from Holland at the beginning of the Second World War, had done their own farming in the 1950s and 1960s, but later had largely abandoned it. In the 1980s they reclaimed some of their agricultural traditions, reread through a feminist and ecological spirituality. They developed a permaculture garden and a solar-heated greenhouse. They added "how to" courses on permaculture and solar heating to their offerings at their retreat center in Loveland, Ohio, using their own practices as demonstration training sites. Other religious orders also underwent their own conversions of their properties to more ecological use. In keeping with their educational missions, many of these orders created training programs in their retreat centers so others could come and learn from their experience.

Although the transformation of mother houses as ecological retreat and teaching centers suggests a rural focus, much of the work of Sisters of Earth integrates rural and urban. Energy conservation, food use, composting, and waste recycling have been applied to urban institutions, hospitals, schools, and parish complexes. Many Sisters of Earth have been science teachers, and ecology has given them a new outlet for their knowledge. Among the projects undertaken by such women at schools and retreat centers have been solar-heated houses and greenhouses, strawbale houses (a cheap and energy-efficient building material), solar ovens, composting toilets, and community gardens. Their vision and skills have also gone out in the mission work of religious orders. Such religious women have taught poor communities in Africa, and Central and South America, how to compost waste, build composting toilets and solar ovens, and use solar electricity to power lighting and pumps for wells.

One of the most important training centers for those interested in the integration of spirituality and ecological practice is Genesis Farm in Blairstown, New Jersey, founded by Sister Miriam Therese MacGillis on the property of her religious order. MacGillis has written extensively on the new universe story promoted by Thomas Berry and Brian Swimme[6] and on ecological spirituality and has lectured on these topics around the world.[7] Genesis Farm offers a six-week and a twelve-week bioliteracy program and does weekend seminars on such topics as "the universe story and bioregionalism" and "simplifying our life styles." These courses include work addressed particularly to religious orders on how they might reenvision their traditional vows of "poverty, chastity and obedience" in the context of an ecological spirituality.

Ecological spirituality and practice shape the daily practical life and the liturgy and prayer practices of Genesis Farm. Genesis Farm has developed a sacred space on their land that is used as an earth meditation walk. The stations of this walk bring together the stages of the universe story with the stages of each person's life cycle story. The cycle of the church year is traditionally rooted in the cycle of the seasons, so it lends itself to a reinterpretation in relation to seasonal change, summer and winter solstices and spring and fall equinoxes. Prayer is integrated into the rhythms of daily life, rising and going to sleep, food preparation, eating and clean-up, times of fasting and times of celebration. Genesis Farm models a holistic community where ecological spirituality and practice have been integrated into every aspect of daily life, its relation to the land, water, air, and the community around them (they also function as a community-supported farm for the area).

These many examples of the integration of spirituality, religious vision, and ecological practice express a contagious energy moving around the world. They suggest a new perspective on the dictum of Lynn White in 1967 that "since the roots of our trouble are so largely religious, the remedy must also be essentially religious."[8] The vision of a transformed relationship of humanity to each other and to the earth demands new nature-conserving technology and organized political work to reform or shut down oppressive institutions. But the motivation for this work cannot just be anger or hatred. It has to be deeply rooted in joy. It must be integrated with a vision of life-giving community and some actual glimpses of what such community might be like. Ecofeminist rereading of religious traditions, with its vision of humanity as part of one life-giving matrix, offers promises of helping to provide the spirituality for such life-giving community.

NOTES

1. On the work of Capacitar-Chile, see Mary Judith Ress, *Without a Vision, The People Perish* (Santiago, Chile: Conspirando Collective, 2003), 119.

2. The website of the Center for Neighborhood Technology is www.cnt.org.

3. See www.nacce.org/1999/earthsibs.html.

4. Thomas Berry, *The Great Work: Our Way into the Future* (New York: Bell Tower, 1999).

5. The website for Appalachia-Science in the Public Interest is www.a-spi.org.

6. Thomas Berry and Brian Swimme, *The Universe Story* (San Francisco: Harper-SanFrancisco, 1992).

7. See Nancy J. Brubaker, "Genesis Farm and a Spirituality of Learning: An Interview with Miriam Therese MacGillis," *Constellation* (Spring 2002), www.tcpc.org/resources/constellation/Spring_02/brubaker.htm.

8. Lynn White, "The Historic Roots of Our Ecological Crisis," *Science* 155 (March 10, 1967), 1207: Reprinted in Roger Gottlieb, *This Sacred Earth: Religion, Nature and Environment* (New York: Routledge, 1996), 193.

WEBSITE RESOURCE LIST

Appalachia—Science in the Public Interest, organization working for environmental protection in Appalachia, www.a-spi.org.

Btselem, the Israeli Information Center on Human Rights in the Occupied Territories, www.btselem.org.

Catolicas por el derecho a decidir, Latin American Catholic women on reproductive rights, www.catolicasporelderechoadecidir.org.

Center for Defense Information, data on military expenditures worldwide, www.cdi.org.

Center for Neighborhood Technology, Chicago, www.cnt.org.

Community-Supported Agriculture, Robyn Van En Center, networks community-supported agriculture farms, www.csacenter.org.

Conscience, Magazine of Catholics for a Free Choice, Catholic reproductive rights group, www.conscience-magazine.org.

Corporate Watch, information on transnational corporations, www.corpwatch.org.

Council of Canadians, Canadians against corporate globalization, www.canadians.org.

The Earth Charter, promotes a global agreement on environmental justice, www.earthcharter.org.

Fifty Years is Enough, movement against the World Bank, www.50years.org.

Focus on the Global South, network of economist Walden Bello on global economic imperialism from an Asian perspective, www.focusweb.org.

Food First/Institute for Food and Development Policy, www.foodfirst.org.

Full Belly Farm, community-supported agriculture farm, Guinda, California, www.fullbellyfarm.org.

Global Action Plan, Alternative Economic development, www.global actionplan.org.

Global Exchange, various campaigns against corporate globalization, www.globalexchange.org.

Grounds for Change, fair trade coffee network, www.groundsforchange. com.

Independent Media Center, www.indymedia.org.

International Forum of Globalization, anti-corporate globalization network, www.ifg.org.

Jubilee USA Network, campaign to forgive global debt, www.jubileeusa.org.

Movimiento Sem Terra, Brazilian landless farmers movement, www.mstbrazil. org.

Natural Step, environmentally sustainable social development, www.natural step.org.

Our Sister Parish, church-related fair trade coffee network, www.oursister parish.org.

Palestinian environmental NGO network (PENGON), www.pengon.org.

Ruckus Society, training in direct action, www.ruckus.org.

Sisters and Brothers of Earth, ecological network of Catholic religious orders in the United States, www.nacce.org.

Sweatshop Watch, organizing network against sweatshops, www.sweatshop watch.org.

Tobin Tax Initiative, project to tax financial speculative transactions, www.ceedweb.org/iirp.

United Students against Sweatshops, university student organization against sweatshops, www.usasnet.org.

Via Campesina, global anti-agribusiness farmers network, www.viacampesina. org.

War Resisters League, information on global militarism, www.warre sisters.org.

World Social Forum, world network for alternatives to globalization, www.forumsocialmundial.org.

World Watch Magazine, major source on global environment, www.world watch.org.

Zapatistas, movement for indigenous rights, Chiapas, Mexico, www.ezln.org.

INDEX

AAEC, 101

abortion rights, 25, 36

absolutization, 38

accumulation, system of, 105

Afghanistan, 9

AFL-CIO, 136, 147

Africa: egalitarian society in, 100;
female genital mutilation in, 29;
Green Belt Movement in, xi, 102–4;
HIV/AIDS funding for, 25–26

African Americans, disenfranchisement
of, 9

African National Congress, 143

agribusiness: biotechnology and, 16–17,
106, 151; control of, x; cost of, 16;
damage by, 16; myths of, 15–16;
pesticides in, 15–16, 106, 151

agriculture: diversification of, 4; global
warming and, 13; subsidies for, 5–6,
10

agriculture, sustainable: cooperatives
for, 132, 156; destruction of, 1,
106–7, 149; nature and, 107, 124

Aguas del Tunari, 142–43

air, environmental ethic toward, 80

All India Council of Christian Women,
108

Allende, Salvador, 10

Alliances for Sustainable Jobs and
Environment, 136

Alliances of Small Island States, 15

Alternatives to Consumerism
(conference), 159, 172n65

amniocentesis, 50

AMOC. *See* Association of Rural
Women Workers of Chinandega

Angola, 2

animal totems, 100–101

animals, factory farming of, 18

Anthony, Susan B., 77

anti-dam movement, xii, 49, 107,
144–45, 173–74. *See also* India

Anti-privatization Forum, 144

antisweatshop movement, xii, 32–33,
131, 146–49

apartheid, 8

*Apocalypse, Now and Then: A Feminist
Guide to the End of the World* (Keller,
C.), 118

apocalyptism, 118

aquifers, 6, 16, 80

Army Corps of Engineers National
Inventory of Dams, 145

ascetic view of religion, 51, 52–53, 56,
75, 78

Ashcroft, John, 24

ABOUT THE AUTHOR

Rosemary Radford Ruether received her M.A. in Roman history and Ph.D. in classics and patristics from the Claremont Graduate School in Claremont, California, in 1960 and 1965. She is the author or editor of thirty-eight books, mostly on feminist liberation theology, theological history, and social justice. She was the Georgia Harkness Professor of Applied Theology at the Garrett-Evangelical Theological Seminary and Northwestern University in Evanston, Illinois, from 1976–2000. She is presently the Carpenter Professor of Feminist Theology at the Graduate Theological Union in Berkeley, California. She is married with three children and two grandchildren.

CPSIA information can be obtained at www.ICGtesting.com
Printed in the USA
LVOW040518020712

288481LV00002B/38/P